EYEWITNESS *TRAVEL GUIDES*

SINGAPORE

LITTLE
INDIA

Kalang River

Geylang River

Singapore River

**KAMPONG GLAM AND
LITTLE INDIA**
See pp70–83
Street Finder map 3

**THE COLONIAL CORE AND
FORT CANNING**
See pp42–59
Street Finder maps 4, 5

**CHINATOWN AND
THE FINANCIAL DISTRICT**
See pp60–69
Street Finder maps 4, 5

DK EYEWITNESS *TRAVEL GUIDES*

SINGAPORE

Main contributor: JILL A. LAIDLAW

DORLING KINDERSLEY
LONDON · NEW YORK · MUNICH
MELBOURNE · DELHI
www.dk.com

DK

LONDON, NEW YORK,
MELBOURNE, MUNICH AND DELHI
www.dk.com

Produced by Editions Didier Millet, Singapore
EDITORIAL DIRECTOR Timothy Auger
PROJECT EDITOR Irene Toh Lay Kuan
ART DIRECTOR Tan Seok Lui
EDITOR Choo Lip Sin
DESIGNERS Norreha Sayuti, Nelani Jinadasa

CONTRIBUTORS
Jill A. Laidlaw, Kathy Khoo, Julia Oh,
Rufus Bellamy, Ben Munroe, Joan Koh, Robert Conceicao

PHOTOGRAPHERS
Lawrence Lim, Colin Koh, Peter Chen, Diana Lynn

ILLUSTRATORS
Anuar bin Abdul Rahim, Lim Yew Cheong, Thomas Sui,
Wong Swee Fatt, Denis Chai Kah Yune, Luanne Tay

MAPS
ERA-Maptech Ltd, Ireland

Reproduced by Colourscan, Singapore
Printed and bound by South China Printing Co. Ltd., China

First published in Great Britain in 2000
by Dorling Kindersley Limited
80 Strand, London WC2R 0RL

Reprinted with revisions 2003

Copyright © 2000, 2003 Dorling Kindersley Limited, London
A Penguin Company

A CIP CATALOGUE RECORD IS AVAILABLE FROM THE BRITISH LIBRARY.

ISBN-13: 978-0-7513-6999-1

FLOORS ARE REFERRED TO THROUGHOUT IN
ACCORDANCE WITH EUROPEAN USAGE; IE THE "FIRST FLOOR"
IS THE FLOOR ABOVE GROUND LEVEL.

**The information in this
Eyewitness Travel Guide is checked regularly**.
Every effort has been made to ensure that this book is as up-to-date
as possible at the time of going to press. Some details, however, such
as telephone numbers, opening hours, prices, gallery hanging
arrangements and travel information are liable to change. The
publishers cannot accept responsibility for any consequences arising
from the use of this book, nor for any material on third party
websites, and cannot guarantee that any website address in this book
will be a suitable source of travel information. We value the views
and suggestions of our readers very highly. Please write to: Publisher,
DK Eyewitness Travel Guides,
Dorling Kindersley, 80 Strand, London WC2R 0RL, Great Britain.

A view of the city skyline

CONTENTS

HOW TO USE THIS
GUIDE 6

**INTRODUCING
SINGAPORE**

PUTTING SINGAPORE
ON THE MAP *10*

CENTRAL SINGAPORE *12*

THE HISTORY OF
SINGAPORE *14*

SINGAPORE THROUGH
THE YEAR *22*

SINGAPORE AT A
GLANCE *26*

SINGAPORE'S BEST:
MUSEUMS AND FAMILY
ATTRACTIONS *28*

Haw Par Villa exhibit

◁ **Boat Quay's shophouses, with skyscrapers in the Financial District looming over them**

MULTICULTURAL
SINGAPORE *30*

RELIGION *32*

PERFORMING ARTS *34*

SINGAPORE'S BEST:
PARKS AND GARDENS *36*

THE SINGAPORE RIVER *38*

SINGAPORE AREA
BY AREA

THE COLONIAL CORE
AND FORT CANNING *42*

Sago Street shophouses

CHINATOWN AND THE
FINANCIAL DISTRICT *60*

KAMPONG GLAM
AND LITTLE INDIA *70*

ORCHARD ROAD *84*

FURTHER AFIELD *90*

FOUR GUIDED
WALKS

A SIXTY-MINUTE WALK
AMONG COLONIAL
HOUSES *110*

A NINETY-MINUTE WALK
THROUGH MOUNT
FABER PARK *112*

A NINETY-MINUTE WALK
THROUGH GEYLANG
AND KATONG *114*

A SIXTY-MINUTE WALK
ALONG EAST COAST
PARK *116*

Ju Ming's *Living World* (1987)

TRAVELLERS'
NEEDS

WHERE TO STAY *120*

WHERE TO EAT *126*

SHOPPING IN
SINGAPORE *142*

ENTERTAINMENT IN
SINGAPORE *152*

OUTDOOR
ACTIVITIES AND
SPECIALIST INTERESTS
162

SURVIVAL GUIDE

PRACTICAL
INFORMATION *168*

Chilli crab

TRAVEL INFORMATION
176

SINGAPORE STREET
FINDER *184*

GENERAL INDEX
194

ACKNOWLEDGMENTS
206

GLOSSARY *208*

TRANSPORT MAP
Inside back cover

Raffles Hotel

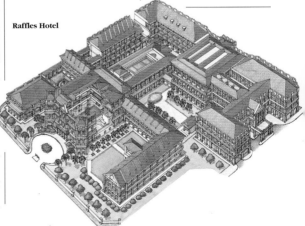

HOW TO USE THIS GUIDE

THIS GUIDE WILL HELP you to get the most out of your visit to Singapore, providing expert reommendations as well as detailed practical information. *Introducing Singapore* maps the city and sets it in its geographical, historical and cultural context, with a quick-reference time-line on the history pages giving the dates of significant events. *Singapore at a Glance* provides an overview of the city's multiculturalism, religions and performing arts and previews its best attractions. *Singapore Area by*

Area starts on page 40 and describes all the important sights, using maps, photographs and illustrations. The sights are arranged in five chapters: those in Singapore's four central areas and those a little further afield. Some neighbourhoods which are best explored on foot are described in *Four Guided Walks*. Hotel, restaurant, shop-ping and entertainment recommen-dations can be found in *Travellers' Needs*, while the *Survival Guide* includes tips on everything from trans-port and telephones to personal safety.

FINDING YOUR WAY AROUND THE SIGHTSEEING SECTION

Each of the five sightseeing areas is colour-coded for easy reference. Every chapter opens with an introduction to the area it covers, describing its history and character. For central districts, this is followed by a

Street-by-Street map illustrating interesting parts of the area; for sights beyond the city limits, by a regional map. A numbering system relates sights to the maps. Important sights are detailed in the following pages.

1 Introduction to the area
For easy reference, the sights are numbered and plotted on an area map, on which MRT stations are shown. The key sights (great buildings, museums and open-air sights) are listed by category.

A locator map shows where you are in relation to other areas of the city centre.

Each area has colour-coded thumb tabs.

Locator map

The area shaded in pink is shown in greater detail on the Street-by-Street map.

2 Street-by-Street map
This gives a bird's-eye view of interesting and important parts of each sightseeing area, with accurate drawings of all the buildings within them. The numbering of the sights ties in with the fuller descriptions on the pages that follow.

A suggested route for a walk is shown in red.

SINGAPORE AREA MAP

The coloured areas shown on this map are the four main sightseeing areas into which central Singapore (*see pp12–13*) has been divided for this guide. Each is covered in a full chapter in the *Singapore Area by Area* section (*pp40–107*). The maps' coloured borders match the coloured thumb tabs on each page of the section. The areas beyond central Singapore are covered in the *Further Afield* chapter (*see pp90–107*).

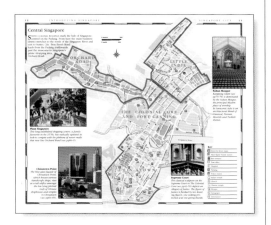

Numbers refer to each sight's position on the area map and its place in the chapter.

Practical information lists all the information you need to visit every sight, including where possible a map reference to the *Street Finder (pp185–9).*

3 Detailed information on each sight
All the important sights are described individually. They are listed to follow the numbering on the area map at the start of the section. The key to the symbols summarizing practical information is on the back flap.

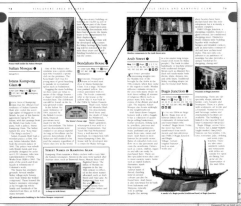

Story boxes highlight unique aspects or historical connections of a particular sight.

Visitors' Checklist provides the practical information you will need to plan your visit.

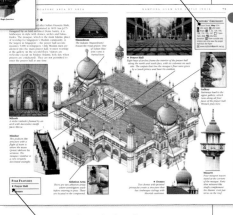

4 Singapore's major sights
These are given two full pages in the sightseeing area in which they are to be found. Buildings of particular architectural interest are dissected to reveal their interiors. Major open-air sights are shown as bird's-eye views.

Stars indicate the best features no visitor should miss.

INTRODUCING
SINGAPORE

PUTTING SINGAPORE ON THE MAP 10-11
THE HISTORY OF SINGAPORE 14-21
SINGAPORE THROUGH THE YEAR 22-25
SINGAPORE AT A GLANCE 26-39

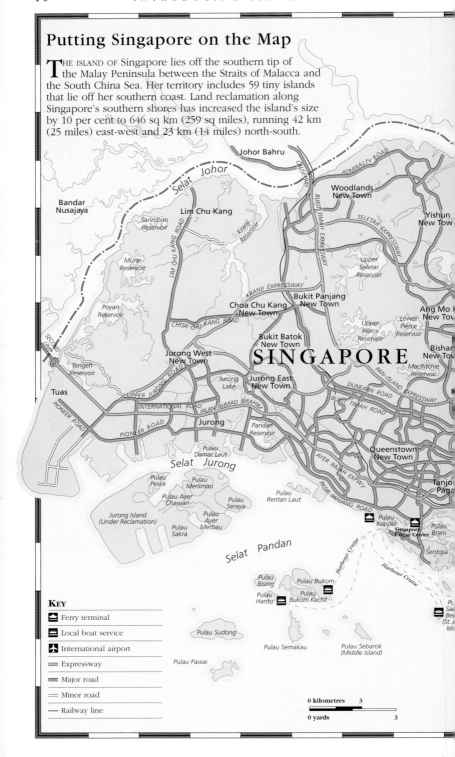

Putting Singapore on the Map

THE ISLAND OF Singapore lies off the southern tip of the Malay Peninsula between the Straits of Malacca and the South China Sea. Her territory includes 59 tiny islands that lie off her southern coast. Land reclamation along Singapore's southern shores has increased the island's size by 10 per cent to 646 sq km (259 sq miles), running 42 km (25 miles) east-west and 23 km (14 miles) north-south.

Johor Bahru

Selat Johor

ADMIRALTY ROAD

Bandar
Nusajaya

Woodlands
New Town

Yishun
New Tow

Lim Chu Kang

Sarimbun
Reservoir

Kranji
Reservoir

BUKIT TIMAH EXPRESSWAY

SELETAR EXPRESSWAY

Murai
Reservoir

Upper
Seletar
Reservoir

LIM CHU KANG ROAD

KRANJI EXPRESSWAY

Bukit Panjang
New Town

Ang Mo
New Tow

Poyan
Reservoir

Choa Chu Kang
New Town

CHOA CHU KANG ROAD

Upper
Pierce
Reservoir

Lower
Pierce
Reservoir

SECOND

Jurong West
New Town

Bukit Batok
New Town

SINGAPORE

Bishar
New Tow

Tengeh
Reservoir

Jurong
Lake

Jurong East
New Town

MacRitchie
Reservoir

PAN-ISLAND EXPRESSWAY

Tuas

UPPER JURONG ROAD

INTERNATIONAL ROAD

JALAN AHMAD IBRAHIM

DUNEARN ROAD

BUKIT TIMAH ROAD

PIONEER ROAD

Jurong

Pandan
Reservoir

Queenstown
New Town

Pulau
Damar Laut

AYER RAJAH EXPWY

Tanjo
Paga

Selat Jurong

Pulau
Pesek

Pulau
Merlimau

PASIR PANJANG ROAD

Pulau Ayer
Chawan

Pulau
Seraya

Pulau
Rentan Laut

Pulau
Keppel

Jurong Island
(Under Reclamation)

Pulau
Ayer
Merbau

Pulau
Brani

Singapore
Cruise Centre

Pulau
Sakra

Sentosa

Selat Pandan

Harbour Cruise

Harbour Cruise

Pulau
Bising

Pulau Bukom

Pu
Sa
Be
(St. A
Isla

Pulau
Hantu

Pulau
Bukom Kechil

Pulau
Bukom Kechil

Pulau Sudong

Pulau Semakau

Pulau Sebarok
(Middle Island)

Pulau Pawai

KEY

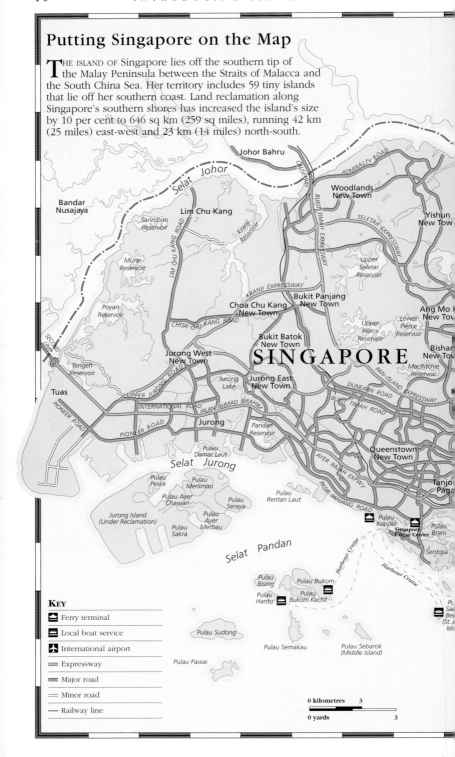	Ferry terminal
	Local boat service
	International airport
=	Expressway
=	Major road
=	Minor road
—	Railway line

0 kilometres   3

0 yards   3

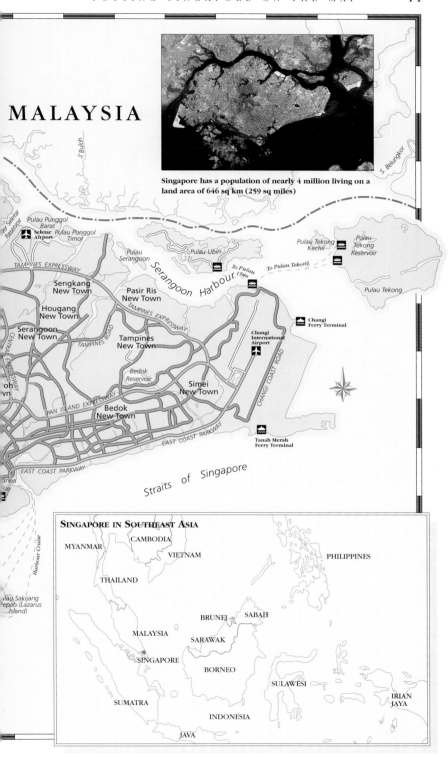

MALAYSIA

Singapore has a population of nearly 4 million living on a
land area of 646 sq km (259 sq miles)

S. Buloh

S. Belungkor

Sungei Seletar Reservoir

*Pulau Punggol
Barat*
**Seletar
Airport**   *Pulau Punggol
Timor*

*Pulau
Serangoon*

Pulau Ubin

Serangoon Harbour

*To Pulau
Ubin*   *To Pulau Tekong*

*Pulau Tekong
Kechil*   *Pulau
Tekong
Reservoir*

Pulau Tekong

TAMPINES EXPRESSWAY

**Sengkang
New Town**

**Pasir Ris
New Town**

**Changi
Ferry Terminal**

**Hougang
New Town**

TAMPINES EXPRESSWAY

**Serangoon
New Town**

**Changi
International
Airport**

CENTRAL EXPRESSWAY

TAMPINES ROAD

**Tampines
New Town**

CHANGI COAST ROAD

*Bedok
Reservoir*

**Simei
New Town**

oh rn

vn

PAN ISLAND EXPRESSWAY

**Bedok
New Town**

EAST COAST PARKWAY

**Tanah Merah
Ferry Terminal**

EAST COAST PARKWAY

arina
Bay

Straits of Singapore

Harbour Cruise

*Pulau Sakijang
epah (Lazarus
Island)*

SINGAPORE IN SOUTHEAST ASIA

MYANMAR

CAMBODIA

VIETNAM

PHILIPPINES

THAILAND

BRUNEI   **SABAH**

MALAYSIA

SARAWAK

SINGAPORE

BORNEO

SULAWESI

**IRIAN
JAYA**

SUMATRA

INDONESIA

JAVA

Central Singapore

STATELY COLONIAL BUILDINGS mark the hub of Singapore, centred on the Padang. From here the main business district stretches to the south of the Singapore River and east to Suntec City. Bras Basah Road leads from the Padang northwards past the museums to Singapore's prime shopping area, Orchard Road.

0 metres   500

0 yards   500

Plaza Singapura
This long-established shopping centre, a family favourite in the 1970s, has radically updated its look to compete with the plethora of newer malls that now line Orchard Road (see pp84–9).

Chinatown Point
The blue glass façade of Chinatown Point, which houses various handicrafts shops, rises as a tall edifice amongst the low-lying pitched roofs of Chinese shophouses and temples in Chinatown (see pp60–69).

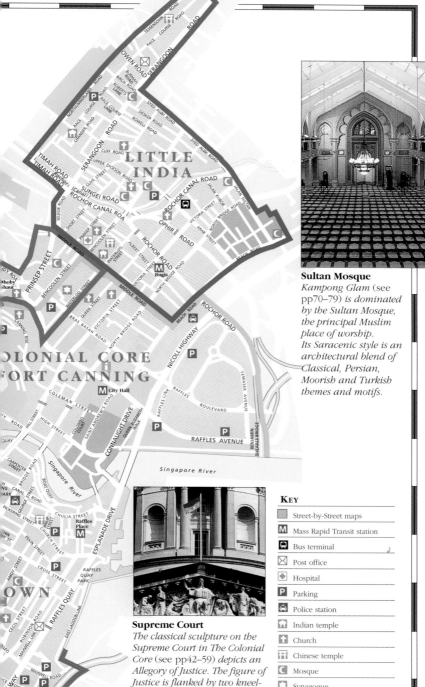

LITTLE INDIA

COLONIAL CORE FORT CANNING

Singapore River

Sultan Mosque
Kampong Glam (see
pp70–79) *is dominated
by the Sultan Mosque,
the principal Muslim
place of worship.
Its Saracenic style is an
architectural blend of
Classical, Persian,
Moorish and Turkish
themes and motifs.*

Supreme Court
*The classical sculpture on the
Supreme Court in The Colonial
Core (see pp42–59) depicts an
Allegory of Justice. The figure of
Justice is flanked by two kneel-
ing figures, one seeking pro-
tection and one giving thanks.*

KEY

	Street-by-Street maps
M	Mass Rapid Transit station
	Bus terminal
⊠	Post office
	Hospital
P	Parking
	Police station
	Indian temple
	Church
	Chinese temple
C	Mosque
	Synagogue
i	Information

THE HISTORY OF SINGAPORE

I N FEBRUARY *1819, Sir Thomas Stamford Raffles signed an agreement with a local Malay ruler that enabled the East India Company to establish a trading post at Singapore. The island was governed as a British colony until 1959. After a brief spell as part of Malaysia from 1963, Singapore became a republic in August 1965.*

Singapore's history goes much further back in time, though, and it reflects the power shifts in the Southeast Asian region over the last few centuries. The island, just 42 km (25 miles) long and 23 km (14 miles) wide, is at the tip of the Malay Peninsula, on the major sea-trading route between the South China Sea, the Indian Ocean and the Spice Islands. Long before the British arrived, Singapore had been a prime trading base successively controlled by seaborne kingdoms such as Sailendra (Sumatra), Majapahit (Java), Siam and Malacca.

That an important trading post existed at Singapore or on one of the nearby islands is implied by several cartographic references. In the 2nd century, the Greek, Ptolemy, located an "emporion" (a trading centre for

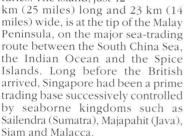

The Singapore Stone, covered in undeciphered script

goods from both the East and West) called "Sabana" near what is now Singapore. The Chinese identified an "island at the end of the peninsula", or "Pu-Luo-Chung", in the 3rd century and Marco Polo made reference to "Chiamassie", which could have been "Temasek", as Singapore was known in the 13th century. Pieces of porcelain and jewellery recovered by archaeologists help to give substance to these references.

JAVANESE CONTROL

From the 7th century, political and commercial power in Southeast Asia was exercised by kingdoms ruling from bases in Sumatra and Java in present-day Indonesia. The strength of these kingdoms lay in their domination of the sea routes between India and China and their control of

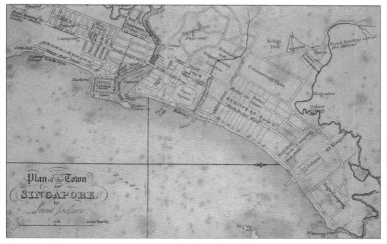

Lieutenant Philip Jackson's map illustrating Raffles' Town Plan of 1822–3

◁ *Canal, Singapore* by Barthélémy Lauvergne (c.1837)

trade in spices such as pepper, nutmeg, cinnamon and cloves, which were prized in China and Europe alike. In 1279, the Majapahit empire was established in Java. Its rule extended throughout Sumatra, Java and Borneo, while Thailand controlled the Malay Peninsula. A little later, the balance of control shifted, and Javanese court records of 1365 refer to a settlement at "Temasek" as a vassal state. By the end of that century, the Majapahit were losing their grip on power. About 1390, Iskandar, a ruler of Palembang, was driven from that place and found asylum in Temasek. Here he seized power, only later to be driven out, possibly by Thai attackers. Iskandar later founded the Malacca sultanate, which in due course extended its authority over Temasek.

The origin of the name, "Singapura", is shrouded in myth. The *Sejarah Melayu,* (Malay Annals) suggests that Temasek was re-named "Singapura" by Sang Nila Utama, a Sumatran king. Utama survived a shipwreck and chanced upon a strange creature on an island. Upon being told that it was a lion, the king named the island "Singapura", or "Lion City".

British residents in the 19th century, dressed in *sarong* **(traditional Malay garment)**

Early Malay dwellings on Pulau Brani

Painting of the Esplanade (1851) by J T Thomson

THE ADVENT OF THE WEST
By the early 1500s, European powers began to look for footholds in Asia to gain direct access to the lucrative spice trade. In 1511, the Portuguese captured Malacca. The Dutch took over in 1641, when they also gained control of the Indonesian islands, later known as the Dutch East Indies. The defeated Malacca sultanate continued to exert its power over Singapore from Johore.

By the beginning of the 19th century, the Dutch East India Company's dominance in the Indonesian Archipelago was being challenged by the British East India Company. The British had a base in Penang at the northern end of the Straits of Malacca. One of the most far-sighted and ambitious officers of the British East India Company was Thomas Stamford Raffles. Raffles had been Lieutenant Governor of the Dutch territories in Java in 1811–16, when they were held by the British following the defeat of the French and their allies, the Dutch, in the Napoleonic Wars.

In 1816, Java was returned to the Dutch, but Raffles had strong ambi-

TIMELINE

c.150 Ptolemy map places the 'emporion' Sabana near Singapore		*Old sailing chart identifying the island of Temasek*		**1365** Javanese records refer to Temasek
AD1	**500**	**1000**	**1200**	
	c.200 Chinese map shows Pu-Luo-Chong	**682–1082** Srivijayan empire in Sumatra		**1279** Majapahit empire in Java

Majapahit jewellery found in Fort Canning

tions to further extend British influence in the region. Early in 1819, he set out with a small exploratory force from Penang and sailed down the Straits of Malacca. At that time, a number of *orang laut* (sea people) were living at the mouth of the Singapore River under the control of the Johore royal family.

Sir Stamford Raffles, Singapore's founder

BRITISH RULE

Raffles landed on Singapore and on 6 February 1819, he signed a treaty with the Malay ruler. Raffles was in Singapore only briefly, but within the first week, he established that there was a safe anchorage and made the crucial decision to declare Singapore a free port, with no tax on trade.

Raffles left Colonel William Farquhar in charge, and encouraged settlers and trading ships to use the new port. Trade grew rapidly. On his second visit a month later, Raffles laid out firmer guidelines for urban development which determined how the older parts of Singapore look even today. Each community was self-governing and lived in segregated areas. These enclaves can still be found in Chinatown (Chinese) *(see pp60–69)*,

Serangoon Road (Indians) *(see pp80–81)* and Kampong Glam (Malays) *(see pp 72–5)*. Streets were planned following standard British East India Company policy – with "five foot ways" (covered sidewalks or passageways).

The Singapore River *(see pp38–9)* was quickly established as the most convenient trading centre, and warehouses or "godowns" were built to protect goods waiting transhipment. In 1822, Raffles returned to take charge of Singapore for six months, before finally leaving the East. He died in London.

News of Raffles' establishment of Singapore as a trading post took six months to arrive in London, and his claims were hotly disputed by the Dutch, but Singapore's early success in attracting trade impressed the British authorities. Eventually, in 1824, an agreement known as the Anglo-Dutch Treaty divided territory along the Straits of Malacca, the British East India Company holding Penang, Malacca and Singapore, which collectively became known as the Straits Settlements in 1826.

IMMIGRANT INFLUX

Singapore grew rapidly, attracting merchants, traders and labourers to the port. The population increased from under 1,000 people in 1819 to 16,000 in 1836 and 81,000 in 1869. The majority of immigrants were Chinese men who came as indentured labour, but there were also European merchants and administrators, many

Bumboats plying the Singapore River in the 19th century

c.1400 Malacca founded	*Col. William Farquhar, first British Resident appointed by Raffles*	**28 January 1819** Raffles lands in Singapore and signs treaty with Malay ruler
	1511 Portuguese capture Malacca	
1400	**1600**	**1800**
	1641 Dutch capture Malacca	**1811–1816** Raffles Governor of Java
1390 Iskandar, a prince from Palembang, flees to Temasek		*One-third cent copper coin issued by British East India Company, 1824*

Indian soldiers and the original Malay inhabitants. These ethnic groups formed the nucleus of Singapore's multicultural society *(see pp30–31)*. Singapore became an entrepôt to other parts of the world. As an outpost of the British East India Company, the administration was kept to a minimum, and lawlessness was common. Piracy was a continual threat, and trade fluctuated wildly. Despite the problems, many who came prospered and left their mark, such as Tan Chee Sang and Whampoa, both Chinese merchants, who operated from large godowns on the banks of the Singapore River.

EARLY DEVELOPMENT

The wooden buildings of Singapore's early days gave way to substantial stone and brick buildings. Private houses, massive godowns and places of worship were built. Terraces of shophouses filled Chinatown and the main trading area to the south of the river around Raffles Place. The older part of Parliament House *(see p46)*, built in 1826, the Armenian Church *(see p58)*, built in 1835, Caldwell House in Chijmes *(see p48)* and the Thian Hock Keng temple *(see pp68–9)*, built in 1841, are still standing. Unlike the mass overcrowding in Chinatown,

wealthy merchants lived on large estates on the surrounding hills. Orchard Road *(see pp84–9)*, Orange Grove Road and Nutmeg Road take their names from the locally grown crops. A Chinese Protectorate headed by William Pickering was set up by the colonial government in 1877 to deal with the Chinese secret societies and oversee the welfare of the Chinese population packed into Chinatown.

Tanjong Pagar docks in the 1890s

THE PORT OF SINGAPORE

The 1860s heralded a new era of prosperity for Singapore. In 1867, the Straits Settlements formally became a British Crown Colony. The opening of the Suez Canal in 1869 consolidated Singapore's position as a major port, securing a key position in the British empire. Singapore became the centre of government for the colony, with Harry St George Ord as the first governor. Impressive colonial buildings housed the administration, including the Supreme Court on the Padang *(see p44)* and Government House (now the Istana).

Postcard showing Colonial-style Singapore Cricket Club, with Victoria Memorial Hall behind it

TIMELINE

Sri Mariamman, Singapore's oldest Hindu temple

1822 Raffles' last visit to Singapore

1826 Straits Settlements formed comprising Penang, Malacca and Singapore

1843 Sri Mariamman Temple built

1824 Anglo-Dutch Treaty establishing British and Dutch territories in Southeast Asia

1832 Singapore becomes capital of the Straits Settlements

1841 Thian Hock Keng temple built

Thian Hock Keng temple, built by Chinese immigrants

1820	1830	1840	1850

Increasing use of steamships led to a dramatic rise in trade in the last quarter of the century, with tin, rubber, oil, copra and sugar displacing traditional trade in exotic wares and spices; English and Chinese interests were dominant. In 1902, an oil storage depot was built on Pulau Bukom, and Singapore became the oil supply centre for the Far East. Port facilities were expanded and a new dock built in Tanjong Pagar.

TURN OF THE CENTURY

Singapore was largely unaffected by World War I, although Germans were interned in the Teutonia Club, now the Goodwood Park Hotel *(see p89)*. The only major incident took place in 1915, in the form of a short-lived mutiny of Indian Sepoy troops guarding captured German prisoners.

Entrepreneur Tan Kah Kee

British commander Gen. A E Percival surrendering to Gen. Yamashita on 15 February 1942

The years following the war, despite periodic slumps in rubber, tin and oil, saw fortunes made: by Tan Kah Kee and Lee Kong Chian trading in rubber; and Aw Boon Haw, who built the Haw Par Gardens *(see p97)* and traded in Tiger Balm, a Chinese ointment.

Immigration of poverty-stricken young men from South China continued unchecked. In 1919, there were violent demonstrations by the Chinese people who were in support of Sun Yat Sen, and Chinese-medium schools became a focal point for Chinese nationalist sentiment. In the 1920s, as communist influences grew in China, Chinese immigration became restricted and Chinese schools closed down.

Dr Sun Yat Sen (centre), with other revolutionary leaders

WORLD WAR II

World War II was a turning point in Singapore's history, as it led to the defeat of the British in Singapore and Malaya, undermining notions of the protection provided by British colonial might. British military leaders, engrossed in the war in Europe, had left Singapore with inadequate defences and no hope of getting reinforcements. Singapore was swiftly overrun by the Japanese within weeks of their landing in Malaya *(see p92)*.

JAPANESE OCCUPATION

In 1942, Singapore became Syonan-To ("Light of the South"). European civilians and prisoners-of-war were interned in Changi Prison *(see p107)* and other camps. Many died building the railway in Burma. Civilians lived in fear of the *kempetai* (Japanese secret police) and in near-starvation conditions. Massacres of Chinese by the *kempetai* took place on several occasions.

1867 Straits Settlements become a British Crown Colony

Straits Settlements coins

1914–18 World War I

Causeway at Woodlands

1923 Causeway to Malaya opens

| 860 | 1900 | 1920 | 1940 |

1877 Chinese Protectorate set up

1902 Oil storage at Pulau Bukom

1939 Outbreak of World War II

1874 Botanic Gardens opens

1915 Sepoy Mutiny

1869 Suez Canal opens

Surrender ceremony in the City Hall chambers

RETURN OF THE BRITISH

After the bombing of Hiroshima and Nagasaki in 1945, the Japanese surrendered. The British returned, and Singapore returned to civil administration as a Crown Colony. But the people of Malaya and Singapore were no longer content to be subject to foreign rule. There was much pressure for independence, even though British rule continued until 1959. In fact a transfer of power to Singapore was planned, and politicians negotiated constitutional reform with the British. The Communist threat in Malaya in 1948 led to a declaration of a 12-year-long state of emergency, and the suppression of left-wing politics.

THE PEOPLE'S ACTION PARTY

Post-war Singapore was a corrupt, dirty and overcrowded city, with a thriving black market. Despite the emergence of political parties and a registered electorate in the 1950s, the slow pace of change resulted in continuing local dissatisfaction. The stage was set for the emergence of the People's Action Party (PAP), formed in 1955 and led by a Cambridge-educated lawyer, Lee Kuan Yew.

In 1955, elections were held to approve a new constitution, which was implemented in 1957. At the elections in 1959, the PAP won a majority of seats and has gone on to win every election since then.

INDEPENDENCE

In 1963, Singapore and Malaya formed an uneasy partnership independent of Britain. This ended on 9 August 1965 when Singapore was expelled from Malaysia and forced to become an independent republic. Although Singapore became a member of the Commonwealth of Nations and was admitted to the United Nations, its

First parliamentary session of Singapore as an independent republic in 1965

leadership was faced with the problem of how to ensure the tiny island's economic viability. Singapore was still a major trading port, with banking, shipping and warehousing facilities, but this was too narrow a base to build on for the future.

In 1967, the British announced the withdrawal of their military presence, which had provided 20 per cent of the national income. But Singapore found new opportunities in rapid industrialization in partnership with multinational firms. Within four years, the economy was booming.

TIMELINE

1940	1950	1960	1970
1942–45 Japanese Occupation	**1948–60** Communist threat, state of emergency	**1957** New constitution implemented	**1963** Merger with Malaysia	**1967** Founder member of ASEAN (Association of South East Asian Nations)
1945 Return of the British	**1955** First municipal elections	**1959** Singapore attains self-government	**1965** Singapore becomes an independent republic	**1971** British forces leave Singapore	**1972** Tanjong Pagar container terminal built

The departure from Singapore of the last British
military vessel on 31 October 1971

MODERN SINGAPORE

In less than 200 years, Singapore has
been transformed from a backwater
to one of the world's "economic mir-
acles". Credit must go to the republic's
former Prime Minister, Lee Kuan Yew.
Lee, who stepped down in 1990, has
led the modern transformation of an
island state without any natural
resources into the developed country
that Singapore is today.

A tough and uncorrupt leadership
shapes policies which focus on sta-
bility and productivity. National
defence, education, housing, infrastructure, civic order, industrialization
and modernization have been prior-
ities. Since independence, Singapore's
economy has grown by an average of
9 per cent each year. Literacy rates
have risen to more than 90 per cent,
and more than 85 per cent of the population own their homes.

The physical landscape of Singapore
has also changed radically. In the last
30 years it has increased its size by 10
per cent through land reclamation
along its southern shoreline. Many of
the older buildings have been torn
down, to be replaced by towering air-
conditioned offices and hotels, and
the majority of the population of
nearly 4 million lives in government-
built high-rise apartments.

Modern Housing Board flats, providing residence
for more than 80 per cent of Singaporeans

Today Singapore braces itself for the
new information technology-based
global economy and plays a part on
the world's financial and political stage
that is disproportionate to its tiny size
and precarious beginnings.

Computerized container facilities at the port

Control tower, Changi Airport

1990 Lee Kuan
Yew steps
down as Prime
Minister

Customs building at Tuas

1980	1990	2000

1981 Changi
Airport opens

1988 Mass Rapid
Transport System
(MRT) opens

1997 Second road
link to Malaysia
opens at Tuas

SINGAPORE THROUGH THE YEAR

Mooncake, a delicacy for the Mid-Autumn festival

As a result of Singapore's multicultural heritage, Singaporeans celebrate a mass of colourful festivals and holidays throughout the year. Many of the religious festivals are based on the lunar calendar, so their dates will vary from year to year. It is worth checking with the Singapore Tourism Board *(see p169)* for exact dates. While some festivities, such as Chinese New Year and Hari Raya Puasa, are celebrated all over the island with street decorations, stalls and entertainment, others are quieter family occasions, or are associated with just one temple. Visitors are welcomed into temples and mosques to enjoy the festivities and food as long as customs of dress are respected. Besides the traditional festivals, the Singapore Festival of Arts provides an exciting month of entertainment with world-class performances.

JANUARY TO MARCH

PONGGAL *(January or February)*. The Sri Srinivasa Perumal Temple *(see pp82–3)* in Serangoon Road should be visited early in the morning (6:30am) to see this Tamil harvest thanksgiving ceremony. To the accompaniment of prayers, music and conch shells, rice is cooked in new pots and allowed to boil over to symbolize prosperity. The rice is then offered to the gods with vegetables, sugar cane and spices, later to be eaten by the celebrants in a cleansing ritual.

Thaipusam *(January or February)*. In honour of the Hindu god Lord Subramaniam, devotees walk from the Sri Srinivasa Perumal Temple *(see pp82–3)* in Serangoon Road to the Sri Thandayuthapani Temple in Tank Road. They carry elaborate colourfully decorated metal frames called *kadhavis*, and their bodies are pierced with hooks. They are fulfilling vows to repay favours from the god, and are in a trance-like state, guided by their many supporters.

Hari Raya Puasa *(variable)*. Hari Raya Puasa is celebrated by the Muslim community to mark the end of Ramadan, the Muslim holy month. The area around the Sultan Mosque, Arab Street *(see pp72–8)*, as well as the Geylang and Joo Chiat areas *(see pp114–15)*, comes alive in the evenings with stalls selling special food and

Children paying their respects to their father on Hari Raya Puasa

sweet delicacies. Families pay their respects to elders and sit down for a traditional meal which includes *ketupat* (rice cakes). Children receive green packets of money from their parents. The rest of the day is spent visiting friends and relatives.

Chinese New Year *(January or February)*. A two-week festival (ending on *chap goh meh*, the full moon of the 15th day) to mark the end of the old year and welcome in the new. Chinatown is a blaze of lights and thronged with stalls and shoppers. Red, the colour of good luck, is everywhere. Debts are settled and families reunite, especially on Chinese New Year's eve. People greet each other with "Gong Si Fa Cai", which means "wishing you great prosperity", and children and

Celebrants in procession during Thaipusam

AVERAGE MONTHLY TEMPERATURE

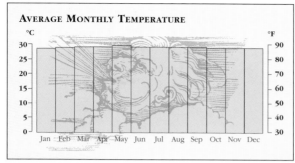

°C
30
25
20
15
10
5
0

Jan Feb Mar Apr May Jun Jul Aug Sep Oct Nov Dec

°F
90
80
70
60
50
40
30

Temperature Chart
Singapore's weather is hot and humid, with little variation throughout the year. The average daytime temperature is 31° C (88° F), dropping to around 24° C (75° F) at night.

Costumed actors adding colour to the annual Chingay Parade

unmarried people are given red packets containing money for luck. Businesses call in the lion dance troops to perform, accompanied by loud drums and waving flags. This is the only time when most shops and restaurants shut in Singapore. Businesses usually reopen after four or five days, but some stay shut for a week or more.
Chingay Parade *(January or February)*. During the Chinese New Year, this

international street parade travels down Orchard Road. Stiltwalkers and lion dancers rub shoulders with baton-twirling cheer-leaders and decorated floats in a Chinese version of *mardi gras*.
Qing Ming Festival *(March or April)*. Chinese families gather to visit the cemeteries and temples for prayers and to offer food and incense to their ancestors.
Hari Raya Haji *(variable)*. This festival is celebrated in honour of those who have made the pilgrimage to Mecca. Sheep are slaughtered as a sacrifice to Allah and the meat is distributed. Muslims go to the mosques to pray and visit their parents to pay their respects.

APRIL TO JUNE

VESAK DAY *(May or June)*. Buddhists celebrate the life of Buddha in temples islandwide. Monks lead chanting, and devotees make

Vesak Day, a Buddhist festival

offerings and pray. Caged birds are set free to symbolize the freeing of souls. In the evening, candlelit processions set out from the temples. Good places to see the celebrations include the Buddhist Lodge at River Valley Road, the Thai Buddhist Temple at Jalan Bukit Merah and Lian Shan Shuang Temple at Jalan Toa Payoh.
Singapore Festival of Arts *(June)*. A varied mix of dance, drama, music and art can be seen. Activities range from grand opera at one end of the scale down to informal street performances.
Dragon Boat Festival and Boat Race *(June)*. The festival commemorates the death of a 4th-century Chinese poet, Qu Yuan.

Spanish dancers at the Arts Festival

Lion Dance, a performance to mark an auspicious Chinese New Year

A magnificent dragon lantern for the Mid-Autumn Festival at the Chinese Garden

Qu Yuan drowned himself in protest against political corruption. Legend says that people threw rice dumplings into the river to stop the fishes eating his body. Rice dumplings in bamboo leaves are on sale at many stalls.

The highlight is the dragon boat competition. Marina Bay comes alive with the beating of drums as international teams compete in special long boats with their dragon-shaped prows.

JULY TO SEPTEMBER

GREAT SINGAPORE SALE *(June or July)*. Merchants everywhere hold attractive sales during this period – the discounts can be extremely enticing, and even draw shoppers from around the region *(see p143).*

National Day *(9 August).* A yearly celebration of Singapore's independence in 1965. It is marked by an evening of spectacular entertainment by mass bands and performers either at the Padang or at the National Stadium. The formality of the military parade contrasts with the cultural performances, while the aerial flypast remains one of the favourite highlights. A laser and fireworks display

Offerings, Hungry Ghost Festival

serves as a magnificent climax to the celebrations.

Hungry Ghosts Festival *(August or September).* The Chinese believe that the seventh lunar month is not auspicious as this is the time when spirits of the dead come back to earth. People offer incense, food and prayers in order to please them, so that they will not bring bad luck to the living. Giant incense sticks are burned. At night, the Chinese street opera troupes *(wayang)* stage colourful and dramatic performances of favourite Chinese legends *(see p153).*

Mid-Autumn Festival *(August or September).* The full moon on the 15th day of the 8th month in the Chinese calendar is celebrated with mooncakes and lanterns. The festival commemorates a 14th-century Chinese patriot who is said to have hidden notes to his companions in mooncakes when he tried to overthrow the Yuan Dynasty.

Mooncakes are sold in hotels and from stalls in Chinatown. Traditionally these pastries contain sweet fillings made of pounded

Fireworks over the Padang during the National Day celebration

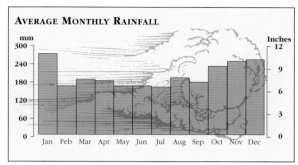

AVERAGE MONTHLY RAINFALL

Rainfall Chart
*Singapore receives
over 2,400 mm (97
inches) of total
rainfall a year. As a
result, humidity
averages 84 per cent.
The northeast
monsoon brings
heavier rainfall
during the months of
October to January.*

**Offerings at the family altar
during Deepavali**

lotus seeds, red beans and
duck eggs, though they now
come in many forms.

The Chinese Garden holds
a lantern competition. Children
carry lanterns – some
with candles, some battery-
operated – under the
evening sky.

OCTOBER TO DECEMBER

DEEPAVALI *(October or
November).* Little India
comes alive with decorations
and lights as Indians celebrate
their Deepavali, and
Hindus mark Lord Krishna's
victory over Narakasura, a
triumph of good over evil,
and light over darkness. The
precise date is established
according to the Indian
Almanacs. Families place oil
lamps outside their homes to
welcome visitors, and family
shrines are decked with
flowers and offerings.
Thimithi Festival *(October
or November).* A procession

travels from the Sri Srinivasa
Perumal Temple in Serangoon
Road *(see pp82–3)* to
the Sri Mariamman Temple
in South Bridge Road.
Crowds gather to watch
devotees walk barefoot
across a bed of glowing
coals that is 3 m (10 ft) long.
They emerge unscathed,
following many days of rites
and preparation.
**Festival of the Nine
Emperor Gods** *(October or
November).* Taoists believe
that the Nine Emperor Gods
will bring good luck and
cure illness during the
festival at Kiu Ong Yiah
Temple in Upper Serangoon
Road. After prayers, feasts
and Chinese opera performances,
images of the gods
are taken in procession in
decorated sedan chairs, led
by temple mediums with
swords and whips. During
this festival, many worshippers
also make a pilgrimage
to the Tua Pek Kong Temple
on Kusu Island to make their
wishes to the god of prosperity
(see p103).
Christmas *(25 Dec).* From
November onwards, Orchard

**A fairyland of Christmas lights
on Orchard Road**

Road becomes a fairyland as
shopping centres vie to be
the best decorated, making a
dazzling backdrop for
Christmas shoppers and
holiday makers. The themed
displays are remarkable for
their creative ingenuity.
Orchard Road is also one of
several rotating venues for
the annual New Year's Eve
street party.

**Walking over hot embers during
the Thimithi Festival**

PUBLIC HOLIDAYS

Local festivals follow the
lunar calendar, and the
dates are variable.

New Year's Day (1 Jan)
Hari Raya Puasa
(variable)
Chinese New Year (Jan
or Feb)
Hari Raya Haji (variable)
Good Friday (Mar or Apr)
Labour Day (1 May)
Vesak Day (May or
June)
National Day (9 Aug)
Deepavali (Oct or Nov)
Christmas Day (25 Dec)

SINGAPORE AT A GLANCE

SINGAPORE IS A COMPACT CITY with one of the world's most modern infrastructures. It is easy to get to shops, parks, hotels and tourist attractions with an ez-link card (which can also be used on buses) in one hand and a street map in the other. This section introduces Singapore's best places of interest, including museums and family attractions, parks and gardens; the Singapore River, which runs through the commercial hub of the city, is featured. There is a description of the strong multicultural nature of Singapore life and the religions practised. Finally there is an overview of the performing arts to be enjoyed in this very cosmopolitan Asian city.

SINGAPORE'S TOP TEN ATTRACTIONS

Raffles Hotel
See pp50–51

Orchard Road
See pp84–9

Chinatown
See pp60–69

Little India
See pp80–83

Singapore Botanic Gardens
See pp98–9

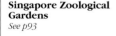

Singapore Zoological Gardens
See p93

Sentosa
See pp104–105

Chijmes
See p48

Boat Quay
See p67

Fort Canning Park
See pp54–5

◁ The Gothic-style former chapel at Chijmes, contrasting with metal-clad Raffles City

Singapore's Best: Museums and Family Attractions

SINGAPORE IS, for its size, rich in museums and a variety of other places for the family to visit. The museums focus on history, cultural traditions, artistic forms brought by the immigrants that made up Singapore's early population, and Asian art in general. Permanent exhibits include Indonesian batik, Chinese ceramics and calligraphy, Malay textiles and Peranakan jewellery. Other attractions include a very impressive zoo and one of Asia's largest bird parks. The Science Centre is rated one of the top ten of its kind in the world. A total contrast is Haw Par Villa, a theme park based on macabre Chinese mythology.

Singapore Zoological Gardens/Night Safari
Over 1,200 animals are kept in natural, open habitats (see p93).

Jurong Bird Park
Huge enclosures house over 8,000 birds of 600 species, amongst which are flamingoes, penguins and hornbills (see pp94–5).

Singapore Science Centre
The centre has over 500 interactive exhibits, ranging from aviation to magnetism, robotics, space travel and natural history (see p96). It also features an Omnitheatre with a 3-D screen.

Haw Par Villa
This Chinese mythological theme park was created by the Aw family (see p97). The "Ten Courts of Hell" are a favourite.

Lim Chu Kang

Choa Chu Kang

Bukit Panjang
New Town

Bukit Batok
New Town

Jurong West
New Town

Jurong East
New Town

Tuas

Jurong

Selat Jurong

Queens
New T

Woo
New

Selat Pandan

Singapore History Museum
The museum's exhibits include dioramas of Singapore's history, a re-creation of a Peranakan house (see p52), rare, old natural history drawings and a secret society lodge.

Asian Civilisations Museum
A well-presented collection contains Chinese, Malay, Islamic and Indian artifacts (see p52), such as this sculpture dating from the Han dynasty (202 BC–AD 220).

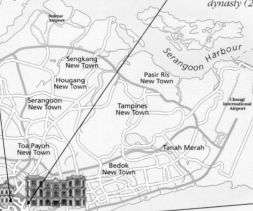

Singapore Art Museum
Pan Shou's Shi ("lion") is an example of Asian art (see pp48–9).

Images of Singapore
Local history, customs, traditions and festivals are showcased through life-like tableaux and special effects (see p105).

The Battle Box
History unfolds as the events leading to the decision to surrender to the Japanese on 15 February 1942 are re-created (see p92). The site is a former British command centre.

Multicultural Singapore

Eurasian Singaporeans

SINGAPORE'S STATUS as a successful melting pot for diverse races is remarkable in that it was achieved within a short time, since the island became a republic in 1965. The government has, to a large extent, succeeded in ensuring harmony between the races by means of legislation, good public housing and education schemes, and compulsory military enlistment for males aged 18. The locals, especially among the younger population, see themselves first as Singaporeans and only secondly as Chinese, Malays, Indians or Eurasians.

Tossing *yu sheng* (raw fish salad), a Chinese New Year ritual

THE CHINESE

THE CHINESE WERE divided in earlier generations by their dialect groups which indicated the province or district in China from which they had come. Most Singapore Chinese today are Hokkiens (42 per cent) and their ancestors came from Fujian province. The other main dialect groups are the Teochews (23 per cent) who were from Guangdong, the Cantonese (17 per cent) from Guangzhou, Hakkas (7 per cent) from central China and the Hainanese (6 per cent) from Hainan Island.

Each dialect group had its own festivities, prayed to its favourite deities in Buddhist, Taoist or Confucianist temples, and enjoyed its own music, literature, operas and cuisine. The Teochews and Cantonese were famous for their street operas, and some opera troupes still perform today. In cuisine, the Hainanese are still noted for their chicken rice; the Hokkiens for their noodle dishes and the Teochews for their rice porridge *(see pp128–9)*.

A more persistent division within the Chinese community is between the Chinese-educated and the English-educated. The latter tend to be regarded as more liberal and Westernized in their outlook while the more conservative Chinese-educated sometimes see themselves as bastions of the preservation of Chinese culture. The government still tries, for example through the "Speak Mandarin" campaign, to balance the need for the Chinese to maintain their Chinese heritage so as to preserve their Asian identity with the need to be proficient in English in order to be able to compete internationally.

THE MALAYS

THE TERM "SINGAPORE Malays" usually refers to Malays who are descended from migrants from the Malay States (mainly Johore and Malacca) and the former Dutch East Indies (present-day Indonesia). The latter included the Bugis from the Celebes, the Riau Malays, the Javanese and the Minangkabau (from Sumatra). The descendants of Arab migrants are sometimes called "Singapore Malays"; they share the same religion, Islam.

Apart from the Kampong Glam enclave to which Raffles assigned the early Muslim migrant community, the Malays eventually gravitated to several *kampung* (villages) in the outlying areas. The areas popular with the Malays were Geylang Serai, Ubi, Eunos, Bedok, Changi and Telok Blangah.

With the introduction in the 1970s of widespread home ownership through government-built housing, the Malay enclaves were dismantled. During the Hari Raya festival *(see p25)*, the apartments which are occupied by Malays can easily be recognized by the decorative lights that adorn their windows. Compared to other groups, the Malays tend to be more traditional, especially in their

Students at a National Day celebration

dress during festivities. Many Malay women wear the *tudung* (Islamic head scarf).

The Malay origins of the island-state are enshrined in the constitution: Malay is the national language and one of the official languages (the others being English, Mandarin and Tamil). The national anthem *(Majulah Singapura)* is in Malay.

An Indian vendor on Serangoon Road

THE INDIANS

THE SINGAPORE INDIANS are not a homogeneous racial group and can be differentiated in terms of languages and religions. About 60 per cent of the Singapore Indians are Tamil-speaking and come from either Tamil Nadu or the Tamil enclave in northern Sri Lanka. Other languages that are spoken by the Indian community include Malayalee (8 per cent), Punjabi, Bengali and Telugu. The government recognizes Tamil as the official language of the Indian community.

Hindu festivals such as Deepavali, Thimithi *(see p25)* and Thaipusam *(see p22)* and the anniversaries of the various deities in the Hindu pantheon are the best occasions to catch a glimpse of traditional Indian culture, and Little India is the place to be on such occasions.

THE EURASIANS

FOR MANY YEARS, the Eurasians (Singaporeans of mixed Asian and European parentage) have struggled to find their rightful place in a society that was dominated by more homogeneous races such as the Chinese, Malays and Indians. Until the 1960s, migration to the West and especially to Australia seemed to be the best option for a number of Eurasians.

Over the course of the 1990s, however, through the efforts of the Eurasian Association and with the government's assistance, the Eurasian community seemed to find their feet and are now firmly entrenched as one of the four main racial categories in Singapore.

Being mainly Christian and Westernized, Eurasians celebrate Western festivals such as Christmas and Easter, but enliven these festivals with their Asian heritage. Eurasian food, for example, is a blend of Western roasts and meat pies with Indian curries such as the Goan "devil curry" and Chinese dishes such as *chap chye* (a vegetable dish). Some older Eurasians speak a local Portuguese dialect, Kristang.

NEW MIGRANTS

SINGAPORE'S transformation from a migrant society to nationhood is entering yet another stage. Concerned that its quite small population might be disadvantaged in competition with the rest of the world in the IT-based global economy, the government has embarked on an active campaign to attract foreign talent from both East and West. Some of the visible signs of the influx of these new migrants are Chinese who speak with Beijing, Hongkong, Taipei or Indonesian accents, and *ang mohs* ("Caucasians") who now live, in increasing numbers, in the heartlands of Singapore's housing estates.

Young Muslims

THE PERANAKANS

Chinese merchants who settled in Malacca during the 18th century and married Malay women are called Peranakans. The word "Peranakan" means "half-caste" in Malay. Male Peranakans are called *babas* and female Peranakans are called *nonyas*. Malacca gradually lost its pre-eminent position as a port to Singapore, and many Peranakan (also called Straits Chinese) families came to Singapore as their businesses demanded it. Today, less than 1 per cent of Singapore's population is Peranakan, but Peranakan culture has had a great influence on the island state.

Peranakans were typically wealthy traders who considered themselves a cut above later Chinese immigrants to Singapore, who were usually labourers. Peranakans had enough wealth to imitate both Chinese and European manners and dress, and were famous for their taste for ornate furniture, fabrics and architecture.

Peranakans straddle Chinese and Malay cultures. Chinese names and religion sit alongside the observance of Malay customs. Peranakan cuisine is a combination of traditional Chinese and Malay recipes and the Peranakan language is a Malay dialect sprinkled with words from the Chinese Hokkien dialect. Peranakan art is a distinctive mixture of Chinese, Malay and (from the early 20th century onwards), European and American influences.

Kebaya-clad *nonya* (female Peranakan)

Religion

A hexagonal mirror to ward off evil

For many Singaporeans, the faiths they profess are usually handed down from their migrant forefathers. The Chinese are mainly Buddhists or Taoists, or they practise a curious mix of the two faiths with Confucianism sometimes added to the alchemy. Almost all Singapore Malays are Muslims. Most Indians are Hindus although some Indians are Muslims, and Punjabis are mainly Sikhs. As in other Asian societies, Christianity is a relative newcomer and made its appearance with the arrival of the European colonists. Most Eurasians are Christians.

Taoist monks performing rites during Hungry Ghosts month

Religion is vibrant in the city-state. Refurbished or new churches, temples and mosques are a common sight. Religious services are usually well-attended. Newer religions or quasi-religious movements such as the Sai Baba movement from India and charismatic Christian groups have found adherents among Singaporeans.

Freedom of worship is guaranteed in the constitution. Mindful of the outbreaks of religious strife in the neighbouring countries, the government takes great pains to ensure that religious harmony exists among the different faiths.

ISLAM

Like most Muslims in Southeast Asia, Singapore's Muslims are mainly of the Sunni sect. Male Muslim devotees, donning white skull caps, can be seen answering the daily call to prayer at mosques throughout the

island, especially at noon on Fridays and during the Muslim fasting month of Ramadan *(see p25)*. During Ramadan, a common sight is the special prayers-cum-religious gatherings that are held in community halls or even on the ground floor of apartment blocks. The two major Muslim festivals are Hari Raya Puasa, which marks the end of the fasting month, and Hari Raya Haji, which commemorates the annual pilgrimage *(haj)* to Mecca that most Muslims aspire to embark on at least once in their lifetime.

The more traditional Muslims send their children to *madrasah* (religious schools) where the curriculum's emphasis is on Islamic studies and the Arabic language. Among the prominent Islamic schools are the *madrasah* next to the oldest Muslim cemetery in Singapore at Victoria Street, and the Alsagoff Arabic School *(see p72)*. The Sultan Mosque is Singapore's most prominent mosque. It was named after Singapore's first sultan, Hussein *(see pp74–5)*.

CHINESE RELIGIONS

Many adherents of Chinese religions practise a colourful mix of Taoism and Buddhism combined with Chinese folklore, *feng shui* (geomancy) and Confucianism, which, strictly speaking, was never intended to be a religion by its founder, the Chinese philosopher, Confucius. In recent years,

attempts have been made to downplay the superstitious and ritualistic elements in the traditional Chinese religions so as to make them more appealing and relevant to the better-educated, younger Chinese, many of whom are turning to Christianity.

There are many rituals in traditional Chinese religions, and the visitor will see many of them still being observed today. They include the burning of joss sticks, joss paper and hell bank notes as offerings, the use of gongs and cymbals as musical accompaniment; and the offering of meats (pork and poultry), sweet cakes, drinks and flowers to deities. High points in the calendars of these Oriental religions are the anniversaries of the many deities who range from the sky god and sea goddess to the humble kitchen god.

Joss stick

Temples of local importance include the oldest in Singapore, the Thian Hock Keng temple at Telok Ayer Street *(see pp68–9)*, dedicated to the goddess of the sea and of special significance to early migrants from Fukien; the Sin Chor Kung Temple which was built by the Teochews from southern China; and the Wak Hai Cheng Bio Temple at Phillip Street which was built by migrants from

Friday prayers at Sultan Mosque

Guangzhou. On Kusu Island, to the south of Singapore, is a shrine to the Tua Pek Kong deity which attracts throngs of devotees during the deity's anniversary *(see p103)*. Devotees visit the shrine to request good health and prosperity and to ask for obedient children.

The Kong Meng San Phor Kark See Temple at Bright Hill Drive is one of the largest Buddhist temple complexes in Southeast Asia, with a crematorium and a columbarium which can hold up to 300,000 urns. Other temples

A reclining Buddha at a Buddhist temple

of note are the 100-year-old Siong Lim San Si Temple at Jalan Toa Payoh, which houses a marble Siamese Buddha and is the largest Buddhist temple on the island, and the Sakya Muni Buddha Gaya or Temple of 1,000 Lights *(see pp80–81)*.

HINDUISM

Hindu temples, like the temples of the traditional Chinese religions, are rich in architecture, decorative art, music and ceremony. Drums, horns and bells, the burning of fragrant incense, the use of blessed fire, and the offering of fruits, grain and sweets to deities are a part of most Hindu temple rituals.

The major Hindu festivals are Deepavali (the festival of lights) *(see p25)*, Thaipusam (a festival of atonement) *(see pp22, 82)* and the various anniversaries of the main Hindu deities. Deepavali is a visual feast of decoration.

Two Hindu temples in the Chinatown area worth visiting are Singapore's oldest Hindu temple, the Sri Mariamman Temple at South Bridge Road *(see p64)*, which is dedicated to the Hindu divine trinity, Brahma, Vishnu, Shiva, and to the goddess, Mariamman, and the Vinayakar Temple.

CHRISTIANITY

Within the city limits, churches belonging to almost all the major Christian denominations can be found. Well worth a visit is the Anglican St Andrew's Cathedral at Coleman Street *(see p46)*, built by Indian convict labour during colonial times. Other notable churches worth a look are the Roman Catholic Cathedral of the Good Shepherd *(see p49)*, not far from Raffles Hotel; St Joseph's Church, known for its unique Iberian architecture; and also the Armenian Church *(see p58)*, which is Singapore's oldest church and full of charm.

Christianity is the fastest-growing religion here. Many converts are young, English-educated Chinese Singaporeans who usually first encounter Christianity through evangelical gospel groups in schools. In many Chinese families, parents adhere to Chinese religions while their children take on

The Neo-Classical façade of the Armenian Church

the Christian faith. It is a testament to Singapore's high level of religious tolerance that this does not seem to cause any particular tension.

SIKHISM

Sikhs, as the followers of Guru Nanak are known, stand at a minority of 15,000. The economic achievements of Singapore's Sikh community, many of whose members traditionally served in the civil service or have a history of success in business, are attested to by the textile shops in the High Street area. Male sikhs sport turbans and do not shave their hair, as a sign of their faith. They have "Singh" ("lion") in their names. Their main place of worship is the Central Sikh Temple, at the junction of Serangoon and Towner Roads.

Hindu worshippers at Sri Veeramakaliamman temple *(see p81)*

Performing Arts

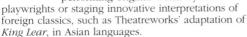

U NTIL RECENTLY, the performing arts in Singapore ran along ethnic lines: Chinese orchestras played to Chinese Singaporeans in community centres and Indian dance groups played to an Indian audience at religious festivals and within communities. Large, well-equipped theatres drew in mostly Western touring musicals, ballets, pop concerts and orchestras. However, a wonderful process of cross-fertilization has begun with Singaporean theatre companies performing original works by local playwrights or staging innovative interpretations of foreign classics, such as Theatreworks' adaptation of *King Lear*, in Asian languages.

A street opera actress

English-language Theatre
The best local theatre is an innovative East/West fusion. Plays such as Theatreworks' Lao Jiu *(above) employ Asian puppetry and masks.*

Western Opera
Western touring companies appear regularly here. Singapore Lyric Opera, Singapore's only professional opera company, presents Western classics such as Carmen *and* Die Fledermaus.

The "water-sleeves", long, white extensions of the sleeves, are typical of the costumes in Chinese opera.

CHINESE OPERA

Performances of Chinese opera take place on the streets of Singapore throughout the year. The Chinese Opera Institute performs pieces from various regions, such as this Huang Mei opera, *The Female Consort*.

Chinese-language Theatre
Theatre performed in Chinese tends to focus on issues particular to the Chinese community. Red Hawk *(above) is about the impact of secret societies on Singapore in the 1950s. Mandarin is the usual medium, with doses of dialect.*

Classical Music
The Singapore Symphony Orchestra performs a wide repertoire of symphonies, recitals and chamber music, holds an annual piano festival and features foreign performers of international standing.

Chinese Orchestral Music

A high standard in Chinese orchestral music is attained by amateur community groups and the professional Singapore Chinese Orchestra (above), which comprises players from around the region and often hosts guest soloists.

Peranakan Theatre

The complex history of the Straits Chinese is brought to life through Peranakan plays that are notable for their wit and humour.

Headgear and make-up emphasize the identity and nature of each character.

The elaborate costume of this actor is worn during a performance of Chinese opera. In the past, intricate embroidery on an official's robe was an indication of his rank and stature.

Chinese Dance

Chinese dance theatre is a good place to encounter integrated choral and instrumental performance. Dance Ensemble Singapore, a semi-professional company, is one of Singapore's finest troupes.

Indian Classical Music

Various local Indian groups teach and perform Indian classical music and instruments such as the sitar (above).

Modern Dance

Singapore Dance Theatre, here performing Giselle, is one of the best companies in the region.

Singapore's Best: Parks and Gardens

Singapore's green areas are concentrated in the central and northern parts of the island. Although urban development is continually chipping away at the natural landscape, 5 per cent of the total land area has been set aside for nature conservation. Over 2,000 species of plants and some 300 species of birds can be found on the island. Justifiably proud of its standing as a "Garden City", Singapore offers the visitor a profusion of trees and flowers. There are many extensive green spaces to visit and enjoy, from beautifully manicured gardens and city parks to expanses of primary and secondary tropical forest, wetland parks and mangrove swamps.

Sungei Buloh Wetland Reserve
Mangroves and exposed mud beds draw over 120 bird species to this wetland park (see p92).

Bukit Timah Nature Reserve
Well-marked trails guide visitors through over 50 ha (125 acres) of primary tropical rainforest (see p94). In this reserve is Bukit Timah Hill, the highest in Singapore.

Woodlands
New Town

Lim Chu Kang

Choa Chu Kang

Bukit Panjang
New Town

Bukit Batok
New Town

Jurong West
New Town

Jurong East
New Town

Tuas

Jurong

Selat Jurong

Queenst
New To

Selat Pandan

Chinese and Japanese Gardens
Pagodas mark the Chinese Garden which lies on an island in Jurong Lake. Their flamboyance contrasts with the minimalism of the nearby Japanese Garden (see p96).

Singapore Botanic Gardens
This oasis has over half a million species of plants and trees. The orchid garden is spectacular (see pp98–9).

MacRitchie Reservoir

The wooded trails around this reservoir provide beautiful views and a chance to see turtles and carp. The park is the habitat of squirrels, monkeys, monitor lizards and birds (see p93).

Pasir Ris Park

Besides a beach and mangrove swamps, the park offers fishing and seafood in a relaxed atmosphere.

Fort Canning Park

Two 19th-century Gothic gates stand in this park which also contains Singapore's earliest Christian cemetery (see pp54–5).

0 kilometres 4

0 miles 4

Mount Faber

Cable cars link Mount Faber to Sentosa. The hill provides a panoramic view of the harbour and southern islands (see p102).

St John's Island

One of the islands southeast of Sentosa, St John's was formerly a quarantine station. There are safe swimming lagoons on the island, and it is a great place for walking and picnicking (see p106).

The Singapore River

**Botero's *Bird*
sculpture**

THE SINGAPORE River was Singapore's earliest trading hub. Long before Stamford Raffles landed on its northern side and signed the treaty with the local Malay ruler, there was a Malay settlement on its banks. Chinese traders following in Raffles' wake built warehouses on the south bank, while the British lined the northern bank with stately colonial buildings.

UOB Plaza's entrance lobby is enlivened with sculptures by Dali and Botero.

Cavenagh Bridge
Signs restricting carriages still stand at Singapore's only suspension bridge.

The Fullerton Hotel's colonial columns dominate the entrance to the river. It replaced Fort Fullerton in 1925.

Asian Civilisations Museum II *(see p47)*

Merlion
This mythical half-fish, half-lion symbol of Singapore guards the river as it opens into Marina Bay.

Raffles' Landing Site
A plaque below a polymarble statue of Raffles marks his original disembarkation.

Anderson Bridge
This was built in 1910 to relieve congestion on Cavenagh Bridge.

Parliament Complex
Opened in 1999, the new Parliament House complements the style of the original parliament building (see p46), dating to 1826, which stands along the river.

Boat Quay
Bars and restaurants bring new life to the restored row of old trading houses lining the southern bank of the river (see p67).

Elgin Bridge
The present bridge was built in 1929 on the site of the first bridge across the river, and named after Lord Elgin, then governor general of India.

Clarke Quay
Refurbished warehouses form a colourful backdrop to this lively shopping and eating venue (see p59).

Merchant Court Hotel

Riverwalk Galleria
is a shopping complex. A sculpture of a boy and his cat sits on the river's edge.

Riverside Point
is a shopping mall that leads to Merchant Square and Central Mall.

River taxi kiosk

Read Bridge

To Robertson Quay

Hill Street Building
(see p58)

0 metres   100
0 yards   100

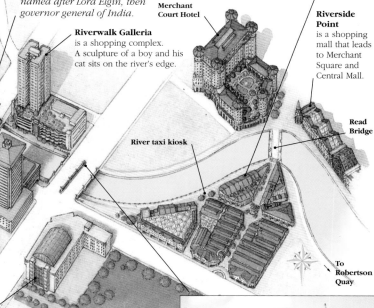

Coleman Bridge
This bridge was named after George D Coleman, an architect who designed many of Singapore's earliest buildings.

SINGAPORE
AREA BY AREA

THE COLONIAL CORE AND
FORT CANNING 42-59
CHINATOWN AND THE FINANCIAL
DISTRICT 60-69
KAMPONG GLAM AND LITTLE INDIA 70-83
ORCHARD ROAD 84-89
FURTHER AFIELD 90-107

THE COLONIAL CORE AND FORT CANNING

THE COLONIAL CORE lies north of the Singapore River. The general layout of the city centre follows Sir Stamford Raffles' plan of 1822 (*see p17*) which specified that the commercial district was to be south of the river with the administrative offices on the north (*see pp38–9*). Today, south of the river lies the Central Business District. For a time, the north bank was the hub of the city's administration. Over the

Tan Kim Seng fountain

years, government offices slowly moved away, leaving behind landmarks of the British era such the Supreme Court. The Padang (*see pp44–5*) and Fort Canning Park (*see pp54–5*) are the focal points of the Colonial Core and have witnessed major events in Singapore's history, from Raffles' landing in 1819 to events of the Second World War, and the birth of modern Singapore in 1959 (*see pp16–20*).

SIGHTS AT A GLANCE

Historic Streets, Buildings and Monuments
Chijmes ❾
Clarke Quay ⓴
Esplanade Park ㉓
Hill Street ⓳
Old Parliament House ❷
Queen Elizabeth Walk ❻
Raffles Hotel pp50–51 ❿
Raffles' Landing Site ❸
Victoria Theatre &
    Concert Hall ❺
War Memorial Park ❼

Churches and Temples
Armenian Church ⓲
Cathedral of the Good
    Shepherd ⓬
Chettiar Temple ⓱

St Andrew's Cathedral ❶

Museums and Galleries
Asian Civilisations Museum I ⓮
Asian Civilisations Museum II ❹
Singapore Art Museum ⓫
Singapore History Museum ⓭
Singapore Philatelic Museum ⓯

Parks and Gardens
Fort Canning
    Park pp54–5 ⓰

Shopping
Marina Square ㉒
Raffles City ❽
Suntec City ㉑

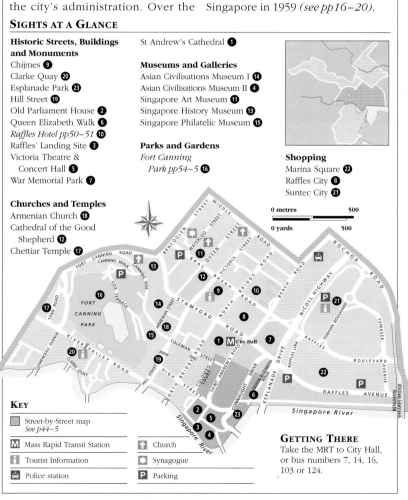

KEY

▨	Street-by-Street map See p44–5
Ⓜ	Mass Rapid Transit Station
ℹ	Tourist Information
🚓	Police station
✝	Church
✡	Synagogue
P	Parking

GETTING THERE
Take the MRT to City Hall, or bus numbers 7, 14, 16, 103 or 124.

◁ **The façade of the Supreme Court, built in 1937–9, and notable for its Corinthian and Ionic columns**

Street by Street: Around the Padang

T HE PADANG is a rectangular playing field where sporting activities from cricket and hockey to soccer and rugby still take place on a weekly basis. The Padang is flanked on most sides by colonial structures such as the City Hall, the Supreme Court, Parliament House and the Singapore Cricket Club. Esplanade Park, on the eastern side of the Padang, once afforded a pleasant walk along the seafront with an excellent view of tall-masted ships attended by thousands of bumboats. Esplanade Park, which sits on reclaimed land, has been developed into a performing arts centre called Esplanade – Theatres on the Bay.

★ Supreme Court
The Supreme Court was the last Classical building to be erected in Singapore.

HIGH STREET

PARLIAMENT LANE

★ Victoria Theatre and Concert Hall
Built in 1862, the Victoria Theatre was originally the Town Hall. The Victoria Memorial Hall was added in 1905 to commemorate the death of Queen Victoria. Its name was later changed to the Victoria Concert Hall **5**

Second Wing of Asian Civilisations Museum

Raffles' Landing Site

To Boat Quay

Old Parliament House
Parliament House (built 1826–7) was originally commissioned as a private residence for a Scottish merchant, John Argyle Maxwell **2**

STAR SIGHTS

★ Victoria Theatre and Concert Hall

★ Supreme Court

★ City Hall

The pyramid in front of Empress Place houses a time capsule which will be opened in 2015 to celebrate Singapore's Silver Jubilee.

★ City Hall
The Neo-Classical façade of City Hall, built in 1929, features a row of 18 Corinthian columns.

To St Andrew's Cathedral & Raffles City

KEY

– – – Suggested Route

| 0 metres | 100 |
| 0 yards | 100 |

LOCATOR MAP
See Street Finder Map 3

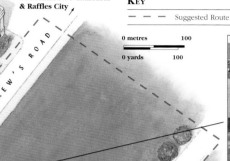

ANDREW'S ROAD

CONNAUGHT DRIVE

QUEEN ELIZABETH WALK

FULLERTON ROAD

To Merlion Park

Memorial Obelisk

To Raffles Place   **Cavenagh Bridge**

The Padang has hosted cricket since the 1830s. Today, sporting events such as the Rugby Sevens happen here.

Lim Bo Seng Memorial is a tribute to the Chinese war hero Lim Bo Seng, who worked with British covert forces until he was captured and tortured to death by the Japanese in 1944.

Singapore Cricket Club (present structure built about 1884) is a distinctive, squat building with dark green bamboo shutters. This members-only club was built for the expatriate community.

Spire of St Andrew's Cathedral

St Andrew's Cathedral ❶

Coleman Street. **Map** 5 E2
📞 *6337 6104.* Ⓜ *City Hall.* 🚌 *7, 32, 51, 81, 124, 145, 197, 603, 851.* 🔲 *daily.* ⛪ *7am, 8am, 11am, 2pm, 5pm, 7:30pm Sun.* 🔲♿🔲🔲
🆆 *www.livingstreams.org.sg*

THE CATHEDRAL of today is the second ecclesiastical building to be erected on the site. The first, built between 1835 and 1837, was designed in the Neo-Classical style by G D Coleman. However, the church was demolished in 1852 following two lightning strikes. The present-day cathedral was begun by Lt-Col Ronald Macpherson in 1856 and completed in 1861, using convict labour sent from India by the British colonial rulers.

Although an Anglican church, St Andrew's was named after the patron saint of Scotland, thanks to Scottish merchants who contributed funds to build the cathedral.

St Andrew's is a good example of English Gothic architectural style as represented in Singapore. Its lancet windows, turret-like pinnacles and decorated spire resemble features of Salisbury Cathedral in England. The outer surface of the cathedral was made from *chunam* plaster, a mixture of egg-white, shell, lime, sugar, coconut husk and water.

Within the church there are artifacts of interest, memorials to soldiers (who lost their lives in the Sepoy Mutiny of 1915 and in World Wars I and II), and brass plaques to families long gone.

Old Parliament House ❷

1 High Street. **Map** 5 D3 Ⓜ *City Hall, Raffles Place.* 🚌 *7, 32, 51, 81, 124, 145, 197, 603, 851.*

PARLIAMENT HOUSE was designed in 1826–7 by G D Coleman (1796–1844), the Irish architect who shaped much of Singapore's colonial built environment. Where Parliament House now stands there was once jungle which was cleared by hand with machetes to make way for the building. This oldest government building in Singapore began life as a mansion for wealthy merchant John Argyle Maxwell. Later it became a courthouse, then the colonial government's Assembly House and in 1962, Parliament House of the independent state of Singapore. The building displays some of the classic features of Neo-Palladian architecture. Large

Elephant sculpture at old Parliament House

windows and doors allow air and light through. The raw materials used include Chinese and Malaccan bricks, tropical hardwood timber, lime plaster from South China Sea corals and granite from Singapore's outlying islands.

Nearby is the new S$80 million Parliament House.

Façade of old Parliament House

Raffles' Landing Site ❸

North Boat Quay. **Map** 5 D3. Ⓜ *Raffles Place.* 🚌 *7, 32, 51, 81, 124, 145, 197, 603, 851.*

A MODERN (1972) polymarble statue of Sir Stamford Raffles gazing upon the flourishing Central Business District, complete with a plinth, marks the spot where he first set foot on Singapore soil, on 29 January 1819 *(see p38)*. This statue is a replica of the original bronze work cast by Thomas Woolner which was unveiled on the Padang on 27 June 1887. The original statue is now in front of the Victoria Concert Hall.

A statue of Sir Stamford Raffles at the original landing site

Asian Civilisations Museum II

1 Empress Place. **Map** 5 D3.
6332 7798. Raffles Place, City
Hall. 75, 540, 608. noon–6pm
Mon, 9am–6pm Tue–Sun, 9am–9pm
Fri (Free adm. from 6pm).
Japanese: 10:30am Tue–Fri,
English: 11am, 2pm Tue–Fri, also at
3:30pm Sat–Sun.
www.museum.org.sg/
ACM/acm.shtml

Home to over 1,600
artifacts, the museum is
the biggest in Singapore and
has 11 galleries and four ACE
(Asian Civilisations Education)
zones: South Asia, West
Asia/Islam, Southeast Asia
and China. It is housed in the
Empress Place Building which
was built in 1864–7. Back
then, it was an emphatic
statement of colonial might
standing tall above tumble-
down shacks and godowns.
The building serviced many
aspects of colonial
administration over the years.
    A reference to Queen
Victoria, Empress Place was
originally the name of the
area surrounding the building,
Singapore's first pedestrian
area. Built by convicts at a
cost of S$53,000, the
building's first function was as
a court house.

Victoria Theatre & Concert Hall

9 Empress Place. **Map** 5 D3.
6338 8283 (theatre), 6338 6125,
6339 6120 (concert hall). Raffles
Place, City Hall. 75, 540, 608. **Box
office:** 10am–6pm Mon–Sat.

Victoria Theatre was built
in 1862 by the British to
house amateur dramatic
productions and Gilbert &
Sullivan operettas. The
Victoria Memorial Hall was
added in 1905 with the help
of private voluntary subscrip-
tions at a cost of S$340,000.
The Memorial Hall was re-
named Victoria Concert Hall
in 1980 when it became home
to the Singapore Symphony
Orchestra (SSO) *(see p154)*.
    The history of the halls is
not entirely pleasant. The

Queen Elizabeth Walk, a coastal park against the city skyline

original bronze statue of
Raffles (1887) at the front of
the building has seen the
conversion of the concert hall
into a hospital during World
War II, the turning of the
clock tower to Tokyo time
during the Japanese Occupation and the holding of war
crimes tribunals after the
Japanese surrender.
    Victoria Theatre & Concert
Hall is a major venue for a
wide range of concerts and
performances *(see p153)*.
Details are posted on the
billboards, and tickets can be
obtained at the box office or
via ticketing outlets in Singapore's main shopping areas.
The halls are served by two
cafés and a shop.

Queen Elizabeth Walk

Connaught Drive. **Map** 5 E2.
Raffles Place, City Hall. 75,
540, 608.

This shady walk stretches
along the east side of the
Padang *(see pp44–5)* and
features several memorials –
the Tan Kim Seng fountain (in
memory of the man who
helped finance the island's
first water works); the Lim Bo
Seng Memorial (built for a
World War II resistance
leader); and the Cenotaph
(commemorating the dead of
World Wars I and II).

War Memorial Park

Junction of Bras Basah and Beach
Roads. **Map** 5 E2. City Hall.
56, 82, 100, 107, 961, 980.

This memorial to the civilian
victims of the Japanese
Occupation *(see pp19–20)*
was built in 1964. The monument is made up of four
white 70-m (231-ft) high

War memorial obelisk

tapering columns, each
seemingly freestanding but
actually joined at the base.
Each column represents a
racial group in Singapore –
Chinese, Indians, Malays and
minorities. The park is a
green space filled with
bougainvillea but it is
corralled by traffic on all
sides. A shopping mall has
been constructed beneath it.

The silver blocks of the Raffles City complex

Raffles City ❽

2 Stamford Road. **Map** 5 E2.
C 6433 2238. **M** City Hall. **▦** 7, 36, 77, 97, 103, 124, 131, 147, 162, 166, 174, 190, 501, 511, 603. **◯** 10am –9:30pm daily. ▣ 🍴 ▣ ▼ ▣ 🚻

Raffles Institution, a school founded by Sir Stamford Raffles, was demolished in 1989 in order to make way for the Raffles City complex, comprising a shopping mall, high-rise offices and two hotels – Swissôtel the Stamford, the world's tallest hotel (73 storeys) and Raffles the Plaza (see p122). The Equinox, one of the world's highest restaurants (see p134), sits at the top of Swissôtel the Stamford. Raffles City was designed by I M Pei, the famous Chinese-American architect who also designed the "calculator tower" (OCBC Building) near Raffles Place. The building has been called the "tin can" because of the metallic appearance of its external cladding.

Raffles City offers four floors of shopping with everything from electronics stores to a Japanese super-market, a depart-ment store,

several cafés, two food courts, medical clinics, a SISTIC ticketing outlet, three jewellers and upscale brands such as Brooks Brothers, Mont Blanc, Polo Jeans and Armani Exchange. Interesting specialist outlets are to be found here, such as stalls selling Thai silk and Chinese handicrafts, as well as a Metropolitan Museum of Art (New York) shop.

Chijmes ❾

30 Victoria Street. **Map** 5 E1.
C 6332 6273. **M** City Hall. **▦** 2, 7, 12, 33, 81, 107, 130, 133, 147, 190, 520, 851, 960. **◯** 11am–1am daily.
▣ 🎵 🍴 ▣ ▼ ▣ 🚻

Chijmes (pronounced "chimes") was once the Convent of the Holy Infant Jesus. The sisters of the convent, which was founded in 1854, ran a women's refuge, orphanage and well-respected school until 1983 when the convent was relocated. The buildings were redeveloped as a series of shops, bars, restaurants and gallery spaces.

Chijmes has something of the atmosphere of London's Covent Garden and still feels like a quiet refuge from the city despite the plethora of popular pubs which now grace its premises. It features cobbled walkways, art and craft shops, upmarket restaurants (everything from fusion to Japanese, Chinese and Austrian), an elaborate fountain and covered Italianate walkways set on different levels. All these elements create a pleasant consumer exper-ience; the complex is well worth a visit.

What was formerly the chapel (built in 1903) is now Chijmes Hall and is used for, among

other things, art exhibitions, fashion shows and weddings. The chapel is capped with a magnificent five-floor-high spire and the supporting columns of the chapel and the walkways are decorated with beautiful carvings of tropical plants and animals.

Raffles Hotel ❿

See pp50–51.

Singapore Art Museum, a former Catholic boys' school

Singapore Art Museum ⓫

71 Bras Basah Road. **Map** 5 D1.
C 6332 3222. **M** City Hall.
▦ 7, 14, 16, 36, 77, 97, 130, 131, 133, 162, 167, 171, 174, 190, 501, 540, 603, 605, 700, 857, 960.
◯ 9am–5:30pm Tue–Sun, 9am–9pm Wed. ● Mon. 🎫 Family tickets available. ♿ ✓ **Japanese:** 10:30am Tue–Fri, **English:** 11am, 2pm daily, also at 3:30pm Sat–Sun. ▣ ▣ ▣ 🚻 ⓦ www.museum.org.sg/ SAM/sam.shtml

A bronze statue of the 17th-century saint John Baptist de la Salle with two school-boy charges stands above the porch of the Singapore Art Museum, an indication that, until 1987, it housed St Joseph's Institution, a Catholic boys' school.

Today the Classical-style building is a showcase for modern Asian art. Since the museum's opening in January 1996, its permanent collection has grown from just under

Façade of the chapel in Chijmes, a former convent school

2,000 art works to over 4,000, making it the largest catalogued collection of 20th-century Southeast Asian art in the region to date.

The museum's collection ranges from sculptures to installations and paintings. The core collection is supplemented by travelling exhibitions from outside Asia, typically featuring 20th-century art from American and European collections.

Artists represented at the museum include Affandi from Indonesia, Georgette Chan, Chua Mia Tee and Tan Swie Hian from Singapore, Wong Hoy Cheong from Malaysia and Tran Trong Vu from Vietnam.

What was once the school chapel is now an auditorium where the paraphernalia of worship, including the stations of the cross, the baptismal font, and the mosaic floor, has been retained. The chapel's central window has been replaced with a modern stained-glass work by the Filipino sculptor Ramon Orlina.

The building's two courtyards are now exhibition spaces arranged either side of the Glass Hall, a converted verandah used as a function room beautifully decorated with blown-glass installations by the American artist Dale Chihuly. The Emage Multimedia Gallery provides information on the history, development and techniques of contemporary art in Southeast Asia. There are 12 exhibition galleries (including the new Queen Street wing), amounting to 3,000 sq m (9,900 sq ft) of gallery space. The museum provides regular educational programmes.

The Dome Café, ensconced in one of the naves of the museums, serves sandwiches, cakes, and a range of coffee drinks.

Renaissance-style exterior of the Cathedral of the Good Shepherd

Chong Fah Chong's *Girl with Folded Arms*, Singapore Art Museum

Cathedral of the Good Shepherd ⓬

4 Queen Street. **Map 5 E1.**
📞 6337 9879. Ⓜ *City Hall, Dhoby Ghaut.* 🚌 *7, 14, 16, 36, 77, 97, 131, 167, 171, 501, 700, 957, 960.* ◑ *daily.* 🕐 *8am, 10am, 6pm Sun. 7am, 1:15pm Mon–Fri. 7am, 6:30pm Sat.*
📷 ♿ ♻ Ⓦ *www.veritas.org.sg*

THE CATHEDRAL is Singapore's oldest Catholic church. Built between 1843 and 1847, it was administered by the French missionary Father Jean-Marie Beurel, who established St Joseph's Institution (now the Singapore Art Museum), and the Convent of the Holy Infant Jesus. The design was the result of a competition between two notable architects of the time, D L McSwiney and J T Thomson. McSwiney won because his design was cheaper. The church, designed in a Latin cross form, features Roman Doric columns. McSwiney's design combines an exterior in the Renaissance style with Palladian porches and a beautifully crafted timber ceiling. The eight-sided steeple by Charles Dyce was a later addition.

Three interesting buildings can be found in the church's compound. They are the **Archbishop's House**, a 19th-century double-storey bungalow with a projecting portico; the **Resident's Quarters**, a U-shaped single-storey building with Doric columns; and the **Priest's House**, which is more ornate. The building achieved cathedral status in 1897.

Stained glass in the Cathedral of the Good Shepherd

Raffles Hotel ❿

Singapore Sling

Rᴀꜰꜰʟᴇꜱ Hᴏᴛᴇʟ consists of an arrangement of white, low-rise, verandah-enclosed, colonial-style buildings with terracotta-tiled pitched roofs. In colonial times, it served as a self-contained island of tranquillity for Europeans amidst the heat and bustle of Southeast Asia. Somerset Maugham, Joseph Conrad, Noel Coward, Charlie Chaplin and Michael Jackson are some of the celebrities who have stayed here. The cool, calm refuges of its courtyards, gardens and covered walkways can be enjoyed by non-residents.

★ Long Bar
The Singapore Sling, the pink drink originally intended for ladies, was created here in 1915 by a Hainanese bartender Ngiam Tong Boon.

★ Ornamental Fountain
The hotel's cast-iron fountain, made in Scotland in the early 1890s, was donated to the hotel in 1990.

Raffles Hotel souvenir shop

Bar and Billiard Room

Tiffin Room

★ Lobby
The lobby is home to the Writers' Bar and it features photographs of some of the writers who have stayed at Raffles.

Writers' Bar

Palm Court
The Palm Court is a beautifully restored space lined with palm and frangipani trees. Collectively, the hotel's gardens house over 50,000 plants representing about 80 different species.

The Raffles Grill is one of Singapore's most prestigious, exquisite and upmarket restaurants (see p135). The Grill looks out on to the Palm Court via French doors.

★ Raffles Hotel Museum

The museum manages to impart a real sense of history and atmosphere via personal mementos, artifacts and archival documents.

Empire Café

Ah Teng's Bakery

Jubilee Hall

VISITORS' CHECKLIST

1, Beach Road. **Map** 5 E1.
📞 *6337 1886.* Ⓜ *City Hall.*
🚌 *56, 82, 100.* ⭕ *daily* 📷 *no tripods;* 🎵 🍴 🛍 🍸 📷 👥
🌐 *www.raffles.com*

Empress Room
The restaurant offers Cantonese food in an old-world atmosphere
(see p135).

Seah Street Deli specializes in New York-style delicatessen food. The portions are authentic, large and reasonably priced.

Raffles Culinary Academy is where the hotel conducts cooking classes by renowned visiting chefs *(see p165).*

The Lawn's tropical foliage combined with a gazebo provides the setting for garden receptions.

STAR FEATURES

★ **Long Bar**

★ **Ornamental Fountain**

★ **Lobby**

★ **Raffles Hotel Museum**

Doc Cheng's
This award-winning theme restaurant offers an exciting fusion of Western and Oriental cuisines
(see p135).

A re-creation of a Peranakan house, Singapore History Museum

Singapore History Museum ❸

93 Stamford Road. **Map** 5 D1.
C 6332 3659. **M** Dhoby Ghaut, City Hall. **▦** 7, 14, 16, 36, 77, 97, 131, 166. ◯ 9am–5:30pm Tue–Sun, 9am–9pm Wed. ● Mon. 🎦 🎟 📷
Japanese: 10:30am Tue–Fri. **English:** 11am, 2pm daily, also 3:30pm Sat–Sun. **Audio-visual show:** 10:15am, 12:15pm, 2:45pm, 3:45pm daily.
🎟 🕍 ⓦ www.museum.org.sg/ SHM/shm.shtml

Sᴵɴɢᴀᴘᴏʀᴇ Hɪsᴛᴏʀʏ Mᴜsᴇᴜᴍ, also known as the National Museum, was originally called the Raffles Museum and Library. Known for its excellent natural history and ethnography collections, the museum moved to its Neo-Palladian premises, complete with stained-glass dome, in 1887 (see p29).

When Singapore gained independence, the museum switched its focus to exhibitions that concentrated on educating people about the history and peoples of Singapore. The natural history collection was transferred to the National University of Singapore. Exhibits include a History of Singapore Gallery, which has a series of 20 model dioramas of Singapore's history from Raffles' landing to the first fully independent parliamentary session in 1965 (see p20); a Peranakan (Straits Chinese) House exhibition; William Farquhar's rare collection of 477 paintings, known collectively as "The Farquhar Collection of Natural History Drawings"; and a Children's Discovery Gallery.

Currently undergoing renovation until 2006, the museum is temporarily housed on the third and fourth floors of Riverside Point shopping mall.

Asian Civilisations Museum I ❹

39 Armenian Street. **Map** 5 D2.
C 6332 3015. **M** City Hall.
▦ 7, 14, 16, 36, 77, 97, 131, 166. ◯ 12pm–6pm Mon, 9am–6pm Tue–Sun, 9am–9pm (Free adm. from 6pm) Fri. 🎫 Family tickets available.
🎟 🎦 **Japanese:** 10:30am Tue–Fri. **English:** 11am, 2pm Tue–Fri, also at 3:30pm Sat–Sun. **Audio-visual show:** 10:15am, 12:15pm, 2:45pm, 3:45pm daily. 🎟 🕍 🏛
ⓦ www.museum.org.sg/ ACM/acm.shtml

Dᴇsɪɢɴᴇᴅ ʙʏ Swan and Maclaren, the Singapore firm of architects who built Raffles Hotel (see p50–51), the first wing of the Asian Civilisations Museum was originally Tao Nan School, established in 1910 by three Chinese philanthropists for the education of boys.

This Neo-Classical building was renovated and opened in 1997. The second wing at Empress Place (see p47) is three times bigger than the first wing. It displays Indian, Chinese, Islamic and Southeast Asian artifacts as well as relics excavated at sites near the Singapore River.

The museum's aim is to educate visitors about the ancestral cultures of Singapore's ethnic groups. Its Southeast Asian collection focuses on artifacts from the region, such as textiles, wood carvings, basketware and

Asian Civilisations Museum, occupying the building of the former Tao Nan School

Singapore Philatelic Museum, where history is told through stamps

lacquerware. There is a permanent showcase of Straits Chinese artifacts, which includes an array of jewellery, beadwork, porcelain and silverwork. Exhibits in the East Asian collection include Chinese jade, ceramics, folk art and bronzes, as well as Chinese paintings and calligraphy. Artifacts from key periods of Chinese history are also displayed *(see p29)*. Seasonal exhibitions are held.

Singapore Philatelic Museum ⓯

23B Coleman Street. **Map** 5 D2.
C *6337 3888.* **M** *City Hall.* 🚍 *2, 12, 32, 33, 51, 103, 124, 147, 166, 174, 190, 197, 851.* ⬤ *9am–4:30pm Tue–Sun.* ⬤ *Mon.* 🖼 🎫 *11am, 2pm daily.* 🔲 W *www.spm.org.sg*

Housed in the former Methodist Book Room building (built 1907), the Singapore Philatelic Museum displays a rare collection of Singaporean and Southeast Asian stamps and postal stationery as well as stamps from over 180 countries.

First impressions indicate that this is a museum for the stamp enthusiast, but an investigation beyond the first floor proves this wrong. An audio-visual presentation explains how stamps are made and, on a more sophisticated level, what they mean to a country, how they can be manipulated for propaganda purposes (such as during the Japanese Occupation) and how they reflect a country's history and social development. The galleries feature numerous interactive displays thoughtfully arranged at a child's height. For those wanting to know more, the exhibition is backed up by free worksheets available in the lobby. The museum also has a resource centre.

Visitors can buy stamps, first day covers and other collectibles at the gift shop.

Fort Canning Park ⓰

See pp54–5.

Chettiar Temple ⓱

Crossing of Tank Road and River Valley Road. **Map** 4 C2.
C *6737 9393.* **M** *Dhoby Ghaut.* 🚍 *14, 32, 54, 65, 139, 195.* ⬤ *8am–noon, 5:30–8:30pm daily.*

The Shivaite Hindu temple currently on this site was built in 1984 and replaced a much older one which was founded by Indian chettiars (moneylenders), from whom the temple takes its name. The temple is dedicated to Lord Subramaniam and it is worth venturing inside

A post box exhibit

(remember to remove your shoes first) to look at the temple's 48 etched glass panels of Hindu deities angled to catch the rising and setting sun.

Craftsmen from southern India were responsible for these and other architectural works of art that were incorporated into the building. They include the *gopuram*, a five-tiered entrance archway, the 72-panelled 6.25-m- (21-ft) high Kamalam-patterned rosewood doors, columns and prayer halls with sculptures of Hindu deities. The temple's main deity, Lord Muruga, is represented in six of his holy abodes. A rarity among Hindu temples, a representation of the rear of an elephant at rest can be found at the back of the sanctuary.

Inside the temple there are two connected rooms, the *mandapam* and the *antarala*, through which the worshipper moves to perform his or her devotions. The *antarala* leads to the most holy part of the temple, the *garbhagrha*, which only priests may enter.

The temple plays an important part in the life of Shivaite Hindus as it is the final point for the procession beginning at Sri Srinivasa Perumal Temple *(see pp82–3)* during the annual Thaipusam festival *(see p22).*

The colourful *gopuram* of the Hindu Chettiar Temple

Fort Canning Park ⑯

Battle Box sign

F ORT CANNING PARK was the seat of the Malay kingdom of Temasek back in the 14th century. It was also the first Christian cemetery on the island. Entry to the park is via either one of the two Gothic gates. Fort Canning has many historical landmarks, with sign-posted walking trails, military ruins, a Malay shrine, Christian gravestones and a spice garden. The old fort gate, built in 1861, is the only remnant of the fort that stood here from 1861 to 1926. From here, there is a view over the Central Business District.

Keramat
The keramat ("holy place") is believed to be the burial place of the last king of the ancient Malay kingdom of Temasek.

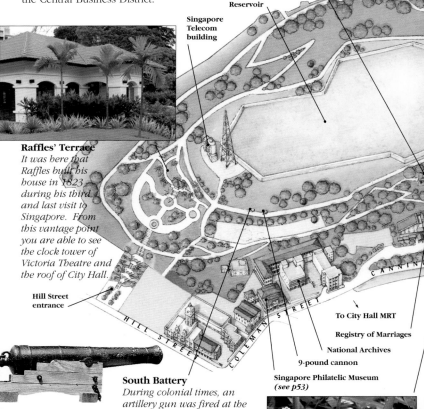

Raffles' Terrace
It was here that Raffles built his house in 1823 during his third and last visit to Singapore. From this vantage point you are able to see the clock tower of Victoria Theatre and the roof of City Hall.

Reservoir

Singapore Telecom building

Hill Street entrance

South Battery
During colonial times, an artillery gun was fired at the South Battery every day.

HILL STREET

COLEMAN STREET

CANNING

To City Hall MRT

Registry of Marriages

National Archives

9-pound cannon

Singapore Philatelic Museum
(see p53)

Spice Garden
Reminiscent of the first botanical gardens Raffles established here in 1822, the garden has plants such as clove, nutmeg and tamarind.

★ **Battle Box**
A guided tour at this former British forces' underground command centre recounts the events of 15 February 1942, the day the British surrendered to the Japanese.

ort Gate   **The Legends at Fort Canning**

Fort Wall

VISITORS' CHECKLIST

51, Canning Rise, Singapore 179872. **Map** 4 C1. 🚇 *6332 1200.* 🖷 *6339 9715.*
Ⓜ *Dhoby Ghaut.* 🚌 *7, 14, 16, 36, 54, 64, 65, 77, 81, 97, 103, 106, 111, 124, 131, 139, 145, 147, 162, 166, 167, 171, 174, 190, 195, 851.* ◯ *10am–6pm, last admission at 5pm Tue–Sun.*
⬤ *Mon.* 🏛 📷 🎫 🛂
Ⓦ *www.nparks.gov.sg*

A sally port is an emergency hidden door created for forces to make a rapid exit. One sally port (of three) survives intact on Fort Canning.

**To Dhoby Ghaut
MRT station**

★ **Fort Canning Centre**
The centre was built as a British army barracks in 1926. After a spell as an office block, it was restored and converted to a gallery and performance space for two local performing arts companies, Theatre Works and the Singapore Dance Theatre (see p34–5) and a culinary school, Academy at-sunrice.

Fort Canning Green

The cupolas were designed by architect George Coleman.

Gothic gate
One of two Gothic gates which date back to 1846, they are believed to have been designed by government engineer Captain Charles Edward Faber.

★ **ASEAN
Sculpture Park**
In the ASEAN Sculpture Park, the inclusion of modern sculptures from each of the ASEAN (Association of South East Asian Nations) countries signifies political and cultural unity.

Interior of the Armenian Church

Armenian Church ⓲

60 Hill Street. **Map** 5 D2. 🔲 *6334 0141.* 🅜 *City Hall.* 🚌 *2, 12, 32, 33, 51, 103, 124, 147, 166, 174, 190, 197, 851.* ⬤ *9am–5pm Mon–Fri, 9am–12pm Sat.* ⬤ *Sun* 📷 ♿

The Armenian Church of St Gregory the Illuminator was the first permanent place of Christian worship in Singapore. The church, which was built in 1835 (the spire was only added in 1850), was able to seat a congregation of only 50 people, which reflected the minority (although influential) status of the local Armenian community then.

Designed by G D Coleman (who also designed several other landmarks of early Singapore such as St Andrew's Cathedral *(see p46)*, the church is a very elegant piece of tropical Neo-Classical architecture with four wide porticoes arranged around a perfectly circular wood-beamed chapel, rather like an overturned bowl. The porticoes were built to provide a space for carriages to deposit their passengers free from the harsh glare of the sun or the torrential down-

pours of the rainy season. The church's interior is decorated with a photograph of the Armenian community here around 1917, portraits of the patriarchs of the Armenian Church and a painting of the Last Supper above the altar. In the church's compound stand a graveyard and a parsonage, a two-storey bungalow which was built in 1905. Among the graves is that of Agnes Joaquim, who discovered an orchid hybrid in 1893 which was later named after her (Vanda Miss Joaquim) *(see p93).* It was adopted as Singapore's national flower.

Hill Street ⓳

Map 5 D2. 🅜 *Clarke Quay.* 🚌 *2, 5, 12, 32, 33, 103, 124, 147, 166, 174, 190, 197, 851.* 📷 🍴 ♿

Stretching from Clarke Quay to Stamford Road, there are several interesting buildings along Hill Street. The Chinese name for Hill Street is "Ong Ke Soa Kha" which means "foot of the Governor's hill" and harks back to the days of the first British Resident, Major Farquhar *(see p17).*

Standing on the site of Singapore's first gaol, the six-storey **Hill Street Building**, built in 1934, was originally a police station and police quarters until 1980. Later, other government offices, including the Archives and Oral History Department,

occupied the building. The building has been renovated to house the office of the Ministry of Information and the Arts. Its Italian-influenced façade has been retained.

Singapore's fire brigade was established in 1900 and the **Central Fire Station** was built as their headquarters in 1906. Its red-and-white brick walls (the "white" bricks are in fact whitewashed plaster) give it a bright presence distinct from the Neo-Classical style of other colonial buildings. The style is typical of English Edwardian architecture. The Fire Station also houses a Civil Defence Heritage Gallery.

The **Singapore Chinese Chamber of Commerce** at No. 47 was built in 1964. It is a slightly incongruous modern building capped by a pagoda roof and fronted with a wall embellished with nine porcelain dragons.

Clarke Quay's refurbished warehouses

Clarke Quay ⓴

Map 4 C2. 🅜 *Clarke Quay.* 🚌 *14, 32, 54, 65, 139, 195, or 3 min. walk from Hill Street.* 📷 🎵 🍴 🛍 🍸 🍴 🛍 *Flea market on Sundays (see p142).* ♿

Clarke Quay was named after Sir Andrew Clarke, the second governor of Singapore. It used to be a strip of delapidated 19th-century warehouses run by predominantly Chinese traders. The area caught the eye of developers in the early 1990s and was converted into a precinct of shops, pubs, floating restaurants, river-boat excursions and craft stalls.

Clarke Quay is a ghost area during the day as most shops

Central Fire Station, the red-and-white landmark on Hill Street

◁ **Night view of the Singapore River, with Boat Quay on the south bank**

and restaurants are closed, but it is very energetic at night and can usually supply a good atmosphere and free entertainment (at the central gazebo). A collection of food stalls, collectively known as the **Satay Club**, remains open until 2am daily.

Suntec City ㉑

Temasek Boulevard. **Map** 5 F1. **C** 6825 2667. **M** City Hall. **🚌** 10, 14, 16, 36, 56, 70, 82, 100. 107, 133, 196, 501. 🄾 🍴 🛗 🍷 🛍 ⚧

SUNTEC CITY, which opened in the 1990s, is a massive complex of buildings that are linked by architectural style as well as underground walkways – it is like a city in itself.
The place comprises four office towers and Southeast Asia's largest exhibition and convention centre, complete with exposed structural elements, rather in the style of Paris' Pompidou Centre. It has the largest shopping mall in Singapore consisting of over 270 retail outlets, a multiplex cinema, Singapore's biggest megamarket, Carrefour, and the world's largest fountain – surrounded by food and beverage outlets to suit every taste. The fountain was built in accordance with *feng shui* principles – symbolically it sits in the palm of a left hand radiating wealth.

Marina Square ㉒

Raffles Boulevard & Raffles Avenue. **Map** 5 F2. **C** 6339 8787. **M** City Hall. **🚌** 36, 133, 501, 857. 🄾 🍴 🛍 🍷 🛍 ⚧

BUILT ON RECLAIMED land, Marina Square was developed in 1984–5 and until recently was the largest shopping mall in Singapore (that honour now goes to Suntec City). It is the venue for some impressive public sculptures, a shopping mall and four major international hotels: the Marina Mandarin, the Oriental, the Ritz-Carlton Millenia and the Pan Pacific (*see pp122–3*). Apart from 2,104 guest rooms and 59,000 sq m (637,000 sq ft) of retail space, Marina Square has 2,300 car-parking spaces. It is linked by a rooftop walkway to the Ritz-Carlton Millenia and Millenia Walk, which has more shops and a food court.

Esplanade Park ㉓

Connaught Drive. **Map** 5 E3. **M** City Hall. **🚌** 10, 70, 75, 82, 97, 100, 130, 131, 167, 196, 608. 🄾

RUNNING ALONG Connaught Drive from the underpass at Anderson Bridge to Stamford Road, the Esplanade Park was one of the most popular outdoor spots for both the European and the Asian communities in the colonial era.

An atrium in Marina Square, the shopping mall

The park contains Queen Elizabeth Walk and landmarks such as the **Cenotaph, the Tan Kim Seng Fountain** built in honour of the philanthropist who set up the settlement's first fresh water supply, and the **Lim Bo Seng Memorial** eulogising the World War II hero who died in Japanese captivity. The park also boasts the Esplanade – Theatres on the Bay, a striking performing arts centre with a wide array of events on offer.
Esplanade Park was the site for a saluting battery known as Scandal Point – due to the frequency with which idle expatriates gossiped at this spot. Hotels used to line this once sea-fronted area, including the Grand Hotel de l'Europe, Raffles Hotel's great rival.

The Esplanade – Theatres on the Bay

CHINATOWN AND THE FINANCIAL DISTRICT

CHINATOWN and Singapore's Financial District lie next to each other, but they present very different faces of the city. Chinatown was created on the recommendation of Sir Stamford Raffles in 1828 and retains much of the architecture and a little of the atmosphere of old Singapore. In contrast, the skyscrapers of Raffles Place and the rest of the Financial District symbolize everything new and dynamic about the modern nation. The division between the two areas is, however, not cut and dried, and one of the most interesting aspects of

Chinese lantern

a visit to this part of Singapore is the way in which the old and new are intimately juxtaposed. Thanks to careful renovation, many old shophouses remain in both quarters and the visitor can get a feel for what life was like in the past. Gracing these streets are many temples and other old buildings erected by the early immigrants not only as places of worship, but also as centres for the different dialect groups which settled in the area. The towering structures of the Financial District are an aggressively modern element in the architectural mix.

SIGHTS AT A GLANCE

Historic Streets and Buildings
Ann Siang Hill **6**
Boat Quay **11**
Lau Pa Sat **7**
Raffles Place **10**
Tanjong Pagar Conservation Area **5**
Telok Ayer Street **8**
Temple Street **2**

Temples
Sri Mariamman Temple **1**
Thian Hock Keng Temple pp68–9 **9**

Shopping
Chinatown Complex **4**
People's Park Complex **3**

| 0 metres | 500 |
| 0 yards | 500 |

KEY

- Street-by-Street map *See pp62–3*
- **M** Mass Rapid Transit station
- Bus terminal
- Police station
- Post office
- **P** Parking
- Church
- **C** Mosque
- Chinese temple

GETTING THERE
Take bus numbers 124, 143, 174 or 190 from Orchard Road or travel via MRT to Raffles Place, Tanjung Pagar or Chinatown.

◁ **A refurbished shophouse in Duxton Road**

Street-by-Street: Chinatown

Tilework, the Majestic Theatre

THE HEART of Chinatown is a colourful cluster of narrow streets running off South Bridge Road, where there are superb examples of shophouse architecture, recalling "old" Singapore. These streets were once a densely packed, bustling warren of shops, tenements, coolie lodging-houses, coffee-houses and opium dens. Today, the area is an official conservation area and has been carefully restored. It is home to antique shops, bars, restaurants and other up-market small-scale enterprises. There is still plenty of local colour, including Chinese medical halls and shops selling temple paraphernalia. The contrast between the terracotta-tiled roofs and their encircling high-rise neighbours makes an unforgettable – and very Singaporean – picture.

To Outram MRT station

EU TONG SEN STREET

SMITH STREET

SAGO STREET

★ **People's Park Complex**
This bustling mall offers good-value shopping and plenty of local products ❸

Chinatown Complex ❹

★ **Trengganu Street**
The street is filled with busy open-air cafés, bars and shops. It has some very distinctive shophouse architecture, with the top overhanging floor being built entirely of timber.

KEY

– – – Suggested Route

0 metres 50
0 yards 50

STAR SIGHTS

★ **People's Park Complex**

★ **Trengganu Street**

★ **Sri Mariamman Temple**

Sago Street, once infamous for its "Death Houses" *(see p65),* is filled with shops that peddle mainly Chinese goods, from lanterns and crockery to foodstuffs such as these Chinese cakes. Chinese operas are staged in the open space.

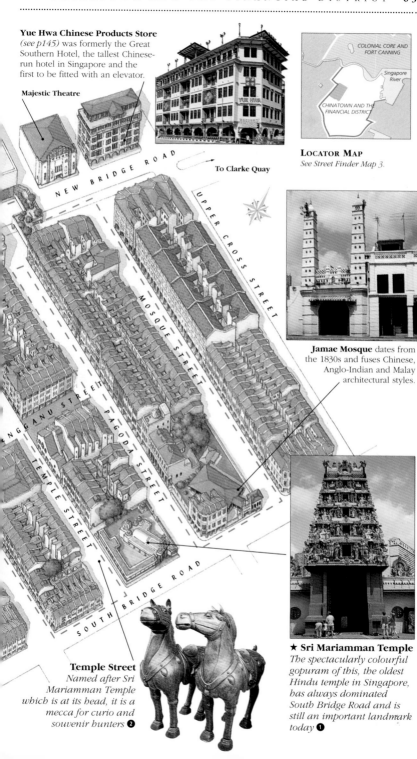

Yue Hwa Chinese Products Store
(see p145) was formerly the Great
Southern Hotel, the tallest Chinese-
run hotel in Singapore and the
first to be fitted with an elevator.

Majestic Theatre

NEW BRIDGE ROAD

To Clarke Quay

LOCATOR MAP
See Street Finder Map 3.

COLONIAL CORE AND
FORT CANNING

Singapore
River

CHINATOWN AND THE
FINANCIAL DISTRICT

UPPER CROSS STREET

MOSQUE STREET

NGGANU STREET

PAGODA STREET

TEMPLE STREET

SOUTH BRIDGE ROAD

Jamae Mosque dates from
the 1830s and fuses Chinese,
Anglo-Indian and Malay
architectural styles.

★ **Sri Mariamman Temple**
*The spectacularly colourful
gopuram of this, the oldest
Hindu temple in Singapore,
has always dominated
South Bridge Road and is
still an important landmark
today* ❶

Temple Street
*Named after Sri
Mariamman Temple
which is at its head, it is a
mecca for curio and
souvenir hunters* ❷

Figurines adorning the gopuram of Sri Mariamman Temple

Sri Mariamman Temple ❶

244 South Bridge Road. **Map** 4 C4.
[6223 4064. **M** Chinatown.
▦ 51, 80, 124, 143, 174, 197, 608.
◯ 7am–12:30pm, 6pm–8:30pm
daily. 📷 ♿

THE SOUTHERN END of South Bridge Road is dominated by the *gopuram* or entrance gateway of the Sri Mariamman Temple. This amazing tower depicts some 72 Hindu deities in vivid colour. The complex is surrounded by a boundary wall topped with figures of sacred cows.

Sri Mariamman is the oldest Hindu place of worship still in use on the island. Although much of the decoration depicts the Hindu divine trinity, Brahma, Vishnu and Shiva, the temple is dedicated to the goddess Sri Mariamman who is known for her powers in curing epidemic diseases. The temple is famous for the annual Thimithi festival, during which devotees walk on hot coals as a sign of their piety *(see p25)*.

The building itself, which replaced an original simple wood and *atap* (thatch) structure, dates from 1843. It was built by Indian convicts and craftsmen from Madras who were skilled in plasterwork. The temple has been repaired and redecorated several times over the years.

Visitors are welcome to explore its numerous courtyards and enjoy its brightly painted ceilings. They should keep noise to a minimum, dress conservatively, and remove shoes before entering. Photography is allowed for a donation of $3.

Tea dispenser, Temple Street

Temple Street ❷

Map 4 C4. **M** Chinatown. **▦** 51, 80, 124, 145, 174, 197, 608. 🍴 ▯ 🍷 🚻 ♿

THE AREA bounded by Mosque Street, Pagoda Street, Temple Street and Smith Street *(see pp62–3)* is the place to come for the Chinatown shopping and eating experience. It features a variety of shops selling souvenirs, antiques, porcelain and clothing, as well as many pleasant cafés and restaurants. The district is a great place to browse and soak up the local atmosphere. During the Chinese New Year festivities, the roads are packed with stalls selling festive food, decorations and gifts.

The shophouses in these streets – ground floors are shops or restaurants and the upper floors are homes – have been well preserved. Many of them are painted in bright, contemporary colours. The area's history is no less colourful, having once been a red-light district. Today, bars and karaoke joints serve as the nightlife.

People's Park Complex ❸

1 Park Road. **Map** 4 C3. **[** 6535 9533. **M** Chinatown. **▦** 2, 12, 32, 33, 54, 62, 63, 81, 124, 961. **◯** 10am–10pm daily. 🍴 ▯ 🍷 🚻

THE FIRST air-conditioned, multi-storey shopping centre on the island, the People's Park Complex was opened in the early 1970s. Today, it retains much of the bustling atmosphere of the old Chinatown, especially in its food court which is set in a central courtyard. A range of department stores, including the characterful Overseas Emporium, and a mix of well-patronized electronics stores, tailors, luggage shops, goldsmiths and travel agents can be found here.

The complex was the forerunner of the modern, air-conditioned shopping centres that dot the island today. It

The Overseas Emporium in People's Park Complex

houses offices and residential units above a level of shopping space. The open space between the complex and the OG Building is used for an open-air market, especially during festivals such as Chinese New Year. Despite the dated, worn-out look of the complex, the textile shops offer great variety and value for money.

Next door is the former Majestic Cinema, which features mosaics of legendary Chinese warriors on its façade.

A stall selling fresh vegetables in Chinatown Complex

Chinatown Complex ❹

New Bridge Road. **Map** 4 C4.
[M] *Outram Park, Chinatown.* 🚌 *2, 12, 33, 54, 62, 63, 81, 124, 147, 961.*
⏰ *10am–10pm daily.* 🍴 ☕ 🛍 🚻

On the corner of Trengganu Street and Sago Street, the Chinatown Complex has one of the most boisterous wet markets in the city. There is a bewildering variety of fresh produce on sale, including fresh fruit and vegetables and some truly amazing seafood. In the morning, freshly skinned frogs and huge fish can be seen. Above the wet market is a range of shops offering everything from jade jewellery to CDs.

Next door is Sago Street, named after the many sago factories which used to operate here. This street was infamous for its "Death Houses", where the terminally ill came to die. Today, rattan mat makers and paper kite sellers operate here.

Restored double-storey shophouses along Duxton Road

Tanjong Pagar Conservation Area ❺

Map 4 C5. [M] *Tanjong Pagar.* 🚌 *80, 145.* 🍴 ☕ 🍸 🛍 🚻

Once a nutmeg plantation, this area boasts some of Singapore's most elegant stretches of renovated shophouses, especially along the impressive sweep of Tanjong Pagar Road and in the area around Duxton Road. One of the first of the old neighbourhoods to be renovated, Tanjong Pagar is now home to many lively bars, clubs, hotels and restaurants, including the beautiful Berjaya Duxton Hotel *(see p123)*.

The former Jinrickshaw Station is at the corner of Neil Road and Tanjong Pagar Road. Jinrickshaws were imported from Shanghai in the 1880s. There were about 20,000 rickshaw pullers and 9,000 rickshaws in 1919.

Shophouse Styles

The shophouse is a memorable feature of the local architectural landscape. Five styles, roughly chronological, have been identified – Early, First Transitional, Late, Second Transitional and Art Deco.

The Early Style (1840–1900) shophouse is a squat, two-storey building. The windows and façade are plain.

The First Transitional Style (early 1900s) shophouse is three storeys high, as shown by this unit at Telok Ayer Street.

The Late Style (1900–1940) shophouse is flamboyantly ornamented, with eclectic styles, as seen at this unit (No. 21) on Bukit Pasoh Road.

The Second Transitional Style (late 1930s) shophouse, such as this unit (No. 10) on Stanley Street, is simplified and less ornate.

The Art Deco Style (1930–1960) shophouse is typified by Classical geometric motifs, as seen in this unit (No. 30) on Bukit Pasoh Road.

Ann Siang Hill ❻

Map 4 C4. **Ⓜ** *Tanjong Pagar, Chinatown.* ▥ *51, 61, 63, 80, 103, 124, 145, 174, 197, 603, 608, 851.*
🎵 🍴 🖵 🍷 📷

The distinctive architecture and clock tower of Lau Pa Sat

Aɴɴ Sɪᴀɴɢ Hɪʟʟ was once a plantation of cloves and nutmegs and was known as Scott's Hill, after its landowner Charles Scott. The land was later acquired by a Malaccan Chinese, Chia Ann Siang, after whom Ann Siang Hill and Ann Siang Road are named.

The informal street layout with its curves and gentle slopes, flanked by highly decorated, double-storey terrace shophouses, makes the area particularly interesting for a walking tour. The houses that line these streets are mainly in the Chinese Baroque style; the Malay influence appears in the half-doors (*pintu pagar*), on some of the houses. Chinese superstitions are given architectural voice in many of these buildings – protective gods are incorporated into door lintels or ceramic roof tiles which direct rainfall over the front of the house to bring prosperity.

Club Street in particular has some fascinating houses, including the Victorian **Chinese Weekly Entertainment Club** at the end of the cul-de-sac. Look for Nos. 33 and 35 that were designed by Frank Brewer, an architect renowned for his striking use of plaster work. The small **Mohamad Ali Lane** has interesting buildings from the 1930s period.

There are many pleasant wine bars *(see pp158–9)* and restaurants, including a few which specialize in fine French cuisine.

Tiled shophouse façade at Ann Siang Hill

Lau Pa Sat ❼

18 Raffles Quay. **Map** 5 D4.
Ⓜ *Raffles Place.* ▥ *10, 70, 75, 82, 97, 100, 107, 130, 131, 167, 186.*
⭘ *24 hours.* 🍴 🖵 📷 🚻

Sɪɴɢᴀᴘᴏʀᴇ's ꜰɪʀsᴛ fish market (Telok Ayer Market), renamed as Lau Pa Sat, is now an architecturally impressive food court offering an extensive variety of Asian fare. Handicrafts are sold at the numerous souvenir stalls.

The elegant octagonal cast-iron structure designed by James MacRitchie was shipped over from Glasgow by the same firm (P & W MacLellan) that fabricated the iron for the nearby Cavenagh Bridge. The market was dismantled during MRT tunnel construction to protect it from vibrations, and later reassembled. After careful renovation, it is now a favourite lunch venue for office workers. An adjacent street is closed off in the evening so that people can enjoy alfresco dining under the stars.

Nagore Durgha, designated a national monument in 1974

Telok Ayer Street ❽

Map 5 D4. **Ⓜ** *Tanjong Pagar, Raffles Place.* ▥ *10, 70, 75, 82, 97, 100, 107, 130, 167, 186.* 🎵 🍴 🖵 🍷 📷 🚻

Cʟᴏsᴇ ᴛᴏ ᴛʜᴇ modern, commercial hub of Singapore's financial district, Telok Ayer Street still retains

Hock Teck Ch'i Temple

much of the feel of 19th-century Singapore, when it was famous as a centre for the Chinese coolie trade. Along the street are a number of traditional businesses at work, some fascinating shophouses, and at least three national monuments. Of these, the most famous is the great Hokkien **Thian Hock Keng Temple** (*see pp68–9*), built in 1842. The other two are **Al Abrar Mosque** and the **Nagore Durgha**. Built in the early 1850s, the Al Abrar Mosque's entrance features two large minarets rising from octagonal columns and two smaller ones rising from circular columns. Nagore Durgha, built in the 1820s by Indian craftsmen, combines classical and Indian Muslim details such as arches and perforated grills. Other sites, such as the **Hock Teck Ch'i Temple** which originally sat on the seafront (*telok ayer* means "water bay" in Malay), are well worth a look. **Fuk**

Tak Chi Museum, now standing on the site of this first temple in Singapore, houses Chinese artifacts. Nearby, **Far East Square** offers a variety of shops, bars and restaurants housed in refurbished shophouses.

Thian Hock Keng Temple **9**

See pp68–9.

Raffles Place **10**

Map 5 D3. **M** *Raffles Place.* 🚌 10, 70, 75, 82, 97, 100, 107, 130, 131, 167, 196. 🎵 🍴 💻 🍸 🏧

T HE MODERN, high-tech hub of commercial Singapore, Raffles Place is hemmed in by skyscrapers which house the headquarters of many well-known multinational corporations. The impressive, 280-m (920-ft) high UOB and OUB bank headquarters were both designed by renowned Japanese architect Kenzo Tange. Together with Republic Plaza, these modern buildings have achieved the maximum height which is allowed by the authorities.

Some striking installations of modern sculpture dot the area. These include Salvador Dali's *Homage to Newton* (1985) and Fernando Botero's

Dali's *Homage to Newton*, Raffles Place

Bird (1990) (*see p38*). On the corner of Battery Road and Flint Street stands one of Southeast Asia's earliest skyscrapers, the **Bank of China** building. Nearby is **Clifford Pier**, which served as inspiration for the story line in Joseph Conrad's *Lord Jim*. Clifford Pier is also the starting point for a number of excellent sightseeing cruises.

Boat Quay **11**

Map 5 D3. **M** *Raffles Place.* 🚌 2, 12, 33, 51, 54, 61, 81, 103, 145, 147, 166, 174, 190. 🎵 🍴 💻 🍸 🏧

H OME TO numerous bars, cafés and restaurants, including the famous Harry's Bar, Boat Quay is where Singapore's workers come to unwind after a hard day on the stock exchange. The bars and restaurants along Boat Quay provide a bewildering variety of cuisines. With outdoor dining, a great view of the Singapore River and the administrative buildings such as Parliament House and the Victoria Theatre on the opposite bank can be had.

There is a river taxi service that plies (only when the tide is in) between Boat Quay and Clarke Quay. Bumboats that used to jostle for position at the quay, ferrying goods from the harbour to the warehouses, now serve as river taxis.

Bars and restaurants lining the riverbank at Boat Quay

Thian Hock Keng Temple

Carving of a gilded Buddha
on temple's roof

Tʜɪᴀɴ Hᴏᴄᴋ Kᴇɴɢ is the oldest Chinese temple (built in 1839) in Singapore. It was the most important centre of worship for Hokkien immigrants. Built on the site of a joss house by Hokkien sailors, it was the place where seafarers gave thanks for a safe passage to Singapore. Today, young and old alike come to this temple to give their thanks to Ma Zhu Po, the goddess of the sea. The temple itself is laid out along a traditional north-south axis and is the home of shrines to numerous deities. Construction was paid for by individual donors, the main one being Hokkien leader Tan Tock Seng (1798–1850). The temple received a major facelift in 2000.

★ Roof Decorations
On the temple's roof ridge stand twin dragons that embody the principles of yin and yang. Between them is the "night-shining pearl", a glass globe which represents the sun.

Rear Hall
This shrine to the moon goddess, Yue Gong Niang Niang, is worshipped alongside Guan Yin, the goddess of mercy, in the rear hall. The other god worshipped here is the sun god, Ri Gong Tai Zi.

★ Secondary Shrines
In the side hall to the left of the main courtyard stand shrines to Kai Zhang Shen Wang (a pioneer) and Cheng Huang (a local deity).

The pagoda
used to house the first Chinese school in Singapore, Chong Wen Ge, built in 1849.

Tourist shop

Sᴛᴀʀ Fᴇᴀᴛᴜʀᴇs

★ **Roof Decorations**

★ **Secondary Shrines**

★ **Ceiling**

VISITORS' CHECKLIST

158 Telok Ayer Street. **Map** 5 D4
▌ *6222 8212.* **M** *Tanjong Pagar.* ◯ *8:30am–5:30pm daily.*

Ancestor tablets
The spirit of ancestors are believed to reside in these tablets, which are venerated.

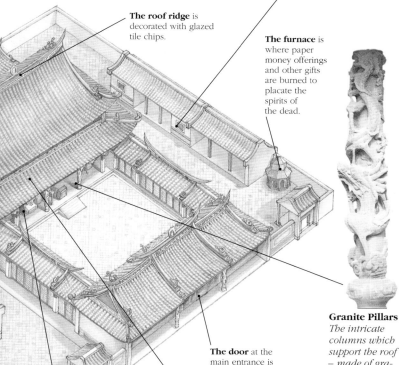

The roof ridge is decorated with glazed tile chips.

The furnace is where paper money offerings and other gifts are burned to placate the spirits of the dead.

Granite Pillars
The intricate columns which support the roof – made of granite from China – are carved with entwined dragons.

The door at the main entrance is decorated with temple guardians from Chinese mythology.

The main hall contains the image of Ma Zhu Po, the sea goddess. She is flanked by Guan Gong, the god of war, and Pao Sheng Da Di, the protector of life.

★ **Ceiling**
Elaborate gilded carvings on the temple's ceiling depict stories from Chinese folklore. These carvings have been painstakingly restored by craftsmen from China in a project that was completed in June 2000.

KAMPONG GLAM AND LITTLE INDIA

Muslim reading the Koran

K AMPONG GLAM AND Little India are two ethnic enclaves that provide some of the best insights into Singapore's Malay and Indian communities respectively. The name "Kampong Glam" is derived from the words "*kampong*" (village) and "*gelam*", a type of tree that once grew in the area. Arab traders were among the earliest settlers here, joining Buginese, Boyanese and Javanese arrivals to create a Muslim enclave. Buildings are predominantly Art-Deco-style shop-

houses and grander colonial architecture with a Middle Eastern feel. Once the seat of Malay royalty, the area still remains an important focal point of Muslim life. Little India is an attractive blend of interesting sights, spicy scents and heady sounds. It is the spiritual heart and the commercial centre of the local Indian community. There are numerous restaurants large and small, traditional shophouses and ornate temples. Crowds flock here, especially at weekends, to worship, shop, eat and socialize.

SIGHTS AT A GLANCE

Historic Streets and Buildings
Arab Street ❹
Bendahara House ❸
Istana Kampong Glam ❷
Little India Arcade ❻
Serangoon Road ⓫

Mosques and Temples
Leong San See Temple ❽
Sakya Muni Buddha Gaya ❾
Sri Srinivasa Perumal Temple pp82–3 ❿
Sri Veeramakaliamman Temple ⓬
Sultan Mosque pp74–5 ❶

Shopping
Bugis Junction ❺
Tekka Centre ❼

KEY

▨	Street-by-Street map *See pp72–3*
Ⓜ	Mass Rapid Transit Station
🚍	Bus terminal
Ⓟ	Parking
⊠	Post office
✚	Hospital
✝	Church
Ⓒ	Mosque
⌂	Indian temple
⛩	Chinese temple

0 metres 500
0 yards 500

GETTING THERE
Take the MRT to Bugis or Little India, or bus numbers 7, 107, 111.

◁ **Mythological carving at Sri Srinivasa Perumal Temple**

Street-by-Street: Kampong Glam

KAMPONG GLAM is the focal point of Muslim Singapore. Two prominent landmarks are the Istana Kampong Glam, the former residence of Sultan Hussein and his descendants, and the premier local mosque, the Sultan Mosque. The 23-hectare (58-acre) Kampong Glam area still bears many traces of its early Muslim settlers, as seen in the buildings, street names, shops and restaurants. This old section of the city provides an invaluable insight into Muslim culture and lifestyle. The famous Arab Street offers a mix of textiles, leather, straw, cane and rattan. Some good Malay food stalls can be found on Kandahar Street.

Alsagoff Arabic School was named after a prominent Arab trader and philanthropist. Built in 1912, it was the first girls' school and first Muslim school to be built in Singapore.

To Malabar Jama-Ath Mosque and old Malay cemetery

| 0 metres | 100 |
| 0 yards | 100 |

★ **Istana Kampong Glam**
Malay motifs combine with the Palladian style in this former royal residence, to become a Malay cultural centre ❷

★ **Sultan Mosque**
The Sultan Mosque dominates the skyline with its golden domes and four corner minarets. It was designed by Irishman Denis Santry ❶

NORTH BRIDGE ROAD

KANDAHAR STREET

MUSCAT STREET

ARAB STREET

Bendahara House
The building, erected in the 1920s, is an example of Palladian-inspired architecture ❸

To Bugis MRT Station

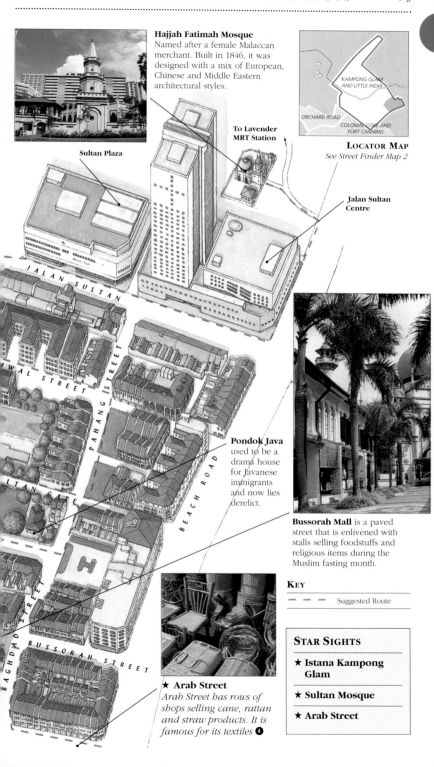

Hajjah Fatimah Mosque
Named after a female Malaccan merchant. Built in 1846, it was designed with a mix of European, Chinese and Middle Eastern architectural styles.

LOCATOR MAP
See Street Finder Map 2

KAMPONG GLAM AND LITTLE INDIA

ORCHARD ROAD

COLONIAL CORE AND FORT CANNING

Sultan Plaza

To Lavender MRT Station

Jalan Sultan Centre

JALAN SULTAN

WAL STREET

PAHANG STREET

TAN GATE

BEACH ROAD

BAGHDAD STREET

BUSSORAH STREET

Pondok Java
used to be a drama house for Javanese immigrants and now lies derelict.

Bussorah Mall is a paved street that is enlivened with stalls selling foodstuffs and religious items during the Muslim fasting month.

KEY

– – – Suggested Route

STAR SIGHTS

★ **Istana Kampong Glam**

★ **Sultan Mosque**

★ **Arab Street**

★ **Arab Street**
Arab Street has rows of shops selling cane, rattan and straw products. It is famous for its textiles ❹

Sultan Mosque ❶

SULTAN MOSQUE IS named after Sultan Hussein Shah, with whom Raffles negotiated in 1819 *(see p17)*. Designed by an Irish architect Denis Santry, it is Arabesque in style with domes, arches and balustrades. The mosque, which is the main Islamic place of worship for Singapore's Muslim community, is the largest in Singapore – the prayer hall accommodates 5,000 worshippers. Only Muslim men are allowed into the main prayer hall; women worship at the gallery on the second floor. Visitors are welcome except on Fridays (Islamic holy day when prayers are conducted). They are not permitted to enter the prayer hall at any time.

Mausoleum
The makam *(mausoleum) houses the royal graves. One of Sultan Hussein's sons is buried here.*

Mihrab
A niche (mihrab) *framed by an arch with decorative motifs faces Mecca.*

Mimbar
This podium-like structure with a flight of stairs is where the imam *(priest) delivers his sermons. The mosque's* mimbar *is a very ornately decorated example.*

STAR FEATURES
★ **Prayer Hall**
★ **Domes**

Ablution Area
There are two ablution areas where worshippers wash before entering to pray. These are located in the compound.

VISITORS' CHECKLIST

3 Muscat Street. **Map** 3 E4.
📞 6293 4405. 📠 6293 2463.
Ⓜ *Bugis*. 🚌 *7, 32, 124, 145,
166, 174, 195, 197*. ⏰ *11am–
7pm daily*. 💰 *voluntary
donation.* 📷 *From outside only.
Visitors can only view the prayer
hall from the foyer.*
🆆 *www.mosque.org.sg*

★ **Prayer Hall**
*Eight bays of arches frame the interior of the prayer
hall along the north and south face, with six columns
on each side. The carpets that line the mosque's floor
were given by a Saudi prince and bear his emblem.*

Gallery
*Stairways lead to the
upper gallery, which
runs along all four
faces of the prayer hall.
Women pray here.*

Minaret
*Four minaret towers
stand at the corners
of the mosque. Forty
slim minaret-like
shafts complement
the Islamic crest pat-
terns on the roof.*

★ **Domes**
*Two domes with pointed
pinnacles create a structure that
has Arabesque stylings with
Moorish overtones.*

Prayer Hall inside the Sultan Mosque

Sultan Mosque ❶

See pp74–5.

Istana Kampong Glam ❷

Sultan Gate. **Map** 3 F4. Ⓜ *Bugis.* 🚌 *107, 961, 980.* ⬤ *Undergoing redevelopment.*

Istana (palace) Kampong Glam was the official royal residence of Sultan Hussein Shah who ceded the sovereign rights of Singapore to the British. As part of this historic agreement *(see p17)*, the Sultan, with his earnings from the British East India Company, built a palace, Istana Kampong Glam. The Sultan named the area "Kota Raja" ("The King's enclave").

Sultan Hussein Shah built a wooden palace at first. His son, Sultan Iskandar Shah, built the present palace in 1840. The palace was rebuilt with British funds and was probably designed by architect G D Coleman, who was superintendent of Public Works from 1828 to 1841. The style of the porch and front façade is reminiscent of Coleman's work.

The Istana has extensive grounds. Several smaller Malay village-style houses were built within the walled compound. These housed the Sultan's extensive entourage as he brought his whole family and hundreds of his relatives from Riau, as well as many servants.

One of the Sultan's descendants was a sports enthusiast who founded a sports club on the premises. The Kota Rajah Club was for young men of good breeding to partake in recreational sports such as badminton.

Hugging the main building on three sides are what remains of the village houses – a cluster of derelict brick and wooden huts. The clubhouse can still be found on the Istana grounds today.

In the Sultan Hussein Ordinance of 1904, enacted by the British Government, financial provisions were made for the Sultan's descendants. The Sultan and his descendants were entitled to an annual stipend. As long as bloodlines can be proved, descendants of the Sultan are still entitled to be paid the annuity regardless of where they live in the world.

The Istana's house sign

This two-storey building on 9,600 sq m (12,000 sq yd) of land is now part of the Kampong Glam conservation area. The sultan's descendants who have had to vacate the Istana were to be compensated for their displacement.

Istana Kampong Glam will be developed into a centre for Malay heritage. The building will be restored over the next few years and a self-funding foundation set up to run the centre.

Bendahara House ❸

73 Sultan Gate. **Map** 3 F4. Ⓜ *Bugis.* 🚌 *107, 961, 980.* ⬤ *Undergoing redevelopment.*

Bendahara (Treasurer's) House is located next door to Istana Kampong Glam. It is a large, old mansion painted yellow, the colour associated with royalty. The locals commonly refer to the house as the yellow villa. It was built in the 1920s by Sultan Hussein Shah's son, Sultan Ali Iskandar Shah. His descendants lived there until the death of Tengku Mahmoud, Sultan Hussein Shah's grandson, whereupon it was sold to a Javanese businessman, Haji Yusof Bin Haji Mohammad Noor, a well-known belt merchant. In conjunction with Istana Kampong Glam, the house will be developed into a centre for Malay heritage.

STREET NAMES IN KAMPONG GLAM

Kampong Glam remains a Malay enclave with a very Middle Eastern resonance. Streets in the area were named after Arabian cities, such as Bussorah Street, Muscat Street and Baghdad Street. The influx of Muslim immigrants in the late 19th century is reflected in the street names allocated, such as Arab Street and Haji Lane. As Kampong Glam was the seat of Malay royalty, streets were named Jalan Sultan and Sultan Gate.

A shop on Arab Street

◁ **Administrative building in the Sultan Mosque compound**

Muslim restaurants in the Arab Street area

Arab Street ❹

Map 3 E4. *Bugis.* 2, 7, 12, 32, 33, 51, 61, 62, 63, 125, 130, 133, 145, 197, 520, 851, 960.

ARAB STREET provides interesting insights into the Muslim way of life brought by the Arabs in the 19th century, when they came to the region to trade. Muslim influence remains strong in the area with many shops on Arab Street selling all manner of religious effects such as prayer mats, holy beads, copies of the *Koran* and skull caps. The majestic Sultan Mosque also looms strikingly in the neighbourhood.

Arab Street draws bargain hunters with a will to haggle. It has a collection of quaint shops selling basketware, leather products, fishing tackle, jewellery, precious and semi-precious gemstones, brass, perfumes and goods made from cane, rattan and straw. Arab Street is most famous for its textile stores. Bales of colourful cloth overflow on to the pavement and cram the storefronts. Fabrics such as cotton, chiffon, organza and silk can easily be purchased here. There are also specialist stores that cater to more esoteric tastes. Items such as ostrich feathers, diamantes, sparkling sequins, various types of thread, dazzling lamé in several colours can also be found here. Arab Street is also renowned for its batik from Indonesia and Malaysia, typically sold in *sarong* lengths (the *sarong*

is a two-metre long wraparound cloth worn by Malay people). The batik is either handmade or machine printed with traditional designs. Shops such as Aljunied Brothers sell ready-made batik shorts, shirts, dresses, ties, and table linen. Traditional Malay wedding shops can also be found in Arab Street.

Bugis Junction ❺

200 Victoria Street. **Map** 3 E4.
6334 8831. *Bugis.* 2, 7, 12, 32, 33, 51, 61, 62, 63, 80, 130, 133, 145, 197, 520, 851, 960, 980.

IN THE MID-1960s in Singapore, Bugis was an infamous district due to its community of transsexuals and transvestites who "worked" Bugis Street. Today, the street has been transformed from seedy motels and dim alleyways into PARCO Bugis Junction and Bugis Village. Certain original features such as stairwells and

shop façades have been incorporated into the redevelopment but it is mainly a modern complex.

PARCO Bugis Junction, a shopping complex, features a glass-covered, air-conditioned shopping street. Distinctive Straits Chinese-style building façades with overhead bridges and detailed cornices add an innovative contrast of old and new architectural styles. This not only contributes to an ambience of nostalgia but also provides a unique backdrop for shopping, dining and

Fountain at Bugis Junction

entertaining. There are 120 specialty shops, sidewalk kiosks, carts, bazaars and boutiques. There is a plaza with sculptures, art works and a fountain. Numerous food and beverage outlets and entertainment facilities are available. The building is linked to the top-end Hotel Inter-Continental *(see p123).*

Bugis Village, across Victoria Street, has a *pasar malam* (night market) *(see p142).* Visitors can buy textiles, CDs, toys, souvenirs, jade, clothing, and even copywatches. There are also entertainment outlets and restaurants with tables set outside for open-air dining, but gone are the transvestites of the mid-1960s.

A model of a Bugis *prahu* (traditional boat) at Bugis Junction

Fragrant handmade garlands on sale in Little India

Little India Arcade ❻

Serangoon Road. **Map** 3 D3. Ⓜ *Little India.* 🚌 *23, 64, 65, 103, 106, 111, 125, 130, 131, 142, 147, 151, 154, 857.* ⭘ *daily.* 📷 ♿ 🍴 🚻

L ITTLE INDIA ARCADE is a collection of conserved shophouses on what was once a Hindu burial ground. Within the arcade are shops which cater mainly to Indians. They sell gaily coloured textiles that are used to make *saris*; fresh onions, potatoes, dried and ground peppers, red chillis, shallots and spices that are used as ingredients in Indian cooking; religious artifacts and garlands that are used as offerings in various Hindu religious ceremonies; Indian music cassettes and videotapes; and an array of handicrafts and souvenirs. The senses of the visitor are aroused by the colours, sights and sounds characteristic of of India.

Ayurvedic medicinal shops offer ancient remedies for a variety of ailments. The betel nut seller often touts his wares in the vicinity. Betel nuts are chopped up and mixed with lime, tobacco and spices, rolled into a betel leaf and chewed to aid digestion. Confectionery stalls sell Indian sweets and snacks, while an air-conditioned food court has stalls offering south Indian, north Indian and Bangladeshi food.

Next to the food court is the **Little India Cultural Corner**, which has an archival display, a video presentation on Indian culture by a local Indian doctor and exhibits of traditional Indian items.

Tekka Centre ❼

Buffalo Road, off Serangoon Road Ⓜ *Little India.* **Map** 3 D3. 🚌 *23, 64, 65, 103, 106, 111, 125, 130, 131, 142, 147.* ⭘ *daily.* 📷 ♿ 🍴 🚻 🚻

T EKKA CENTRE is reputed for its wide array of spices and fresh ingredients, some of which may not be easily available elsewhere. The market is popular with Indians and Malays. Prices here are also comparatively cheaper. Unlike other wet markets which close by noon, the stalls here open until late in the evening.

There is a food centre selling a wide variety of cooked food. On the second floor is a maze of shops offering household goods, jewellery, clothing, bed-linen and artifacts.

Tekka in Teochew dialect means the "foot of bamboo shoots", an allusion to the bamboos which used to grow by the Rochor River. The centre is also known as Kandang Kerbau (meaning "buffalo pen") Market, or KK Market. In the 1870s, the area was a centre for cattle rearing.

Dried food products sold at Tekka Centre

Leong San See Temple ❽

Race Course Road. **Map** 3 E1. Ⓜ *Farrer Park.* 🚌 *23, 64, 65, 111, 130, 131, 133, 139, 147.* ⭘ *6am – 6pm. daily* 📷

M EANING "DRAGON Mountain", the Leong San See Temple was first built in 1917 by a Buddhist monk. Both Taoists and Buddhists worship at the temple.

In the main hall, there is an altar dedicated to the Goddess of Mercy and Compassion, Kuan Yin, and to the

Sakyamuni Buddha. The temple's roof is ornately decorated with fine carvings of dragons, phoenixes, chimeras and flowers. At the back of the temple, there is a wide courtyard containing many ancestral tablets.

Gilded seated Buddha at Leong San See Temple

Sakya Muni Buddha Gaya ❾

366 Race Course Road **Map** 3 E2. 📞 *6294 0714.* Ⓜ *Farrer Park.* 🚌 *23, 64, 65, 106, 111, 125, 130, 131, 142, 147, 151, 857.* ⭘ *7:30am–4:30pm daily.* 📷 ♿

T HIS BUDDHIST TEMPLE is commonly known as the "Temple of 1,000 Lights", from the coloured electric lights that illuminate a 15-m (50-ft) high, 300-tonne seated Buddha statue. The

Towering statue of Buddha at Sakya Muni Buddha Gaya

Komala Villas Restaurant in Serangoon Road

temple was built by Vuttisasara, a Thai monk, in 1927, which accounts for the Thai *wat* style design with a mixture of some Chinese and Indian influences. Vuttisasara made the Buddha statue and an ebony and mother-of-pearl replica of what is believed to be Buddha's footprint.

Another relic in the temple is a piece of bark that is believed to have come from the *bodhi* tree under which Buddha sat in his quest for enlightenment. In a chamber behind the Buddha statue is an image of a reclining Buddha with important events in Buddha's life portrayed at its base. A pair of lions guard the temple's entrance. Visitors have their fortune told near the prayer hall.

Sri Srinivasa Perumal Temple ❿

See pp82–3.

Serangoon Road ⓫

Map 3 D3. Ⓜ *Little India.* 🚌 *23, 64, 65, 106, 111, 125, 130, 131, 142, 147.* 🔽 ⅋ 🅿 ⚑

THE EARLY INDIAN migrants to Singapore in the 19th century settled along the banks of the Rochore Canal. The area eventually became a cattle-breeding and trading centre. This is reflected in the names of some of the streets in the area – Buffalo Road, Kerbau (meaning "buffalo") Road, and Race Course Road, where horseraces were held. Over time, with more Indian arrivals in Singapore, Serangoon Road became

"Little India", the religious, cultural and economic centre for the local Indian community. Today foreign Indian workers add to the local population congregating here.

Serangoon Road, the heart of Little India, is one of the oldest roads in Singapore. At meal-times, the cafés and restaurants in the area are packed with mainly male Indians who normally use their fingers to eat from the banana leaves that serve as plates. The more famous Indian restaurants are the **Komala Villas Restaurant** (for vegetarian food) and **Muthu's Curry** (for fish-head curry). Serangoon Road is well-known for its Hindu temples, shops that sell Indian spices, jewellery and textiles, restaurants, small hotels, fortune-tellers and swing-door bars. Fortune-telling parrots and street pedlars mingle amid the ornate fronts of shophouses, remnants of a traditional plaster-work technique. Mirrors are hung above the doors of many shops on Serangoon Road and its side streets. These are believed to deflect evil influences. Behind ornate temple doors, age-old prayer rituals are being practised. Senses cannot help but be overwhelmed by the scent of heady spices, very important in Indian cuisine. Fresh flower shops painted pink, for good luck, and green, to

symbolize spring, can be found in abundance. Flowers play an important role in the daily lives of Indians – as offerings to deities, as garlands worn on auspicious occasions and as hair decoration.

Sri Veeramakali-amman Temple ⓬

Serangoon Road **Map** 3 D3. 📞 *6293 4634.* Ⓜ *Dhoby Ghaut, Bugis.* 🚌 *23, 64, 65, 103, 106, 111, 125, 130, 131, 142, 147, 151, 857.* 🔽 *daily.* ● *12:30–4pm.* 📷 ⅋ 🅿

THIS TEMPLE IS dedicated to the Hindu goddess Kali, the consort of Shiva the Destroyer in the Hindu Trinity. Veeramakaliamman means "Kali the courageous". The temple, which was built in 1881 by Bengali labourers, represents the goddess with many arms and legs, each holding on to a weapon of war. Kali is symbolic of power and epitomizes the struggle against evil.

The main altar has a black statue of Kali with her sons, Ganesh, the elephant god, and Murugan, the child god riding a peacock, on either side. The temple is crowded on Tuesdays and Fridays, holy days when devotees come to pray and worship.

Sri Veeramakaliamman Temple, a temple in honour of the Hindu goddess, Kali

Sri Srinivasa Perumal Temple ❿

Lotus symbol on ceiling

THIS HINDU TEMPLE is devoted to the worship of Vishnu (also known as Perumal), and is one of the most important in Singapore. It is the starting point in the annual Thaipusam festival *(see p22)*. Built in 1855, the temple was originally a simple structure with a prayer hall *(mandapam)* and a pond, which was later filled in for environmental reasons. In 1966, when Sri Srinivasa Perumal Temple was consecrated, an impressive six-tier tower *(gopuram)* was built, funded by a merchant, P Govindasamy Pillai. Major reconstruction work was carried out on the temple in the 1990s.

★ **Mandapam**
The main prayer hall (mandapam) *has a decorated ceiling supported by ornately carved columns.*

The inner sanctum is where the main idol lies. Only priests can enter.

★ **Subsidiary Shrines**
There are several subsidiary shrines dedicated to different deities. This one is in honour of Ganesh, the elephant-headed god who removes obstacles.

STAR FEATURES

★ *Mandapam*

★ *Subsidiary shrines*

★ *Gopuram*

Vimanams
Decorated domes (vimanams) *mark the position of the temple's subsidiary shrines.*

THAIPUSAM FESTIVAL

This Hindu festival begins at dawn at the temple. Male devotees enter a trance-like state, carrying ornately decorated *kavadis* (portable shrines), attached by metal hooks to their torsos, with skewers pierced through their tongues and cheeks. This is done in penance for sins and in honour of Lord Murugan, the god of bravery, power, beauty and virtue. Women carry milk pots, also fulfilling vows relating to penance. Accompanied by chanting and singing, they walk to Sri Thendayuthapani Temple *(see p53)* on Tank Road, about 3 km (2 miles) distant.

Devotee carrying an ornately decorated *kavadi*

Main Shrine
Here, devotees make offerings of ghee, flowers and fruit, to the accompaniment of music and chants. They touch their heads with holy water.

Vishnu
This sculpture of Vishnu shows him with four sacred instruments – the conch shell, club, lotus and sabre.

★ Gopuram
The 20-metre- (60-ft-) high entrance tower has six tiers of sculptures.

The office provides information on temple activities.

Main Entrance
Statuary stands guard on either side of the massive, wooden door. Devotees ring the bells before entering, asking the gods to grant their prayers.

Hanuman
This shrine is dedicated to Hanuman, the monkey god. According to Hindu epic, he helped rescue Sita from the demon, Ravana.

ORCHARD ROAD

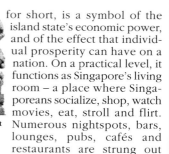

Stone guardian at Ngee Ann City

I N THE 1840s, Orchard Road was a sleepy 2.5 km- (1.5-mile-) stretch of dirt road crossed by a railway, dotted with burial grounds and lined with orchards, nutmeg plantations and the occasional home. Today, it is Singapore's most famous shopping street *(see pp86–9)*. Orchard Road is now lined with numerous shopping malls selling designer goods from around the world. Everything from Swiss watches to state-of-the-art Japanese electronics, Italian furniture, and American designer clothing can be found in lavish flagship stores in gleaming air-conditioned malls.

Even for those who are not interested in shopping (a national pastime in Singapore), it is worth visiting Orchard Road just to see some of the most modern mall architecture in the world; the red (an auspicious colour to the Chinese) temple-like form of Ngee Ann City *(see pp88–9)* is an unashamed shrine to consumerism. "Orchard", as it is commonly called

for short, is a symbol of the island state's economic power, and of the effect that individual prosperity can have on a nation. On a practical level, it functions as Singapore's living room – a place where Singaporeans socialize, shop, watch movies, eat, stroll and flirt. Numerous nightspots, bars, lounges, pubs, cafés and restaurants are strung out along the entire stretch from Tanglin Road right down to Dhoby Ghaut. Orchard Road is the major location for international hotels, such as the Hilton, the Singapore Marriott, the Grand Hyatt, the Mandarin Singapore and Le Meridien *(see pp124–5)*.

Spectacular lights are switched on for Christmas and Chinese New Year, drawing thousands of locals and tourists. The Chingay procession *(see p23)* is held here.

The entrance to the Istana, the Neo-Palladian presidential palace, is on Orchard Road. The Istana is open on some public holidays.

SIGHTS AT A GLANCE

Historic Streets and Buildings
Dhoby Ghaut **1**
Goodwood Park **6**
Peranakan Place/ Emerald Hill **2**

Shopping
Centrepoint **3**
C K Tang **5**
Ngee Ann City **4**
Tanglin Shopping Centre **7**

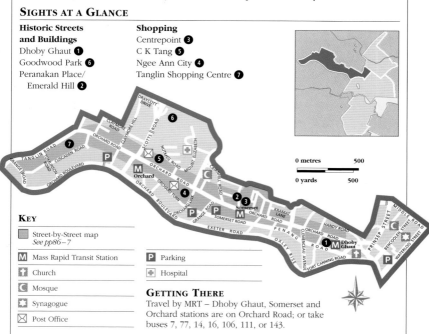

KEY

▢	Street-by-Street map See pp86–7
Ⓜ	Mass Rapid Transit Station
✚	Church
Ⓒ	Mosque
✡	Synagogue
✉	Post Office
Ⓟ	Parking
✚	Hospital

0 metres 500
0 yards 500

GETTING THERE

Travel by MRT – Dhoby Ghaut, Somerset and Orchard stations are on Orchard Road; or take buses 7, 77, 14, 16, 106, 111, or 143.

◁ **The interior of Shaw House, one of the many shopping centres along Orchard Road**

Street by Street: Orchard Road

Shop display

S O GREAT is the profusion of shops on Orchard Road – stretching from Tanglin Mall to Plaza Singapura – that it is easy to be daunted by the sheer range and scale of the retail outlets. Each mall seems bigger and more luxurious than the one before. In many cases, the same brands are carried in different shopping centres so it is possible to see a great deal in a short visit without missing too much. However, each mall along Orchard Road does have a character, so it is good to wander around a few in a leisurely way and enjoy shopping to the full.

★ Ngee Ann City

Ngee Ann City is one of the largest malls in Southeast Asia with seven floors. It has numerous restaurants, a post office, banks, a Japanese department store and more than 120 shops (see p88–9) ❹

Wheelock Place
Shaped rather like a glass and steel Christmas tree, Wheelock Place houses a major bookshop, a few restaurants and a department store.

Paragon shopping centre's interior boasts a vast, cool, shop-lined atrium. Its five floors contain gift, fashion and lifestyle stores.

Delfi Orchard

The Promenade

Liat Towers

Forum Galleria is packed with shops selling clothes and toys for children.

C K Tang *(see p89)*

★ Tanglin Shopping Centre
Tanglin Shopping Centre is a paradise for lovers of antiques, bric-à-brac, old maps, books, furniture carpets and art (see p144).

Wisma Atria
The blue-coloured Wisma Atria houses Isetan, a Japanese department store. All kinds of merchandise, from fashion to electronics, can be found here.

★ Peranakan Place

Beyond Peranakan Place's Baroque Chinese shophouse façade are cafés, pubs and restaurants **2**

LOCATOR MAP
See Street Finder Map 1

STAR SIGHTS

★ **Ngee Ann City**

★ **Tanglin Shopping Centre**

★ **Peranakan Place**

Centrepoint Shopping Centre
Centrepoint's flagship store, Robinson's, has an excellent range of household goods. Cold Storage in the basement has one of the best supermarket selections **3**

0 metres   200

0 yards   200

The Heeren

Cuppage Centre

Plaza Singapura
One of the first malls on Orchard Road, Plaza Singapura was refurbished in the 1990s. Besides a department store, it houses a number of specialist outlets.

Specialist Shopping Centre
John Little department store is the anchor tenant.

Park Mall
Furniture and interior decoration is the emphasis of Park Mall, from the traditional to avant garde displays of state-of-the-art kitchens and other furniture from Europe and Asia.

Dhoby Ghaut ➊

Map 2 C5. **M** *Dhoby Ghaut.*
🚌 *7, 14, 16, 36, 64, 65, 77, 85, 106, 111, 123, 124, 139, 143, 167, 171, 174, 190.* 🍴 🍸 🚻 👨‍👩‍👧

T HE AREA KNOWN AS "Dhoby Ghaut" was named after the *dhobies* (Indian laundry-men) who worked here many years ago. The *dhobies* used to collect the clothes door-to-door from residents, record-ing the items in a book. They washed them in a nearby stream and left the laundry to dry at the place where the YMCA now stands.

The YMCA sits on the site of detention and interrogation rooms used by the Japanese during World War II. Beside it is the white Presbyterian church, established by Scot-tish settlers in 1877. It was used as a supply base for Japanese civilians.

Peranakan Place/ Emerald Hill ➋

Emerald Hill Road. **Map** 2 B4.
M *Somerset.* 🚌 *7, 14, 16, 65, 77, 106, 111, 123, 124, 143, 167, 171, 174, 190.* 📱 🍴 🛍 🍸 🚻 👨‍👩‍👧 🎵

P ERANAKAN PLACE is a group of modern air-conditioned shops thriving within the shell of Peranakan-style shophouses. Renovated in 1984, this is the only piece of old shophouse architecture left on Orchard Road. There is an interesting mix of East and West retailers, with a French café, a Chinese

barbecued meat shop, an outdoor pub and restaurant, and a Mediterranean restaurant and wine cellar. Further along, a row of restored shophouses at Cuppage Terrace houses bars and sidewalk cafés.

Despite the distinctly historical feel to the area, Peranakan Place is a good example of the country's rise to a wealthy, developed nation. Elitist establishments such as boutiques and plush eateries abound, and the sight of sleek, expensive cars is not an uncommon one. Inevitably such develop-ments are reflected in the prices of many of the goods on offer at retail outlets.

Most buildings on Emerald Hill are residential houses built by 30 different owners between 1900 and 1930. An interesting feature are wooden *pintu pagar* (half doors), often quite elaborately carved, across conventional doorways. Richly coloured, ornamental ceramic tiles and architectural elements reflect the ancestor worshipping beliefs of their original occupants, the Peranakans. These include mirrors above doors to ward off evil spirits, incense stick holders worked into external supporting columns and animal reliefs gambolling across brightly-painted façades to invite good luck.

Al fresco dining and drinking near Peranakan Place

Centrepoint ➌

176 Orchard Road. **Map** 2 B4.
📞 *6235 6629.* **M** *Somerset.*
🚌 *7, 14, 16, 65, 77, 106, 111, 123, 124, 143, 167, 171, 174, 190.*
🕐 *10:30 am – 8:30 pm Sun –Thur, 10:30 am – 9:30 pm Fri –Sat.*
🍴 🛍 🚻 👨‍👩‍👧

C ENTREPOINT SHOPPING Centre is dominated by Robinson's five-floor department store. The store claims to put on the best seasonal sales in Singapore, one of which coincides with the Great Singapore Sale in June *(p142)*. A large supermarket is open in the basement, along with a few food and drink outlets. Western fashion is on the

Centrepoint, in the heart of Orchard Road

upper floors in branded shops and also the largest Marks & Spencer store in Singapore, while new Asia is represented by various jewellery shops, a Japanese discount food shop, and Singaporean and Hong Kong fashion outlets.

The top two floors house interior decoration and furniture shops.

Ngee Ann City ➍

391A, Orchard Road. **Map** 2 A4.
📞 *6738 1111.* **M** *Orchard.* 🚌 *7, 14, 16, 65, 77, 106, 111, 123, 124, 143, 167, 171, 174, 190.* 🕐 *10am –9:30 pm daily.* 🍴 🛍 🍸 🚻 👨‍👩‍👧

N GEE ANN CITY is easily the most imposing mall on Orchard Road. Its twin towers and the connecting block are clad entirely in marble; its main entrance is punctuated with two enormous silver columns and guarded by two huge hand-carved *foo* dogs imported from China to bring prosperity. The building's atrium is five floors high,

The modern sculpture and fountain in front of Ngee Ann City

1930s, the hotels competed for famous guests – Raffles boasted Charlie Chaplin as a guest while the Goodwood Park would namedrop the Duke of Windsor as a patron.

The Goodwood houses over 200 rooms which look over lush lawns and gardens *(see p125)*. Its elegant public corridors are lined with original works of art and antique furniture. The Tower Wing, distinguished by its gable ends with ornamental plasterwork, was gazetted a national monument in 1989. For a civilized escape from the heat, try the excellent high tea at the Café Espresso.

zigzagged with escalators, and lined with luxury goods shops. The world's most prestigious retailers are represented – Tiffany, Gucci, Cartier, Harrods, Salvatore Ferragamo, Louis Vuitton, and Bulgari, to name but a few.

Other facilities include a post office, a ticket booking office, a bookstore, a library, banks, a private health club, a discothèque and a coffee shop with a great view over the Civic Plaza.

C K Tang ❺

310 & 320 Orchard Road. **Map** 2 A3.
🅲 6737 5500. Ⓜ Orchard. 🚌 7,
14, 16, 36, 64, 65, 77, 106, 111, 123,
124, 132, 139, 143, 167, 171, 174,
190, 502, 700. 🕙 11am–9pm
Mon–Fri, 11am–9:30pm Sat,
noon–8:30pm Sun. 🔢 🔼 🔽

UNDER THE green-and-red tiled Chinese roof and columns, C K Tang touts itself as Singapore's "Harrods", offering everything from rice

cookers and cosmetics to specialist Chinese foods. It carries mainstream fashion labels and supports local designers such as Arthur Yen. Tang's has a wide selection of silk garments and scarves from China, and ethnic fashions from the region.

The distinctive tower of the elegant Goodwood Park

Goodwood Park ❻

22 Scotts Road. **Map** 2 A3.
🅲 6737 7411. Ⓜ Orchard. 🚌 54,
105, 124, 132, 143, 167, 171, 190,
700. 🔼 🔽 🔲
🆆 www.goodwoodparkhotel.com.sg

THE GOODWOOD PARK Hotel was originally the Teutonia Club, a club for German expatriates. The building and its extensive landscaping was begun in 1900 and the hotel was designed by J Bidwell, who was also the architect of the Goodwood's famous rival, Raffles Hotel. During the

Tanglin Shopping Centre ❼

19 Tanglin Road. **Map** 1 E2.
🅲 6737 0849. Ⓜ Orchard. 🚌 7,
77, 105, 106, 111, 123, 132, 174,
502. 🕙 11am–7pm Mon–Fri,
10:30am–10pm Sat, 10:30am–8pm
Sun. 🎵 🔼 🔲 🔽 🔲 🔼

HERE AT THE far end of the Orchard Road shopping corridor, the pace seems slower with chatty shop owners, a high concentration of non-label-orientated stores, and no piped music. Tanglin Shopping Centre, a favourite haunt of expatriates, is the ideal place to get a suit or dress made, buy an antique, old prints, a carpet or Southeast Asian art *(see p144)*.

Tanglin houses some of the "firsts" and "bests" of Singapore shopping. Antiques of the Orient, the best-stocked antique map and secondhand bookseller in Singapore, has many fascinating prints, postcards and photographs. Select Books, a specialist bookstore and publisher, has an excellent range of titles on Southeast Asia.

Steeple's Deli, the first European/American-style sandwich joint in Singapore, and still one of the most authentic, can be found tucked away in a cramped corner of the second floor and is well worth a visit. Anywhere, a pub, with its house band, Tania, is also popular with expatriates.

Entrance to C K Tang

FURTHER AFIELD

Camping tents at Pasir Ris

S OME OF the most inter-esting sights lie out-side the city limits. They include places of natural beauty and several man-made attractions. West of the city, overlooking the port, is Mount Faber. Tourist attractions located in the west include Haw Par Villa and the Singapore Science Centre. North of the city lie remnants of the original forest at Bukit Timah. The surround-ing nature reserve encompasses the main water reservoirs on the island. The Kranji War Memorial lies in the north, as do the Singapore Zoo-logical Gardens. The east is noted for its beaches at the East Coast Park and Changi Village. Off the coast lie floating fish farms and the rustic Pulau Ubin. To the south, besides Sentosa, there are several un-spoilt islands (Hantu, Sisters, St John's and Kusu islands), which are good spots for picnics and water sports.

SIGHTS AT A GLANCE

Parks, Gardens, Nature Reserves and Reservoirs
Bukit Timah Nature Reserve **6**
East Coast Park **25**
Jurong Bird Park **8**
Jurong Reptile Park **9**
Japanese and Chinese Gardens **10**
MacRitchie Reservoir **5**
Mandai Orchid Gardens **3**
Mount Faber **18**
Singapore Botanic Gardens pp98–9 **16**
Singapore Zoological Gardens **4**

Sungei Buloh Wetland Reserve **1**

Historic Streets, Buildings and Monuments
Changi Village and Prison **26**
Holland Village **14**
Kranji War Memorial **2**
Sun Yat Sen Villa **15**
Tiong Bahru **17**

Themed Attractions
Haw Par Villa Tiger Balm Gardens **13**
Ming Village **12**

Singapore Discovery Centre **7**
Singapore Science Centre **11**

Exhibitions
HarbourFront Centre **19**

Outlying Islands
Kusu Island **21**
Lazarus and Sisters Island **24**
Pulau Hantu **22**
Pulau Ubin **27**
Sentosa pp104–5 **20**
St John's Island **23**

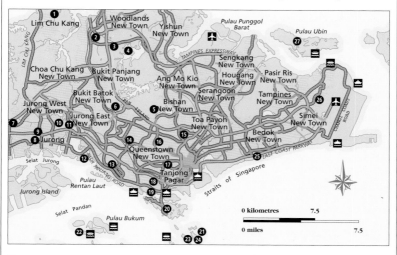

KEY

Street Finder	═ Ferry terminal	Ferry terminal
Built-up area	═ Major road	Local boat service
Airport	— Railway line	

◁ **Pagoda in the Chinese Garden**

A boardwalk at Sungei Buloh Wetland Reserve

Sungei Buloh Wetland Reserve ❶

301 Neo Tiew Crescent. 🄲 6794 1401. Ⓜ Kranji. 🚍 925. Alight at Kranji Dam car park and walk for 15 min, Mon–Sat. The bus stops at the entrance on Sun and public hols. ◯ 7:30am–7pm Mon–Sat, 7am–7pm Sun and public hols. (Last adm: 6pm). 🅳 📷 🍴 🏠 ♿ 🌐 www.sbwr.org.sg

Lying at the confluence of three rivers is this 87-ha (218-acre) mangrove and wetland park. The area was used for prawn and fish farms until 1989, when the farmers were resettled and work commenced to turn it into Singapore's first and only wetland reserve.

The park, which opened in 1993, is a seasonal stopover for migratory birds. The birds flock here from September to April, this being the last stopover in the migration path southwards from the Malay peninsula. More than 126 bird species are found here. Birdwatchers can delight in observing shorebirds and waders such as sandpipers and plovers scavenge for food in the mudflats (see p95). Resident birds, such as herons, kingfishers and sunbirds, also nest in the area. The wetland sites provide rich feeding grounds for the birds

and reptiles. The variety of local wildlife that can be observed in their natural habitat includes mudskippers, tree-climbing crabs, water snakes and monitor lizards.

For close-ups of the flora, such as water plants, without getting muddy or wet, there is a boardwalk through the mangroves. There are also many trails that can be hiked. Specially constructed towers offer-discreet, bird's eye views of the territory.

At the visitors' centre, there are permanent exhibits and an audio-visual show.

Kranji War Memorial

Kranji War Memorial ❷

9 Woodlands Road. 🄲 6269 6158. Ⓜ Kranji. 🚍 170, 178, 960 from MRT station. ◯ 8am–6:30pm daily. 📷

The Kranji War Memorial was built in honour of allied servicemen who lost their lives in battle during the fall of Singapore in World War II and the subsequent Japanese Occupation. This peaceful and beautifully landscaped area, with its levelled lawns and lined trees, is a fitting tribute to those fallen soldiers who defended Singapore, and an interesting place to walk. Their names are inscribed on the walls of the memorial set in the middle of the cemetery. The memorial's design represents the three arms of the service – army, air force and navy. A register of names is available for viewing. Some of Singapore's late past presidents are also buried here.

The Fall of Singapore

On 1 December 1941, a state of emergency was declared in Singapore. At the time, although the situation had worsened in Malaya, Singapore was confident it would not fall to the advancing Japanese forces. By 31 January 1942, through a combination of land and seaborne attacks, British troops were forced to withdraw fully across the causeway to Singapore. The battle for Singapore had begun. On 8 February 1942, Japanese artillery and aircraft started shelling Singapore heavily and Japanese assault boats assailed the coastline. Fierce fighting broke out. By 14 February 1942, the Japanese controlled all the military airfields and main reservoirs. The Malay Regiment made a heroic last stand, but the situation became hopeless. Sir Winston Churchill gave permission to the commanders on the ground to surrender. On 15 February 1942, Singapore fell as Lieutenant-General Arthur Percival, the General Officer Commanding, Malaya, surrendered to the Japanese (see p20). After the surrender, the prisoners-of-war were interned in Changi Prison (see p107) and other camps.

Drawing depicting life in Changi Prison by Haxworth, a British prisoner-of-war

Mandai Orchid Garden ❸

Mandai Lake Road. 🅒 6269 1036.
Ⓜ Ang Mo Kio. 🚌 138, from MRT
station. ◯ 8am–5:30pm daily. ●
public hols. 🖼️ 📷 🚻 🎁 🚼
🌐 www.singaporeorchids.com.sg

T HIS 4-HA (10-ACRE) hillside
garden is covered with
orchids blooming in the open
next to a landscaped water
garden in a valley. The
Mandai Orchid Garden is
the largest commercial
orchid farm in Singa-
pore. Over 200
varieties of orchid
species are found
here, including
Vanda Miss Joaquim,
Singapore's national
flower, which is
named after an
Armenian woman
who discovered
the hybrid in her garden in
the 1800s. Fresh orchids can
be purchased on site.

Vanda Miss Joaquim, the national flower

Singapore Zoological Gardens ❹

80 Mandai Lake Road. 🅒 6269 3411.
Ⓜ Ang Mo Kio, Choa Chu Kang.
🚌 138 from Ang Mo Kio, 927 from
Choa Chu Kang, 926 from Woodlands
bus interchange (Sun and public hols),
or 171 from the city (alight at Mandai
Road, then take 138 from across the
road). ◯ 8:30am–6pm daily. 🖼️ 📷
♿ 🎞️ optional. 🚻 🎁 🚼
🌐 www.zoo.com.sg

T HE ZOO IS SET in 100 ha
(250 acres) of refreshingly
green and peaceful surroundings, and houses over 240
species of animals, 40 of
which can be found on the
world endangered species list,
such as the Malayan tiger.
Over 2,000 animals live in
open concept enclosures
designed to allow them to
breed, interact and flourish in
the most natural setting possible. Natural barriers such as
streams, rocks and vegetation
are used to separate the animals from visitors. Some
animals, such as monkeys
and peahens, move around
freely. In the Fragile Forest

enclosure, butterflies, bats
and birds can be observed in
a rainforest setting.
 This world-famous, award-
winning tourist sight is well
worth a full day's visit. Visitors can have breakfast or tea
with orang utans. There are
special animal feeding times
and shows featuring sea lions,
elephants, primates and
reptiles. The children's section
features animals close at
hand, a playground, a fountain area and a train ride.
 The zoo's breed-
ing programme is
well-known. It has
witnessed a
world's first – the
tropical birth of a
polar bear. A regular
tram service with
recorded informa-
tion covers the
entire grounds.
 For fuller appre-
ciation, follow up with a
walking tour.
 The **Night Safari** is a
unique 40-ha (100-acre) site
and is a night zoo and
wildlife park combined. The
nocturnal activities of over
1,200 animals, numbering
some 110 species, can be
observed from the comfort of
a conducted tram ride. Designated trails can be followed
for closer moonlit encounters.
Subtle lighting allows the
creatures to be watched without disturbing their routines.
Animals are grouped into
their native jungle habitats,
and different geographical
zones are re-created, such as

the Asian rainforest, the
Nepalese river valley and the
Burmese jungle.

🗡️ Night Safari

◯ 7:30pm–midnight daily (Last
adm: 11pm). 🖼️ 🚫

The band stand at the MacRitchie Reservoir

MacRitchie Reservoir ❺

Off Lornie Road. 🚌 74, 93, 130, 132,
167. ◯ daily. 📷 🚻 🚼

C OMPLETED IN THE LATE
1860s, MacRitchie Reser-
voir is a 12-ha (30-acre) park
with two exercise areas and a
playground. It is a favourite
spot for strolls, jogs, picnics
and family outings. Many
paths branch off from the
main 10-km (6-mile) track,
and lead to longer routes into
wooded areas. Refreshment
kiosks, fountains and distance
markers are located among
the lush foliage, where
monkeys and other wildlife
abound. On most Sundays,
local bands and orchestras
perform at the band stand.

White-handed gibbon in the Singapore Zoological Gardens

A gallery in Singapore Discovery Centre, an interactive "edutainment" complex

Bukit Timah Nature Reserve ⑥

177 Hindhede Drive.
📞 6468 5736. Ⓜ Newton. 🚌 171
🕐 8am–6pm daily. 📷 🚻 🚹

This 164-ha (410-acre) nature reserve contains a cornucopia of flora and fauna. One of only two rainforests in the world within city limits, it is about 12 km (7 miles) from the city centre. It boasts Singapore's highest point, **Bukit Timah Hill**, which is about 164 m (540 ft) above sea level. Well sign-posted paths lead the visitor through the reserve, where exotic birds, butterflies, monkeys, squirrels and flying lemurs live. The view from

A disused quarry at Bukit Timah Nature Reserve

the disused quarry lake is not to be missed. The reserve is popular with trekkers and rock climbers. Free brochures and trail maps are available.

Singapore Discovery Centre ⑦

510 Upper Jurong Road.
📞 6792 6188. Ⓜ Boon Lay. 🚌 193
from Boon Lay. 🕐 9am–7pm
Tue–Fri, 9am–8pm Sat, Sun and
public hols. ⬤ Mon. 📷 🚹 🚻
🚹 🚻 🌐 www.sdc.com.sg

The Singapore Discovery Centre is all about learning and having fun through state-of-the-art, high-tech interactive exhibits. Situated next to a military academy, this "edutainment" centre provides a multi-sensory experience with 6-DOF (Degree-of-Freedom) motion simulator rides (which enable the rider to experience a missile in flight). Other attractions are a shooting gallery, virtual reality games, and three-dimensional cinema with laser and film shows played on a five-storey-high large-format screen. There are galleries in which one can relive the experience of Singapore's past, displays that keep one in touch with technology today and glimpses of what is possible in the future. For military buffs, there is an outdoor Singapore Armed Forces military hardware

exhibition that shows off the fighting machines and weapons of the army, navy and air force. There is a section on tactics, a shooting gallery with computer-generated enemies, a gallery showing the development of military technology, and a jungle survival area.

The centre also runs educational programmes for school children. Students can arrange to have guided tours, participate in general knowledge quizzes, and attend talks and camps. They can learn about Singapore's past achievements and ongoing development through live performances. Guides gamely don period costume and act out skits and shows. There is also a children's outdoor adventure playground.

Jurong Bird Park ⑧

2 Jurong Hill, off Ayer Rajah
Expressway. 📞 6265 0022. Ⓜ Boon
Lay. 🚌 194, 251 from Boon Lay.
🕐 9am–6pm Mon–Fri, 8am–6pm
Sat, Sun and public hols. 📷 🚹
🚻 🚹 🚻 🌐 www.birdpark.com.sg

Over 8,000 birds of more than 600 species, including numerous exotic and endangered birds, inhabit this 20-ha (50-acre), beautifully landscaped setting. A panorail (so named because of the panoramic views it offers) courses around the park for elevated views of the various exhibits. There are well-marked paths for a walking tour to see the stunning aviaries, pools and designed habitats. The park boasts the highest man-made waterfall in the world.

Exciting bird shows held at the amphitheatre, featuring flamingoes, macaws, hornbills and cockatoos, are both spectacular and captivating. Birds of prey such as eagles, falcons and hawks demonstrate natural hunting skills and instincts in falconry displays. The birds' feeding times should not be missed.

It is a delight to wander casually in the aviaries amid more than 100 species of free-flying birds from the equatorial jungles of Southeast Asia. The birds' natural habitats are carefully re-created within each enclosure, including simulated tropical thunderstorms. The penguin enclosure has a re-created Antarctic environment that is home to more than 200 penguins of five species as well as other seabirds such as puffins. Owls

Scarlet macaws in Jurong Bird Park

Green iguana at Jurong Reptile Park

can be found in the nocturnal bird house along with night herons and kiwis. Parrot Paradise is a commotion of colours. The largest bird park in the Asia-Pacific region; it's considered one of the world's finest.

The man-made waterfall at the Jurong Bird Park

Jurong Reptile Park ⑨

241 Jalan Ahmad Ibrahim/Ayer Rajah Expressway. 6261 8866.
Boon Lay. 194, 251 from Boon Lay. 9am–6pm daily.
10am, 11am, 3pm and 4pm.

PREVIOUSLY JUST A crocodilarium, this 2-ha (5-acre) revamped park now houses around 400 reptiles and amphibians in a lush natural environment setting. It is one of Southeast Asia's largest reptile theme parks. The venomous, the exotic and the just plain strange are all here in a spine-chilling world containing over 50 different species. The park's inhabitants include 15- to 18-ft (4.6- to 5.5-m) crocodiles, king cobras, giant tortoises, chameleons, iguanas and anacondas.

The park holds a special, yet morbid, appeal for children. The daily reptile shows are thrilling and the hand-feeding sessions are not for the squeamish, as crocodiles leap and snatch wildly for their meal.

Guided tours provide comprehensive educational information on the reptilian inhabitants. For close-up views, capture unforgettable memories at a "Touch 'N' Feel/reptile photography session". The latest addition is a "Kidz Fish 'N' Play" corner, where children can catch fish and take them home.

Although the emphasis is on fun and nature study, the centre is also committed to research and conservation.

BIRD WATCHING IN SINGAPORE

About 350 bird species are found living wild in Singapore. There is no need to venture far in order to enjoy birds in all their varied splendour and melody. In Orchard Road, one shares the thoroughfare with black-naped orioles, Javan mynahs and Asian glossy starlings. The Singapore Botanic Gardens (see pp98–9) is a good place to get acquainted with birds of parks, including pink-necked green pigeons and long-tailed parakeets.

Migratory birds can be found at coastal wetlands such as Sungei Buloh Wetland Reserve (see p92), Singapore's first bird sanctuary. Between September and March, thousands of shorebirds, terns and egrets can be seen here in peaceful co-existence with residents such as collared kingfishers and Pacific swallows. The more adventurous can also visit Bukit Timah Nature Reserve (see p94) for rainforest birds, Pulau Ubin (see p107) for rural birds and Mount Faber (see p102) for migrating birds of prey.

Long-tailed parakeet

Beautiful landscaping in the Japanese Garden, with a pagoda in the neighbouring Chinese Garden in the background

Japanese and Chinese Gardens ⑩

1 Chinese Garden. 【 6261 3632. FAX 6265 8133. M Chinese Garden. 🚌 154. ⭘ 9am–7pm Mon–Sun. Festivals from time to time.

AT THE JAPANESE and Chinese gardens, there is a contrast of horticulture and two distinct styles of architecture. The pleasantly landscaped gardens are situated on two islands linked by a 65-m (215-ft) bridge. The Japanese Garden focuses on simplicity with Zen rock gardens, stone lanterns, summer houses and *koi* (carp) ponds.

The 13-ha (33-acre) Chinese Garden characterizes the Imperial Sung Dynasty style and mirrors the resplendence of Beijing's Summer Palace. It has twin pagodas, a stone boat and a classical tea room. The Chinese Garden also has an interesting collection of *bonsai* (miniature trees) and herbs. The herbs found here have medicinal value and are used as ingredients in traditional recipes.

Confucius' statue at the Chinese Garden

Singapore Science Centre ⑪

15 Science Centre Road, off Jurong Town Hall Road. 【 6425 2250. M Jurong East. 🚌 66, 178, 198, 335. ⭘ 10am–6pm Tue–Sun and public hols. W www.science.edu.sg

ACCLAIMED as one of the world's top ten science centres, the Singapore Science Centre has more than 650 exhibits and hands-on displays *(see p28)*. It opened in 1977 and since then, has been busy promoting knowledge of science and technology.

The Science Centre building was designed by Raymond Woo who won an architectural design competition organized by the Science Centre Board in order to select a suitable building design for the building.

The emphasis of the displays in the Singapore Science Centre is on education and interactive fun, making the world of science accessible and enjoyable. The exhibits illustrate the physical sciences, life sciences, applied sciences, technology and industry, all in an entertaining manner. Hands-on exhibits create an environment where visitors can indulge in participatory learning. The aviation gallery explores the principles of flight.

Next door, the **Omnimax Theatre** offers spectacular visuals and sound on huge 3-D screens occupying entire walls and the ceiling.

Omnimax Theatre ⭘ 9:30am–8:30pm Tue–Sun and public hols. Regular show times.

Ming Village ⑫

32 Pandan Road. 【 6265 7711. FAX 6266 2465. M Clementi. 🚌 78 or free shuttle from Orchard, Mandarin, Raffles and Pan Pacific Hotels (morning only). ⭘ 9am–5:30pm daily.

MING VILLAGE is a tribute to the heritage of the Ming and Qing Dynasties of China, when the art of porcelain-making reached its peak. Chinese porcelain-making is considered a dying art in the modern world of mass production. Ming Village is the largest pottery centre in Asia and one of the very few

Singapore Science Centre, a place to explore science and technology

surviving places where this Chinese art is still being promoted. It produces excellent handmade replicas of the finest pieces of the Ming and Qing eras using traditional techniques. Age-old processes and methods of mould-making, glazing, hand-throwing, hand-painting and firing are used. No two pieces are identical as each piece is created and painted by a single artist. Visitors can watch the skilful porcelain craftsmen at work and take home a reproduction of a Ming masterpiece.

There is also a pewter museum, run by Royal Selangor, which has pewter antiques. Some rare pieces date back 100 years. There is a showroom of pewter products which are on sale.

Replicas of Ming porcelain on display at Ming Village

Haw Par Villa Tiger Balm Gardens ⑬

262 Pasir Panjang Road. 🄲 6872 2780. Ⓜ Buona Vista. 🚌 200 from MRT station, or 10, 30, 51, 143. ◯ 9am–6pm daily. 🈯 🍴 🛍 👪

THIS INTERESTINGLY landscaped park is famous not only for its picturesque surroundings and carp ponds but also for its statues and tablets depicting aspects of Chinese folklore and mythical creatures. Haw Par Villa is a unique theme attraction *(see p28)* based on Chinese legends and myths, portrayed in

Exhibit at Haw Par Villa Tiger Balm Gardens

graphic detail using over 1,000 figurines. Visitors can descend into the underworld and experience the Ten Courts of Hell. The moral tales and stories told impart valuable lessons such as the consequences of greed and the importance of filial piety.

Holland Village ⑭

Jalan Mambong, off Holland Road. Ⓜ Buona Vista. 🚌 7, 61, 75, 77, 106 and 165. 📷 🍴 🛍 🛒 🍸

HOLLAND VILLAGE, an area bounded by Lorong Liput, Lorong Mambong, Holland Road and Holland Avenue, is a popular meeting place for expatriates and locals alike. Tucked amidst public housing estates, it offers a slice of vernacular Singaporean life, where urbanites indulge in the unique suburban milieu without having to travel very far. It is a self-contained community, with shops, coffee shops, pubs, cafés and

restaurants, and still has the feel of a small village about it.

There is a distinct mix of the old and the new, as coffee shops, cobblers, markets and hawker centres dwell side by side with wine bars, cafés, fast food outlets and alfresco restaurants. Diners are spoilt for choice with the variety on offer, from cheesecake and ice cream to sushi and North Indian food.

Rows of shophouses sell a varied mix of wares from cane furniture to electronic goods. There are also stores selling antiques, art works and handicrafts. Holland Village Shopping Centre *(see p144)* has a supermarket, and the upper floors are a myriad of curio and clothes shops where bargains can be had on batik and souvenirs. There is also a roof garden café next to a furniture showroom. The newsagent at the corner of the shopping centre is a virtual institution. It has one of the best selections of magazines in town.

The news vendor at suburban Holland Village

Singapore Botanic Gardens ⑰

Dendrobium Sonia

THE SINGAPORE BOTANIC GARDENS is located close to the bustling city and serves as a peaceful sanctuary. This idyllic garden sits on 52 ha (130 acres) of land. Swans, ducks and turtles inhabit the lakes. Refrains of orchestral music can sometimes be heard from outdoor concerts *(see p154)*. The park is excellent for strolling and boasts serene lakes, pretty waterfalls, landscaped fountains and well-situated rest spots. It has both primary jungle and manicured lawns as well as a newly-created Prehistoric Garden. The gardens' orchid breeding programme, begun in 1928, has produced more than 2,000 hybrids, with more being added each year.

★ National Orchid Garden
The beautifully landscaped garden has a spectacular showcase of over 2,000 orchid hybrids and over 400 species.

VIP Orchid Garden
In 1928, the government started breeding hybrid orchids, and after 1957 started naming selected ones after distinguished guests.

Burkill Hall was home to many of the Garden's past directors, including Isaac Henry Burkill and his son.

Band stand
This octagonal band stand was popular in the 1860s when a promenade in the gardens, listening to music played by a band, was a fashionable pastime.

Swan Lake is home to a host of swans as well as a variety of pond flora.

Sculptures
Girl on a Swing *is the first of a series created by Sydney Harpley.*

★ **Yuen-Peng McNeice Bromeliad Collection**
The collection of 20,000 bromeliads, which come from the forests of Central and South America, was donated by Lady Yuen-Peng McNeice. More than 700 species and 500 hybrids can be seen.

0 metres 100
0 yards 100

Towards
Eco Lake

EJH Corner House
This has been converted into a restaurant with a pleasant view of the idyllic surroundings.

The Tan Hoon Siang Mist House
contains rare orchid blooms.
Cultural artifacts particular to the
orchid's country of origin are
displayed alongside.

Visitors' Centre
The centre has an information counter, a café, a shop and restrooms, with ample parking space. It has its own main entrance access from Evans Road.

Symphony Lake
On an islet in the middle of Symphony Lake is the Shaw Foundation Symphony stage. Concerts and performances are regularly held in the pavilion.

STAR FEATURES

★ **National Orchid Garden**

★ **Bromeliad Collection**

Sun Yat Sen Villa ⑮

12 Tai Gin Road. **C** 6256 7377.
M *Novena*. **▦** 21, 54, 56, 130, 131,
139, 145, 186. **◯** 9am–6pm daily.

Century-old Sun Yat Sen's Villa, also known as Wan Qing Yuan

SUN YAT SEN VILLA is a Victorian villa named after prominent Chinese nationalist, Dr Sun Yat Sen *(see p19)*, who used it as a headquarters to conduct anti-Manchurian activities outside China. He is reported to have stayed at the villa on three occasions.

Built in 1900–02, the two-storey villa features verandahs, a covered entrance porch and arches surrounded by Doric and Corinthian columns and pilasters. It recently underwent major restoration. A new Sun Yat Sen Nanyang Memorial Hall pays a photographic and documentary tribute to Dr Sun Yat Sen's life. A statue of the man stands on the front lawn.

Singapore Botanic Gardens ⑯

See pp98–9.

1930s Art Deco apartment block in Tiong Bahru housing estate

Tiong Bahru ⑰

Tiong Bahru Road. **M** *Tiong Bahru*.
▦ 16, 32, 33, 63, 64, 75, 123, 132,
145, 195, 851.

TIONG BAHRU is one of the oldest suburban residential areas in Singapore and is noted for its Art Deco-style apartment blocks. It is well-known for its fresh produce wet market and open-air alley restaurants. However, what it is most famous for is its bird-singing corner. Since the 1970s, bird fanciers have been bringing their prized birds to this spot for the legendary bird-singing sessions. The best time to visit is on Sunday morning when owners bring along their songbirds in beautiful ornate cages. The cages are hung up on wires strung between trees or under verandahs. The birds are not mixed randomly. Birds of the same species sing together. The bird owners will then sit around the coffee shop (junction of Tiong Bahru and Seng Poh Roads) sipping drinks, showing off their pretty birds and listening to the sweet melodious tunes.

Bird-singing at Tiong Bahru

Mount Faber ⑱

Kampong Bahru Road and Telok Blangah Road, leading up to Mount Faber Road. **M** *HarbourFront*. **▦** 10, 61, 65, 124, 143, 147, 166, 167, 196, 197, 855, 865, 961. **◯** *daily*. **W** *www.nparks.gov.sg*

MOUNT FABER, standing at 105 m (345 ft), offers a breathtaking panoramic view of Singapore, especially of the harbour and the southern islands. The view of the city skyline at night is most spectacular. One of the oldest ridge parks in Singapore can be found here. The lush 56-ha (140-acre) secondary rain-forest is filled with palm trees, rhododendrons, planted bougainvillea and red flame trees. The park is designed to preserve the area's topography. The vegetation helps stabilize the terrain, and look-out points on various sides of the ridge have been created to offer the best possible views *(see pp112–13)*. There is a big rain tree on Faber Point, marking the peak of Mount Faber. As well as a tea house and a souvenir shop, visitors will find a sculpture of a merlion (half-lion, half-fish) statue looking across the sea channel. Cable cars taking visitors across to Sentosa island *(see pp104–5)* can be boarded here.

A view of the harbour and cable cars from Mount Faber

◁ **Lush tropical vegetation at the Singapore Botanic Gardens**

HarbourFront Centre ⓳

Maritime Square, off Telok Blangah Road. 🄲 *6377 6111* 🄼 *HarbourFront* 🚌 *10, 30, 61, 65, 80, 93, 97, 100, 131, 143, 145, 166, 855, 963.* 🄾 *10:30am–6:30pm Tue–Fri, 10:30am–8:30pm Sat–Sun.* 📷 🍴 🖥 🚻
🆆 *www.theharbourfront.com.sg*

FORMERLY THE World Trade Centre, HarbourFront Centre forms part of a larger leisure precinct, the 24-ha (60-acre) HarbourFront Development, which is aimed at transforming the entire Maritime Square area into a waterfront leisure destination and is scheduled to be ready in 2006. Included in the new development will be Singapore's largest retail mall, which will feature a unique attraction – Canal Village – as

Gateway leading to HarbourFront Centre's exhibition halls

well as boast a rail link to the resort island, Sentosa (*see pp 104–5*), to add to existing road, ferry and cable car links.

East of HarbourFront Centre stands the old St James Power House. No longer in use, this is one of the earliest power houses that was built in Singapore. Although no restoration work has been done on it, its red brick exterior remains intact and is still architecturally stunning.

Regional ferries and cruise ships depart from Singapore Cruise Centre frequently – right next to HarbourFront Centre. Boat lovers will enjoy watching sea-going vessels. From here, ferries bring visitors across to Sentosa. Cable cars linking the main island to Sentosa can be seen transporting people overhead.

Taoist temple on Kusu Island, site of a yearly pilgrimage

Sentosa ⓴

See pp104–05.

Kusu Island ㉑

🄲 *6270 7888 for ferry times.* 🚢 *From HarbourFront Centre.* 🎫 *Includes ferry ticket.* 📷 🚻

KUSU ISLAND IS also known as "Turtle Island". As legend has it, the island was actually a giant turtle which transformed itself into land to save two shipwrecked sailors, one Chinese and one Malay.

Kusu Island receives the most visitors during the ninth lunar month (October or November), when Taoist and Muslim devotees flock to the island on an annual pilgrimage. Taoists visit Tua Pek Kong ("*Da Bo Gong*" in Mandarin) Temple, which has a turtle pond, to pray to the god of prosperity for good luck and wealth with joss sticks, candles and offerings of flowers and food (*see p25*).

Muslim devotees climb 122 steps up a steep hill to visit a Malay shrine, Keramat Kusu. Childless couples mark their prayers by tying pieces of cloth around trees on their way up to the shrine.

On the island are two swimming lagoons, picnic facilities, toilets and public telephones.

Pulau Hantu ㉒

🄲 *6275 0388 (Sentosa Development Corporation) for camping permit.* 🚢 *Chartered bumboat from Clifford Pier.* 📷 🚻

PULAU HANTU means "Ghost Island" in Malay. The island got its name from locals who thought it was haunted. Legend has it that pirates hid loot on the island and left lights flickering to scare people away. The flickering lights led locals to believe there were spirits on the island.

Despite its sinister name, the island has one of Singapore's cleanest beaches. The waters off the island are home to coral reefs rich with marine life to tempt divers, snorkellers and fishermen. There is a clear lagoon for swimming and a smaller adjacent islet that is accessible at low tide. Pulau Hantu is also a popular camping site. A camping permit is required. There are bathroom and shower facilities on the island but no phones or food outlets.

Sandy shoreline at Pulau Hantu

Sentosa ⑳

Paddling at Siloso Beach

Sₑₙₜₒₛₐ Iₛₗₐₙᴅ started life as a fishing village and was ominously called Balakang Mati (Back of the Dead) as it was used as a burial site. The British used the island as a military base until 1967. Today, Sentosa has been transformed into a recreational playground for people of all ages. Sun, sea and sand aside, its attractions include museums, historical sights, adventure theme parks, a musical fountain, nature trails and sporting activities. All the sights can be reached by the island's monorail. Sentosa has two major hotels (*see p125*) as well as chalets. The island can be reached by cable car, ferry, bus or taxi.

Dragon Trail/Nature Walk
This nature trail meanders through tropical secondary rainforest to a number of scenic vantage points. Monkeys, squirrels and birds can be spotted.

★ Underwater World
In this tropical fish oceanarium, a moving walkway transports visitors through an 83-metre- (274-feet-) tunnel to see over 2,500 species of marine life.

Shangri-la's Rasa Sentosa

★ Fort Siloso
This last bastion of the British during World War II, built in the 1880s, is an intriguing complex of bunkers, cannons and underground passageways.

Butterfly Park
Over 1,500 live butterflies of more than 50 species fly around in an enclosed garden. There is also an insect museum.

STAR SIGHTS

★ Underwater World

★ Fort Siloso

★ Musical Fountain

★ Images of Singapore

VISITORS' CHECKLIST

33 Allanbrooke Road. ☎ 6275 0388. FAX 6275 0161. ⎇ Service E Orchard Road; Sentosa bus A World Trade Centre, or Sentosa bus C Tiong Bahru MRT station.
⬛ ◯ 9am –9pm daily. 📷 📷
♿ ☎ ⑪ ⬜ ⬜ ⚹⚹
W www.sentosa.com.sg

★ Musical Fountain
The show is a high-tech spectacle featuring fiery flames, lasers and music. A 122-feet- (37-metre-) high Merlion complements the fountain display.

Ferry Terminal

Orchid Garden
Admire rows of colourful tropical orchid varieties here. Within the garden is a koi pond and a restaurant.

0 metres	200
0 yards	200

Volcanoland
A magical themed adventure re-creates a journey into the centre of the earth, including a multi-sensory show which culminates in a sensational volcanic erup-tion. Outdoor performances in a themed setting are staged.

★ Images of Singapore
The museum tells Singapore's history through wax figures and showcases local cultures.

Mangrove, St John's Island

St John's Island ㉓

[6270 7888. 🚢 *From HarbourFront Centre.* 🏖 📷 🚻 *Chalets available for rent.*

Sᴛ Jᴏʜɴ's Iꜱʟᴀɴᴅ was Sir Stamford Raffles' first stop when he arrived in Singapore. In the late 19th century, it was a quarantine centre for Chinese immigrants suffering from cholera. In the 1930s, it was the world's largest quarantine centre for leprosy. It became a deportation holding centre in the 1950s, and later a rehabilitation centre for drug addicts. Despite its chequered past, this unlikely place for a day trip is today a serene place with grassy areas to picnic, paths for strolling, soccer fields for a match and a clear lagoon for swimming.

Lazarus and Sisters Islands ㉔

🚤 *Hire water taxi from Jardine Steps or Clifford Pier.* 📷 🚻

Lᴀᴢᴀʀᴜꜱ and Sisters Islands, unlike many of the other islands to the south of Singapore, are relatively unspoilt. There are two islands in the Sisters group, Pulau Subar Darat and Pulau Subar Laut. Here, off the beaten track, the ambience is relaxed, and will appeal to visitors who just want to find a quiet spot on the beach. As there are no amenities on the islands, it is advisable to bring a picnic and plenty of water. The sea is ideal for swimming and snorkelling. Offshore, scuba divers can enjoy the coral reefs which are rich with marine life, but the currents tend to be strong. Visitors must bring their own dive equipment.

East Coast Park ㉕

Off East Coast Parkway (ECP).
🚌 *13, 16, 196, to Marine Terrace and take underpass across ECP.* 📷
🍴 💺 🍸 🏖 🚻

Tʜᴇ ꜱᴛʀᴇᴛᴄʜᴇꜱ of beach along East Coast Park are considered among the best in Singapore. The park lasts for more than 10 km (6 miles) along the coast from Changi Airport to Marina Bay. The seafront is lined with swaying palm trees, shady rest stops and park benches. For the fitness-conscious, there are walking and jogging paths, and cycling and in-line skating tracks. Bicycle hire shops in the area rent out bicycles, with choices ranging from racers and mountain bicycles to tandems for couples. There is even an in-line skate rental and repair store. Strategically placed cafés, kiosks and snack shops provide refreshments for passers-by. Fishing enthusiasts can spend lazy hours with their rods; picnickers can pitch tents on the beach; health buffs can work out at the outdoor fitness stations; and birdwatchers can take a walk through designated bird sanctuaries *(see p95)*.

The pleasing sea breeze and scenic views on the East Coast make it a fashionable place to live. The area is well-provided with bars, chic restaurants and a host of recreational facilities. The food on offer ranges from fast food and hawker fare to seafood and Western snacks. At the East Coast Recreation Centre, indoor activities can be enjoyed, such as bowling,

snooker and children's games. For outdoor sports, the Europa Sailing Centre offers windsurfing and sailing. Facilities for tennis players *(see p164)* and golfers are also available.

Holiday chalets can be rented for short-term stays. These resorts on the beach front offer integrated facilities such as spas, swimming pools and barbecue pits. On weekends, the East Coast can get very crowded with family outings *(see pp116–17)*.

Gallery of old prints and memorabilia at Changi Museum

Changi Village and Museum ㉖

Upper Changi Road North.
[6214 2451 Ⓜ *Tanah Merah, Tampines.* 🚌 *2, 29.* **Changi Museum:**
🕙 *10am–4:30pm daily.* ✝
5:30pm–7pm Sun. 📷 🛍 💺 🏖
🚻 🆆 www.changimuseum.com

Cʜᴀɴɢɪ Vɪʟʟᴀɢᴇ is a relaxed sanctuary by the beach. Visitors can enjoy a leisurely drink at one of the outdoor bars or dine at the hawker centre, coffee shops or restaurants. Alfresco dining is

Family fun on level and well-marked cycling tracks at East Coast Park

Bumboats plying the Southern Islands at the jetty of Changi Village

available. Changi's sleepy village-like atmosphere contrasts sharply with the busy, ultra-modern international airport nearby. It is an ideal spot for lazy weekends and for aeroplane spotting. Changi beach is good for swimming and picnicking.

Changi Prison is not just a penitentiary, but is also noteworthy for its association with World War II. A prisoner-of-war (POW) camp was based in Changi where many allied troops were incarcerated. Although it was designed to hold a maximum of 600 prisoners, at one point during the war, it held as many as 3,000 POWs.

The **Changi Museum** has, over the years, amassed a good collection of paintings, photographs and personal effects donated by former POWs, which are on display. A series of sketches by a POW named Haxworth made during his internment provide valuable insights into the daily life and work of the prisoners in the camp during the Japanese Occupation *(see p92)*.

Within the Museum is a simple chapel with outdoor pews and a thatched roof over a raised platform. A wreathed altar with a cross is decorated with candles. It is a replica of a small chapel that the allied prisoners originally built and stands as tribute to the men who died in captivity.

Pulau Ubin ㉗

Ⓜ Tanah Merah, Tampines. 🚌 2, 29.
⛴ From Changi Village. ⭕ daily. 📷
🍴 🏪 🏕 ♿

Ⓢingapore's SECOND largest offshore island, Pulau Ubin, which sits in the Johor Strait between Changi and the mouth of the Johor River, is perhaps the last place left for a peek into the rustic atmosphere of Singapore in the 1960s. A Malay and Chinese community used to engage in farming, granite quarrying and fishing on the island. Today, only about 200 people live on the island. Measuring 8 km (5 miles) across and 1.5 km (1 mile) wide, Pulau Ubin houses a traditional Malay fishing

Jackfruit grown in Pulau Ubin

village. The remnants of rural *kampung* (village) life can be seen – attap (thatch roof) and zinc-roofed wooden houses that stand on stilts, *sampans* (wooden fishing boats), fishing nets being dried in the sun, chickens running around and fruit (coconut, durian, rambutan and jackfruit) trees.

The island's flora and fauna include those that once existed on the mainland and that can now only be found here. Wild berries and wild orchids perch on trees; the insect-trapping pitcher plant, various medicinal plants and herbs and mangrove flora still thrive on the island. The island's wildlife includes monkeys, monitor lizards, water-hens, squirrels and snakes such as pythons and cobras. The waters around the island teem with fish, crabs and prawns. Pulau Ubin is also a good spot for bird-watchers *(see p95)* as birds of prey such as eagles, kites and hawks, as well as fruit bats and migratory birds nest here during the northern winter months.

Bicycles can be rented from the jetty. The community centre nearby has a good collection of photographs of life on the island during its heyday. There are a few seafood restaurants, old-style coffee shops and sundry shops that offer necessities for the visitor, such as insect repellent, sun-block, hats, canned drinks and snacks. A couple of run-down taxis ply the gravel tracks. Campsites, chalets and lodges provide overnight accommodation.

Rustic Malay *kampung* (village) houses on Pulau Ubin

FOUR GUIDED WALKS

To GET A real feel for Singapore it is good to explore on foot – many of the city's hidden treasures and most interesting neighbourhoods can only be discovered by the walker who leaves the air-conditioned comfort of a taxi or public transport.

Sign at East Coast Park

The whole of Singapore is compact in scale, and so even outside the central area there are many less well-known gems easily accessible to the inquisitive visitor.

As a walker, you will find that there is much more to Singapore than the shopping malls and high-rise buildings for which it is best known today. Small though the island is, it offers much variety of atmosphere, and fascinating details on a local scale.

To help you find your way around the centre of the city, the Singapore Tourist Board has produced a number of brochures outlining walks that take in some of the most rewarding sites. These include itineraries around Chinatown, Little India and along the Singapore River.

On the following pages are four walks that will take you through some areas of Singapore not generally covered in other guides. They include a glimpse of an important part of Singapore's colonial architectural heritage, a visit to the lush greenery and superb views of Mount Faber, a stroll through the island's most colourful historic neighbourhoods, Geylang and Katong, and a trip to the East Coast.

The climate of Singapore is hot and humid throughout most of the year. It is therefore best to walk in the relative cool of the morning or in the late afternoon when the heat of the day has passed. Whenever you go out into the sun, it's advisable to take a plentiful supply of water, a hat, sunglasses and sunscreen.

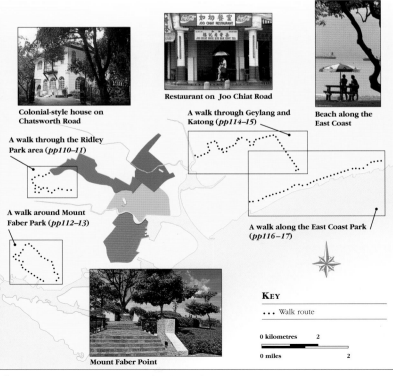

Restaurant on Joo Chiat Road

Colonial-style house on Chatsworth Road

A walk through the Ridley Park area (pp110–11)

A walk around Mount Faber Park (pp112–13)

A walk through Geylang and Katong (pp114–15)

Beach along the East Coast

A walk along the East Coast Park (pp116–17)

Mount Faber Point

KEY

••• Walk route

| 0 kilometres | 2 |
| 0 miles | 2 |

◁ The "black-and-white" style of many colonial-period houses in Singapore

A Sixty-Minute Walk among Colonial Houses

Public buildings such as Raffles Hotel (*see pp50–51*) are familiar symbols of Singapore's colonial era, but the island's "black-and-white" mansions – named after their black-painted timbers and white-painted walls – give a more intimate feel of the period. A good number of them survive. Set in pleasant grounds, they were built from the 1920s onwards with the tropical weather in mind, generally for senior business and military personnel and colonial administrators. Their high ceilings, shaded verandahs and bamboo blinds gave protection from the tropical climate before air-conditioning was common. This walk leads through the Chatsworth Road and Ridley Park area, where some excellent examples of this architecture remain. Other such areas include Cluny Road, Nassim Road and Mount Pleasant Road.

Doorway of no. 24 Chatsworth Road

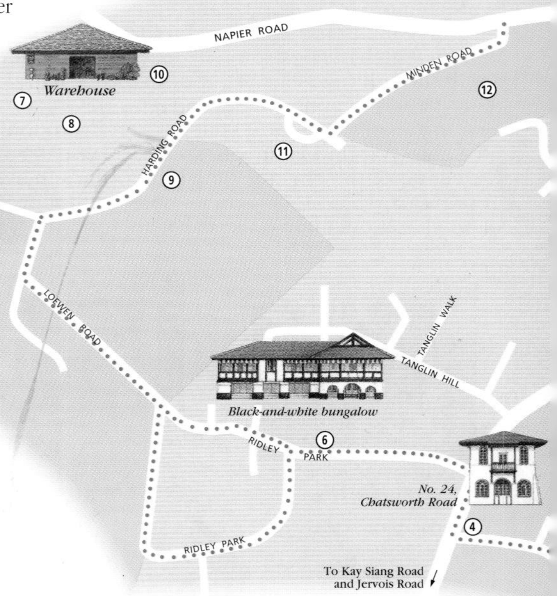

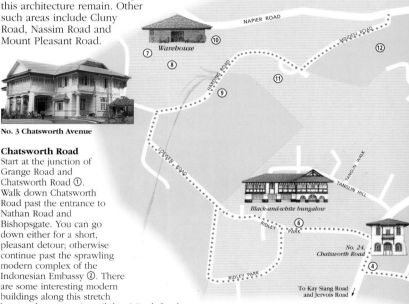

No. 3 Chatsworth Avenue

Chatsworth Road

Start at the junction of Grange Road and Chatsworth Road ①. Walk down Chatsworth Road past the entrance to Nathan Road and Bishopsgate. You can go down either for a short, pleasant detour; otherwise continue past the sprawling modern complex of the Indonesian Embassy ②. There are some interesting modern buildings along this stretch but you have to wait until the junction of Chatsworth Road and Chatsworth Avenue before you get to a couple of the large villas the area is noted for (no. 3 and no. 4) ③.

No. 4 Bishopsgate

Look for the old red fire hydrant near the start of the avenue, just beyond the roundabout, before turning back into Chatsworth Road. Here you will see several impressive properties on the hillside to your right. On the left, just after the turning to Chatsworth Park, make sure you take a look at the stone tigers pacing the lawn of no. 17, which has some particularly fine gable details and an interesting chimney on its outhouse. Walk further along the road and take a look at the imposing houses on the right (nos. 20 and 24). At the junction with Tanglin Road, you will see no. 23 ④. Note how the servants' quarters are connected to the main house by a covered walkway – a common feature of this style of house. If you have time to wander, turn left here to explore the houses along Kay Siang Road and Jervois Road, further down Tanglin Road. If not, turn right and walk past the Singapore Scout Association headquarters ⑤ on your right. Turn left into Ridley Park.

Ridley Park and Beyond

After the the first stretch of Ridley Park (taken over by condominiums), the road narrows and takes on a more rural character. Here are some of the more substantial of Singapore's "black-and-whites", set in beautiful wooded surroundings ⑥. The park is named after "Mad" Henry Ridley, the famous pioneer of the rubber industry in the region and director of the nearby Botanic Gardens in the late 1880s. You can either carry straight up the park or, better, walk around the loop which starts

No. 14 Chatsworth Road

opposite the Mexican Embassy. Many of the houses you can see, which were built in the 1920s and 1930s, were privately owned by firms such as Cable & Wireless. Where Ridley Park becomes Loewen Road, you find yourself walking through an area occupied by the army. It is, however, lush with forest vegetation, with some fine trees (beware of falling fruit). At the end of Loewen Road, there is an expanse of

playing field. On the far side of the field is the Civil Service Club's Dempsey Road Clubhouse ⑦. If you have time, it is well worth exploring the maze of warehouses that surrounds it ⑧. These contain some of the best antique and carpet shops on the island. Otherwise, turn right along Harding Road, to pass an antique centre next to the Ebenezer Chapel ⑨. Opposite it is the brightly painted Youth Flying Club ⑩. Continue on past the playing fields to your right and you will come to a bigger church, St George's ⑪. Follow the road down past a golf course ⑫ to Holland Road. From here, it is a short walk to the gates of the Botanic Gardens and on to the western end of Orchard Road.

St George's Church

| 0 metres | 300 |
| 0 yards | 300 |

KEY

∗∗∗ Walk route

A black-and-white bungalow in Ridley Park

TIPS FOR WALKERS

Starting and finishing points: Junction of Grange Road and Chatsworth Road; Holland Road entrance to the Botanic Gardens
Length: About 4km (2.5 miles).
Getting there: Bus 75, or taxi.
Stopping-off points: There is a café and restaurant near the Dempsey Road Clubhouse and a food court near the entrance to the Botanic Gardens; but no refreshment stops along the actual walk route itself.

A Ninety-Minute Walk through Mount Faber Park

Telescope at Faber Point

Tower of the Danish Seaman's Mission [3]

ALTHOUGH LITTLE MORE than a hillock, Mount Faber offers superb views of Keppel Harbour, the outlying islands and the city centre itself. A signal station in the 19th century and originally called Telok Blangah Hill, it was renamed in 1945 after a government engineer, Captain Charles Edward Faber. Heavily wooded with lovely park areas, it is popular with walkers and joggers escaping from the bustle of the city. There are two ways up – you can either take the cable car from the HarbourFront Centre or Sentosa, or you can walk up from Telok Blangah Road.

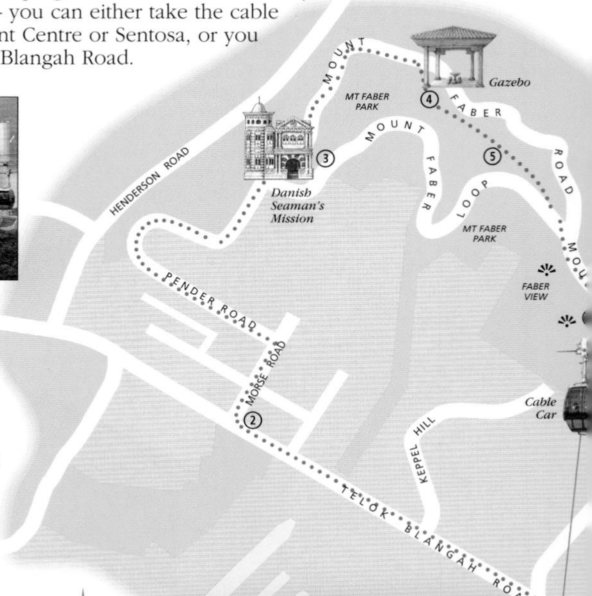

HarbourFront Centre [1]

Going Up

Start from the HarbourFront Centre [1] (*see p103*), gateway to Sentosa and embarkation point for many cruises. Go over the footbridge crossing Telok Blangah Road, turn left and walk past the hawker centre next to the bus station. Continue along Telok Blangah Road. Pass the striking modern architecture of the Grace Methodist Church [2] and turn right up Morse Road (following the sign for Mount Faber Park). Walk up Pender Road, along which you'll catch glimpses of some colonial "black-and-white" houses between the trees. The road twists up the hillside – be careful of traffic. Follow the road to a crossroads, above which stands the lovely house of Tan Boon Liat or "Golden Bell" (now the Danish Seaman's Mission) [3], where Dr Sun Yat Sen is said to have stayed in 1911. If you have time to kill, you can take a detour round the little park to your left. If not, press on straight ahead along Mount Faber Road, following the signs to Faber Point.

Grace Methodist Church [2]

Lookout area at Faber Point [5]

Up to Faber Point

The road plunges you into forest which cloaks this flank of the hill and in which there are splendid specimens of bougainvillea and many other shrubs and trees. After a few minutes, you will see a path going into the trees on the right-hand side of the road. Cross the road and take the path. Climb through the dense undergrowth, ignoring the small track which branches right, until you reach a gazebo ④, where you can break for a rest. Here you will catch a first glimpse of the views that await you at the top. Once you have got your breath back, follow the path along the ridge up some steep red-brick steps and you will find yourself at Faber Point ⑤. Take a look at the relief pictures depicting various facets of Singapore life and history which surround the base of this lookout point. Walk round the base and climb up the steps for some breathtaking views along the coast and out to the surrounding islands and nearby Indonesian archipelago. To the northeast is a stunning view of the city's business district (spectacular at night when the skyscrapers are lit up). Telescopes and interpretation boards are provided.

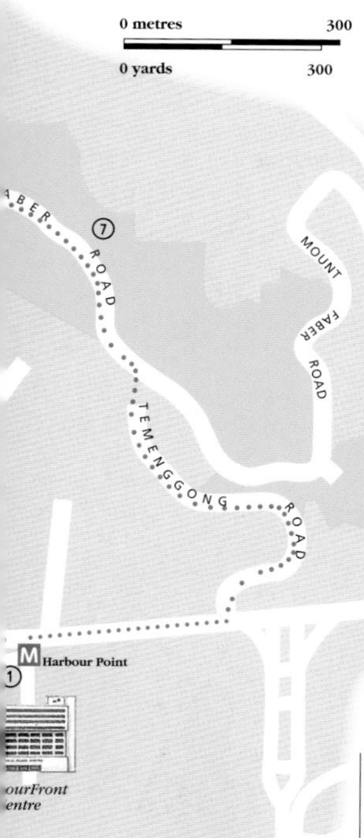

KEY

- ••• Walk route
- ✲ Good view point

Ornamental pond at Cable Car Station

To Cable Car Station and down

From Faber Point, continue along the ridge. The path drops down to the road, where toilets are provided. Continue along the road to the cable car station ⑥. Here there is another excellent viewing platform, as well as a pretty ornamental pond, a bar and the opportunity to buy souvenirs. If you have had enough walking, you can board the cable car, which will take you down to the HarbourFront Centre. If not, continue along the road – here the footpath has been turned into a "floral walk", overhung with a trellis on which grow many beautiful tropical blooms. This route takes you down to the Marina Deck ⑦, a slightly surreal reconstruction of a two-masted ship.

From here the road drops down the side of the hill. After a few hundred metres, take the path that cuts off through the trees on your right. This joins Temenggong Road – it is named after the officials who helped control Singapore in the early 19th century, two of whom are buried close by. Walk down to Telok Blangah Road. Turn left and walk back to the HarbourFront Centre, where you can have a drink or snack.

Tips for Walkers

Starting point: *HarbourFront Centre.*
Length: *3.8 km (2.4 miles)*
Getting there: *To the HarbourFront Centre by bus 10, 30, 61, 65, 80, 93, 97, 100, 131,143, 145, 166, 855.*
Stopping-off points: *There are several cafés and snack shops on top of Mount Faber, including a bar at the cable car station. The HarbourFront Centre has a large number of cafés and restaurants. Along the walk there are many pleasant places to stop and eat food taken with you.*

A path through dense foliage, Temenggong Road ⑧

Marina Deck ⑦

A Ninety-Minute Walk through Geylang and Katong

GEYLANG AND KATONG are arguably the best places to get a glimpse of "old" Singapore. Historically the home of Malay and Straits Chinese communities, these districts present the visitor with a colourful mix of traditional styles of architecture in various states of repair. The walk winds through these old backstreets to show an atmospheric part of Singapore very different from Orchard Road and the modern business district.

From Kallang MRT station to Aljunied Road

At Kallang MRT Station ① take the right-hand exit, cross Sims Avenue and walk past the bus terminal ② to reach Geylang Road. Turn left and walk along this road which is full of interesting shops and restaurants. On your right is the site of the old Gay World amusement park ③. Do not miss the cinema on the right, with its colourful posters advertising the latest Indian films. Turn left down Lorong 9 taking in the Pugilistic Association's headquarters ④ and the Buddhist religious outfitters. Then turn right into Sims Avenue, where a street barber has his stall. On either side of the avenue you'll see an amazing variety of fruit and vegetable stalls. Turn right down tree-lined Lorong 17 and then left to rejoin Geylang Road. Walk past the petrol station and cross the footbridge. Turn right down Lorong 18 to get a glimpse of Singapore's red-light district, then walk along Westerhout Road and up Lorong 20. Continue right down Geylang Road.

Along Geylang Road

The next stretch of Geylang Road features a variety of restaurants and hawker centres in the traditional "shophouse" style. Explore Lorong 29 where you will find an interesting temple ⑤. At its end, turn right into Sims Avenue. On the right-hand side, you'll catch sight of an unusual modern sculpture above Tomlinson's antique shop. Turn right down Lorong 33, a pleasant back street of pastel mansion blocks which also has a temple ⑥. When you reach Geylang Road, cross over and walk to your left

Traditional Chinese temple – with modern refreshments ⑥

until you reach Lorong 38. Walk down this road until you reach a canal, which you follow to the right past the playground – try the reflexology path. Walk up Lorong 40 and continue along Geylang Road, past City Plaza shopping centre ⑦.

Geylang Serai

After you cross Tanjong Katong Road you will see the Malay Village ⑧ on your left. Stop and have

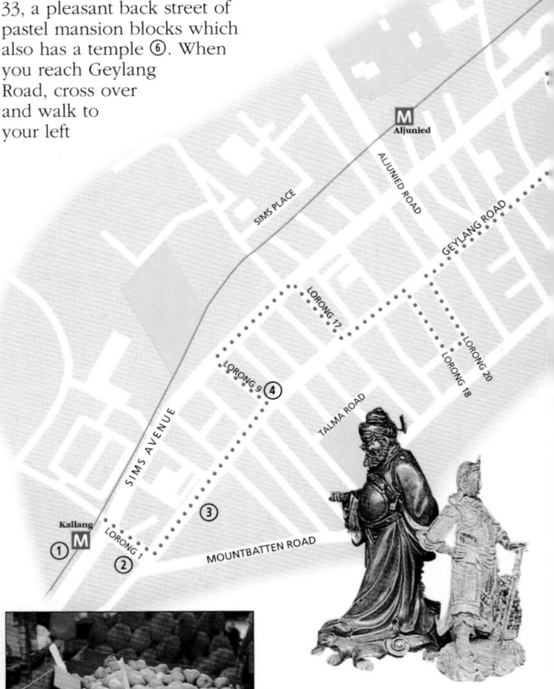

Antiques on sale on Sims Avenue

KEY

... Walk route

[M] MRT station

Entrance to Gay World, formerly a famous amusement park

Fruit stall on Sims Avenue

The Malay Village, a showcase for Malay arts and crafts ⑧

Joo Chiat Road

Follow Joo Chiat Road down on the right-hand side. Browse among the amazing variety of shops which spill out on to the covered walkway. All along this road are wonderfully ornate old Peranakan-style terrace houses and interesting lanes to explore. If you are interested in *nonya* food, try the Guan Hoe Soon restaurant (no. 214). A detour down Joo Chiat Lane will take

0 metres 400

0 yards 400

Traditional Malay headscarves on sale at Geylang Serai market ⑨

a look around the exhibits and shops. Turn the corner after the Malay Village and walk up Geylang Serai, then turn right along Jalan Pasar Baru. You will see Geylang Serai Market ⑨ on your right. Retrace your steps back to Geylang Road and cross over to the Joo Chiat Complex ⑩. Here you'll find an excellent range of textiles for sale.

you to the Hup Hin Bakery, built in 1930 ⑪. Or look left down Koon Seng Road, to see an attractive row of pastel shophouses. When you reach East Coast Road, turn left and walk along to the "Red Bakery", more correctly known as the Katong Bakery & Confectionery ⑫. The bakery, an evocative legacy of prewar Singapore, still makes its own bread and cakes.

A row of colourfully painted shophouses, Koon Seng Road

A Sixty-Minute Walk along the East Coast Park

Cyclists at the East Coast

THE EAST COAST PARK is typically one of Singapore's major planned recreation areas, complete with barbecue pits and "fitness parks". Built on reclaimed land, the park is home to a number of leisure attractions and some great seafood restaurants. It is not all regimented, however, with a number of "long grass" bird sanctuary sections set aside to encourage wildlife. On weekends and holidays, the beach is busy with locals, and it is good to join them for a walk or bicycle ride. You can even hire in-line skates.

Sign marking a bird sanctuary

From Benjamin Sheares Bridge

The East Coast Park actually starts under the western end of Benjamin Sheares bridge. Walk along the East Coast Park Service road until you see a walking off, marked by two, large yellow footprints. In front of you is a canal and a stretch of reclaimed land, and beyond that, the sea. Turn left, sticking to the path, but watch out – passing cyclists

keep an eye on where you are going - don't cross the lines! The route runs for some 10 km (6 miles) along almost the full length of the park. You will see distance markers every so often. The path is lined with coconut palms, so heed the signs warning of falling coconuts! On your left-hand side, beyond the expressway, is an almost unbroken line of

area ② on the left of the path. Then you will find yourself right next to the sea. Here the beach curves away into the distance and offers a

Swimming at the Big Splash ③

A beach outing at the East Coast beach

and skaters can be dangerous. Although the path is divided up into designated areas for cyclists, skate–boarders and walkers, it is advisable to

condominiums. But once you get going, the tower blocks quickly disappear behind the trees, and after about ten minutes you will catch your first sight of the sea. If you want, stop for a rest at one of the picnic tables ① and enjoy the sea view with its array of shipping.

Beaches and a Big Splash

Soon after the picnic site, you will pass the first bird sanctuary

whole series of pleasant places to sunbathe and have a barbecue. There is even a tent-pitching area (*see p106*). Unfortunately, the water quality does not invite bathing, except by the hardy. However, this does not deter locals from settling down for the day with food and drink, and even throwing the odd beach party. A little further on is the Sea Breeze Adventure Club, famous for its Big Splash water chute ③. Stop for refreshments or a slide. Carry on and you will pass the Singapore Road Safety

School ④ – complete with working traffic lights – through the fence. After the next bird sanctuary area, you will see a rather striking yellow observation tower ⑤. Climb up and enjoy the views along the coast and out to sea, where the ships anchor.

Ornamental pond in East Coast Park

Seafood and Seasports

From the observation tower, the path follows the beach. When you get to the sign for the East Coast Park Police Post, you will see the East Coast Recreation Centre ⑥ on your left. Here there is a wide range of amusements, restaurants and snack bars – even a bowling alley. It is one of a number of places along this stretch where you can hire bikes and skates. As you walk down the beach, you will pass a number of other amenities set back from the sea, including a tennis centre and the Costa Sands holiday chalets ⑦. Beyond the chalets there is a pretty ornamental pond ⑧, where the path offers you a number of options – keep near the sea and you will find yourself at the East Coast Seafood Centre ⑨. This place is popular with locals and offers some excellent eating, including a variety of specialist dishes such as crispy baby squids, steamed seabass, or their highly renowned Indonesian crab recipes. If you have more time, you can walk beyond the lagoon ⑩ and explore the Seasports Centre ⑪ and try local delights at another excellent open-air food centre.

> **Tips for Walkers**
>
> ***Starting Point:*** *Benjamin Sheares Bridge.*
> ***Length:*** *About 4.8km (3 miles).*
> ***Getting there:*** *Bus 401 (Sun and public holidays) or taxi.*
> ***Stopping-off points:*** *There are covered rest areas all along the route. Refreshments are available at East Coast Recreation Centre and East Coast Seafood Centre and various stalls in between.*

Key

- ••• Walk route
- Underpass

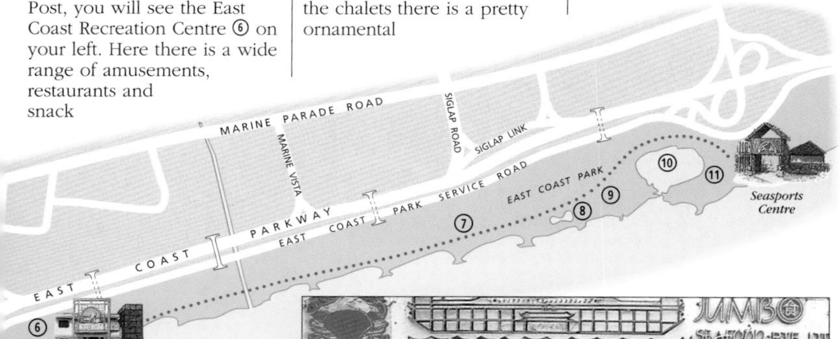

Diners at East Coast Seafood Centre ⑨

Dinghy sailing in the waters off the East Coast Park

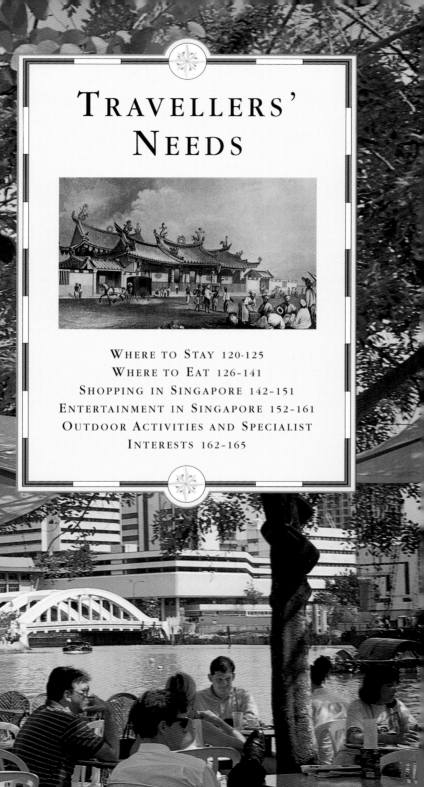

TRAVELLERS' NEEDS

WHERE TO STAY 120-125

WHERE TO EAT 126-141

SHOPPING IN SINGAPORE 142-151

ENTERTAINMENT IN SINGAPORE 152-161

OUTDOOR ACTIVITIES AND SPECIALIST
INTERESTS 162-165

WHERE TO STAY

**Doorman at
Raffles Hotel**

For an island that is merely a dot on the world map, Singapore boasts a very large number of hotels. The largest and best-known chains are all represented here. Standards are generally very high. Many of these places are luxurious and comfortable, though most are at the upper end of the price range. However, good affordable accommodation can still be found a little outside the city centre. Most hotels, including the mid-priced ones, would have business facilities, cable television, in-room IDD telephones and computer ports. Budget travellers may be frustrated by the lack of cheap motels and hostels, though they are not entirely non-existent. Finding accommodation should not be a problem, although June and December are peak periods. Hotels in the Marina Bay area are often well-booked whenever there is a large convention at the Singapore International Convention and Exhibition Centre nearby.

HOTEL RATINGS

Hotels in Singapore are classified by the "star" rating. Accommodation in the Orchard and Marina vicinity starts from three stars. Boutique hotels claim to be a class of their own and refuse to be categorized. The rating system is a reliable guide to the level of service you will expect to receive.

FACILITIES

Due to Singapore's year-round high temperatures and humidity levels, hotels are almost all air-conditioned. Even the most basic hotels have at least one good

**Singapore Marriott, located at a busy
intersection on Orchard Road**

restaurant, in some cases so popular with the locals it is impossible to get a table without a reservation, though priority is often given to hotel guests. Hotels generally provide 24-hour room service.

Rooms usually have at least a telephone, a television and an attached bathroom with hot-and-cold shower. Safes within hotel rooms are common, but although crime levels are low, valuables can and should be deposited at the front desk if necessary.

Most hotels in the city have sports facilities – a basic gymnasium, if not also a swimming pool. Many cater to business travellers, so you can expect the usual business trappings, including e-mail facilities. If the business centre is closed in the evening, the front desk will usually help you to send faxes.

WHAT TO EXPECT

A night's stay in a luxury or even mid-priced hotel typically includes a generous international buffet breakfast and free use of the gymnasium and swimming pool. Other than in pubs, bars and dance clubs, it is an offence to smoke in air-conditioned public places. Non-smoking floors and rooms are common and you can request to be given one when you check into your hotel.

LUXURY HOTELS

There is no lack of luxury, or "five-star" hotels on the island. Many of them belong to international chains – so you can expect appropriate standards, and prices to match. Some of the most expensive and elegant – Four Seasons, Grand Hyatt and Shangri-La – are located around Orchard Road.

Some of the city's best hotels are located at the Marina district, near the eastern end of Orchard Road. Hotels in this area offer stunning views of the harbour and the sea. The Oriental and Ritz-Carlton Millenia are among the best here. Swissôtel the Stamford, the world's tallest hotel, has a stunning view, particularly from Equinox restaurant at the top.

Luxury hotels offer air-conditioned rooms, with comfortable bathrooms, cable television and a mini-bar. Other standard facilities are a swimming pool, health and business centres and a variety of coffee shops, restaurants and well-stocked bars.

MID-PRICED HOTELS

Those who do not wish to pay for luxurious accommodation are turning to mid-priced hotels which offer mostly the same kind of facilities but deliver them with fewer frills – the price (expect to pay S\$100–S\$200), as always, is a good reflection.

Though often a little off the hub, mid-priced hotels are generally well located and serve the needs of most business and leisure travellers perfectly.

BUDGET HOTELS

THE ISLAND does not cater well to budget travellers, but east of the city centre, in Geylang, there are cheap hotels. Be aware – some are disreputable, and charge "by the hour". Many places on Bencoolen Street offer a night's stay for less than S$50. These are very basic and can be poorly kept. The Bugis area is becoming popular, with cheap and clean places to stay. Little India is popular with backpackers who enjoy immersing themselves in the sights and scents of the South Asian subcontinent.

The Royal Peacock Hotel, a boutique hotel

BOUTIQUE HOTELS

TRAVELLERS KEEN to experience the more authentic flavours of the city are turning to boutique hotels. Hoteliers have turned decades-old buildings into fine establishments that are cosy and comfortable. Many are pre-war shophouses painstakingly restored and converted. Some of them provide basic business facilities. Always ask if the room has windows; some do not and the effect can be claustrophobic. Most rooms are small. Chinatown has become a fashionable place to stay, Pagoda Street/Tanjong Pagar fast becoming an alternative entertainment area *(see*

Shangri-La's Rasa Sentosa Resort, a stone's throw away from the beach

pp160–61). Singapore's Chinatown is clean and very well maintained, and while detractors label it "sterile", certain pockets are charming.

RESERVATIONS

FOR ONLINE BOOKING, you could visit this website: www.hotels.online.com.sg (Singapore Hotel Comprehensive Tourist Information Guide and Reservation Service). Alternatively, you can book a room through your travel agent or call the hotel direct. Your credit card number (to which a cancellation fee may be charged) will be needed.

HOTEL PRICES

PUBLISHED ROOM RATES are quoted on the high side but many hotels give attractive discounts from time to time. If they are not advertised, it is still worth "shopping around", or asking for a "corporate rate". Generally, you can expect about 20 to 30 per cent off rack rates. Unless otherwise stated, room rates may not include extras, which include 10 per cent service charge, 5 per cent GST and 1 per cent tax.

SPECIAL NEEDS

MANY FIVE-STAR hotels have rooms specially designed for the disabled, while most hotels are accessible to a wheelchair.

For those travelling with children, extra beds and baby cots will be provided for a fee. Baby-sitting services are usually available, but you will have to arrange for them at least one day in advance. Some hotels, such as the Beaufort, have clubs which run programmes to keep young ones occupied.

SERVICED APARTMENTS

POPULAR with those who are planning a longer stay, serviced apartments, though very expensive, come with many conveniences. Many are equipped with kitchen facilities and offer all the provisions of a good hotel – swimming pool, gymnasium and security guards. You may just rent a room in one of these private apartments.

CAMPING

YOU CAN CAMP in designated parks and islands. Better locations include the East Coast beach, Pasir Ris beach, Pulau Hantu and Pulau Ubin *(see pp103, 106 – 7).* For permission, call the National Parks Board at 6391 6874.

Camping at Pasir Ris Park

Choosing a Hotel

THE HOTELS in this guide have been selected across a wide price range for their good value, excellent facilities and location. The chart lists these hotels by area. The colour code of each area is shown on the thumb tab. The rooms in most of these hotels have air-conditioning, a television set, a minibar and an in-room safe. Major credit cards are generally accepted.

	SWIMMING POOL	GARDEN/TERRACE	BUSINESS CENTRE	CHILDREN'S FACILITIES

THE COLONIAL CORE AND FORT CANNING

	SWIMMING POOL	GARDEN/TERRACE	BUSINESS CENTRE	CHILDREN'S FACILITIES
MARINA MANDARIN Map 5 E2. $$$ 6 Raffles Boulevard. (6338 3388. FAX 6845 1001. W www.marina-mandarin.com.sg This hotel has nice rooms, some of them overlooking the harbour and bay. The lounge is inviting, and the Italian restaurant is famous. 24 ⊞ 📺 🍸 *Rooms: 575*	●		●	■
RAFFLES THE PLAZA Map 3 D4. $$$ 2 Stamford Road. (6339 7777. FAX 6336 6210. W www.rafflestheplazahotel.com This hotel is very conveniently located. It shares a complex with a busy shopping centre *(see p48)* and a MRT station. 24 ⊞ 📺 🍸 ⚘ *Rooms: 769*	●		●	■
SWISSÔTEL THE STAMFORD Map 3 D4. $$$ 2 Stamford Road. (6338 8585. FAX 6338 2862. W www.raffles.com When this hotel was built, it had the distinction of being the tallest hotel in Asia, and still is today. Every room has a superb view. 24 ⊞ 📺 🍸 ⚘ *Rooms: 1,262*	●		●	■
CARLTON Map 3 D5. $$$$ 76 Bras Basah Road. (6338 8333. FAX 6339 6866. W www.carlton.com.sg The hotel is within easy reach of the historic district. Its lobby is not the most attractive, but the rooms are comfortable. 24 ⊞ 📺 🍸 ⚘ *Rooms: 629*	●		●	■
CONRAD INTERNATIONAL CENTENNIAL Map 5 F2. $$$$ 2 Temasek Boulevard. (6334 8888. FAX 6333 9166. W www.conradhotels.com An opulent hotel with particularly good service. Breathtaking harbour views from its luxuriously furnished rooms, and big bathrooms. 24 ⊞ 📺 🍸 *Rooms: 509*	●		●	■
GRAND PLAZA PARKROYAL Map 5 D2. $$$$ 10 Coleman Street. (6336 3456. FAX 6339 9311. @ grandplaza@sin.parkroyalhotels.com Contemporary art fills the sun-lit lobby of this hotel which retains an old-world charm. It has a large spa, with marine-based treatments. 24 ⊞ 📺 🍸 ⚘ *Rooms: 330*	●		●	■
MERCHANT COURT Map 4 C3. $$$$ 20 Merchant Road. (6337 2288. FAX 6334 0606. W www.swissotel.com Overlooking the Singapore River *(see p39)*, the hotel is part of the Raffles International group, and offers good service. 24 ⊞ 📺 🍸 *Rooms: 476*	●		●	■
NEW OTANI Map 4 C2. $$$$ 177A River Valley Road. (6338 3333. FAX 6339 2854. W www.newotanisingapore.com The hotel is situated next to Clarke Quay *(see p59)*. There is a multimedia personal computer in every room. 24 ⊞ 📺 🍸 *Rooms: 408*	●		●	■
PAN PACIFIC Map 5 F2. $$$$ 7 Raffles Boulevard. (6336 8111. FAX 6339 1861. W www.panpac.com Rooms look across the harbour, and the Chinese restaurant at the top has a panoramic view. The central atrium is spectacular. 24 ⊞ 📺 🍸 *Rooms: 784*	●	■	●	■
THE ORIENTAL SINGAPORE Map 5 F2. $$$$ 5 Raffles Avenue. (6338 0066. FAX 6339 9537. W www.mandarinoriental.com A warm and quietly opulent interior awaits. The service is also personable. Rooms overlook the harbour and Marina Bay. 24 ⊞ 📺 🍸 *Rooms: 527*	●		●	■
RAFFLES Map 5 E1. $$$$$ 1 Beach Road. (6337 1886. FAX 6339 7650. W www.raffleshotel.com A Singapore institution, symbol of tropical style for a century *(see pp50–1)*. This superbly restored suite-only hotel is furnished in colonial style, and is set around landscaped courtyards. 24 ⊞ 📺 🍸 *Rooms: 107*	●	■	●	■
RITZ-CARLTON MILLENIA Map 5 F2. $$$$$ 7 Raffles Avenue. (6337 8888. FAX 6338 0001. W www.ritzcarlton.com This "six-star" hotel is architecturally imposing. Butler service is a recent innovation. A key feature is the unobstructed view of the city skyline from the bathrooms. 24 ⊞ 📺 🍸 *Rooms: 610*	●		●	■

Price categories for a standard double room per night, inclusive of breakfast, service charges and any additional taxes such as Goods and Services Tax (GST):
Ⓢ under S$100
ⓈⓈ S$100–200
ⓈⓈⓈ S$200–300
ⓈⓈⓈⓈ S$300–400
ⓈⓈⓈⓈⓈ Over S$400.

SWIMMING POOL
Hotels with an indoor or outdoor swimming pool.
GARDEN/TERRACE
Hotels with a garden, landscaped courtyard or terrace.
BUSINESS CENTRE
Message service; fax for guests; desk and telephone in each room; meeting room within the hotel.
CHILDREN'S FACILITIES
Child cots and baby-sitting service available on request.

	Price	Swimming Pool	Garden/Terrace	Business Centre	Children's Facilities
CHINATOWN AND THE FINANCIAL DISTRICT					
DAMENLOU Map 4 C4. 12 Ann Siang Road. ☎ 6221 1900. FAX 6225 8500. A very small but charming hotel housed in a red-painted pre-war building. The coffee shop run by its owner is an institution not to be missed. One room does not have a window. No non-smoking rooms available. **Rooms: 12**	Ⓢ				▪
THE INN Map 4 C4. 36 Temple Street. ☎ 6221 5333. FAX 6225 5391. W www.theinn.com A friendly, no-frills boutique hotel in renovated Chinatown, surrounded by traditional shophouses. The rooms are basic but clean. **Rooms: 42**	Ⓢ				
ROYAL PEACOCK Map 4 C4. 55 Keong Saik Road. ☎ 6223 3522. FAX 6221 1770. @ rpeacock@cyberway.com.sg Although in Chinatown's red-light district, this boutique hotel converted from a former pre-war house has plenty of charm. Not all rooms have windows, and some are very small; non-smoking rooms are not available. **Rooms: 76**	Ⓢ				
AMARA Map 4 C5. 165 Tanjong Pagar Road. ☎ 6224 4488. FAX 6224 3910. W www.amarahotels.com This business hotel gives very easy access to the financial district and is close to an MRT station. There is a good shopping centre, and the hotel's Thai restaurant, while not cheap, is justifiably popular with locals. **Rooms: 368**	ⓈⓈ	●			▪
CONCORDE Map 4 A3. 317 Outram Road. ☎ 6733 0188. FAX 6733 0989. W www.concorde.net The friendly staff and the hotel's Chinese restaurant are plus points. Rooms are arranged around an impressive central atrium. **Rooms: 515**	ⓈⓈ	●		●	▪
BERJAYA DUXTON Map 4 C4. 83 Duxton Road. ☎ 6227 7678. FAX 6227 1232. W berjayaresorts.com.my Well-located for the business district, this elegant, small hotel in a conservation area was formerly a trading house (from 1860). The French restaurant is one of the best (see p136). There are no non-smoking rooms. **Rooms: 48**	ⓈⓈⓈ			●	▪
NOVOTEL APOLLO Map 4 B2. 405 Havelock Road. ☎ 6733 2081. FAX 6733 1588. W www.novotelapollo.com Situated not far from the city centre, this hotel has a jacuzzi and decent rooms. The Indonesian restaurant has a good buffet. **Rooms: 480**	ⓈⓈⓈ	●		●	▪
KAMPONG GLAM AND LITTLE INDIA					
ALBERT COURT Map 3 D4. 180 Albert Street. ☎ 6339 3939. FAX 6339 3253. W www.albertcourt.com.sg This hotel located at the fringe of colourful Little India has a distinctive colonial façade and a warm ambience. The restaurants and pubs downstairs can get loud sometimes, although the rooms are peaceful enough. **Rooms: 136**	Ⓢ				▪
PERAK LODGE Map 3 D3. 12 Perak Road. ☎ 6296 9072. FAX 6392 0919. W www.peraklodge.net This small hotel is basic but well-maintained and provides great value for money. The atmosphere is cosy and friendly. It is definitely one of the best places to stay in colourful Little India. Several rooms have no windows. **Rooms: 34**	Ⓢ				
PLAZA PARKROYAL Map 3 F4. 7500 Beach Road. ☎ 6298 0011. FAX 6296 3600. W www.plazaparkroyalhotels.com The hotel is only a five-minute drive from the city centre. It has a splendid spa, with beauty treatments provided. **Rooms: 342**	ⓈⓈⓈ	●		●	▪
INTER-CONTINENTAL Map 3 E5. 80 Middle Road. ☎ 6338 7600. FAX 6338 7366. W www.intercontinental.com Colonial charm pervades the hotel's Peranakan-style rooms. Good Mediterranean, Cantonese and health food restaurants. **Rooms: 406**	ⓈⓈⓈⓈ	●		●	▪

For key to symbols see back flap

Price categories for a standard double room per night, inclusive of breakfast, service charges and any additional taxes such as Goods and Services Tax (GST):
S under S$100
SS S$100–200
SSS S$200–300
SSSS S$300–400
SSSSS Over S$400.

SWIMMING POOL
Hotels with an indoor or outdoor swimming pool.
GARDEN/TERRACE
Hotels with a garden, landscaped courtyard or terrace.
BUSINESS CENTRE
Message service; fax for guests; desk and telephone in each room; meeting room within the hotel.
CHILDREN'S FACILITIES
Child cots and baby-sitting service available on request.

ORCHARD ROAD

Hotel	Swimming Pool	Garden/Terrace	Business Centre	Children's Facilities
ASIA Map 2 A2. (SS)				■
ANA Map 1 E2. (SSS)	●		●	
GRAND HYATT SINGAPORE Map 2 A3. (SSS)	●	■	●	■
ORCHARD PARADE Map 1 F2. (SSS)	●		●	
PHOENIX Map 2 B4. (SSS)	●		●	
THE ELIZABETH Map 2 A3. (SSS)	●		●	■
TRADERS Map 1 E2. (SSS)	●		●	■
CROWN PRINCE HOTEL Map 2 B4. (SSSS)	●		●	
HILTON SINGAPORE Map 1 F2. (SSSS)	●		●	■
HOLIDAY INN PARK VIEW Map 4 B4. (SSSS)	●		●	■
LE MERIDIEN SINGAPORE Map 2 B4. (SSSS)	●		●	■
MERITUS MANDARIN Map 2 A4. (SSSS)	●		●	■

ASIA Map 2 A2. (SS)
37 Scotts Road. 6737 8388. FAX 6733 3563. W www.hotelasia.com.sg
This small hotel boasts comfortable rooms and helpful staff. It has a great Chinese restaurant. 24 Y *Rooms: 146*

ANA Map 1 E2. (SSS)
16 Nassim Hill. 6732 1222. FAX 6732 2222. W www.anahotel.com.sg
Tucked away in a quiet, tree-lined corner off busy Orchard Road, this hotel caters adequately to business travellers and provides a welcome respite from the downtown crowd. 24 Y Y *Rooms: 457*

GRAND HYATT SINGAPORE Map 2 A3. (SSS)
10 & 12 Scotts Road. 6738 1234. FAX 6732 1696. W www.singapore.hyatt.com
Grand, luxurious and opulent, the hotel boasts an international restaurant with an extensive Martini menu, a popular Italian restaurant and a hot nightclub. 24 Y Y *Rooms: 683*

ORCHARD PARADE Map 1 F2. (SSS)
1 Tanglin Road. 6737 1133. FAX 6733 0242. W www.orchardparade.com.sg
Mediterranean is the keynote in this newly refurbished hotel. The rooms are comfortable and the restaurants in the area are good. 24 Y Y *Rooms: 387*

PHOENIX Map 2 B4. (SSS)
277 Orchard Road. 6737 8666. FAX 6732 2024. W www.hotelphoenixsingapore.com
This hotel houses a sizzling night club in its basement. Most rooms have a personal computer and a stepper machine. 24 Y Y *Rooms: 394*

THE ELIZABETH Map 2 A3. (SSS)
24 Mount Elizabeth. 6738 1188. FAX 6739 8005. W www.theelizabeth.com
Just a short walk away from the shopping district, this hotel has an extremely pleasant lounge. A small hotel staffed by friendly people. 24 Y Y *Rooms: 256*

TRADERS Map 1 E2. (SSS)
1A Cuscaden Road. 6738 2222. FAX 6831 4314. W www.shangri-la.com
A no-frills but comfortable business hotel at the quieter end of Orchard Road, it is near the Botanic Gardens and next to a shopping mall. 24 Y Y *Rooms: 547*

CROWN PRINCE HOTEL Map 2 B4. (SSSS)
270 Orchard Road. 6732 1111. FAX 6732 7018. @ cphs@cmihotels.com
In the centre of a prime shopping district, this hotel lacks the grandeur of other more expensive hotels in the area but is very comfortable. 24 Y Y *Rooms: 311*

HILTON SINGAPORE Map 1 F2. (SSSS)
581 Orchard Road. 6737 2233. FAX 6732 2917. W www.singapore.hilton.com
The stylish Hilton has some of the charm of a gentleman's club. It has a good continental restaurant and a pool on the rooftop. 24 Y Y *Rooms: 423*

HOLIDAY INN PARK VIEW Map 4 B4.
11 Cavenagh Road. 6733 8333. FAX 6734 4593. W www.holidayinn.com.sg
Located in peaceful surroundings, the hotel is a short walk to Orchard Road. The North Indian restaurant is famous. 24 Y Y *Rooms: 312*

LE MERIDIEN SINGAPORE Map 2 B4. (SSSS)
100 Orchard Road. 6733 8855. FAX 6732 7886. W www.lemeridien-asiapacific.com
Behind a slightly forbidding exterior, the hotel offers comfortable accommodation very close to the centre of town and its shopping facilities. 24 Y Y *Rooms: 400*

MERITUS MANDARIN Map 2 A4. (SSSS)
333 Orchard Road. 6737 4411. FAX 6732 2361. W www.mandarin-singapore.com
Located at the heart of Orchard Road, this is an established hotel with an air of sobriety. It has a revolving restaurant on the top floor. 24 Y Y *Rooms: 1,068*

ORCHARD Map 1 F2. $$$$ 442 Orchard Road. ☎ *6734 7766.* [FAX] *6733 5482.* [W] *www.orchardhotel.com* An efficiently run hotel with all the usual facilities at the quieter end of Orchard Road and a lively restaurant scene. [24] ▦ 🍸 🍷 ♿ ***Rooms:*** *674*	●		●	■
ROYAL PLAZA Map 1 F2. $$$$ 25 Scotts Road. ☎ *6737 7966.* [FAX] *6737 6646.* [W] *www.royalplaza.com.sg* Surrounded by busy shopping malls, this hotel has a peaceful lobby and a popular Italian restaurant *(see p137).* [24] ▦ 🍸 🍷 ♿ ***Rooms:*** *495*	●		●	■
SHANGRI-LA SINGAPORE Map 1 E1. $$$$ 22 Orange Grove Road. ☎ *6737 3644.* [FAX] *6733 1029.* [W] *www.shangri-la.com* The hotel is set amid an immaculately manicured garden. Its rooms are arranged in three distinct wings, all with their own luxurious characters. While not right in the heart of the city, it is perfectly accessible. [24] ▦ 🍸 🍷 ***Rooms:*** *547*	●	■	●	■
SINGAPORE MARRIOTT Map 1 F2. $$$$ 320 Orchard Road. ☎ *6735 5800.* [FAX] *6735 9800* [W] *www.marriotthotels.com/sindt* The lobby is impressive and the rooms well-furnished *(see p120).* The hotel's Sidewalk Café is the place to see and be seen. [24] ▦ 🍸 🍷 ***Rooms:*** *373*	●		●	
THE REGENT SINGAPORE Map 1 E2. $$$$ 1 Cuscaden Road. ☎ *6733 8888.* [FAX] *6732 8838.* [W] *www.regenthotels.com* An immensely stylish hotel, with great service and large, luxurious rooms, set in leafy surroundings. [24] ▦ 🍸 🍷 ***Rooms:*** *441*	●		●	■
FOUR SEASONS SINGAPORE Map 1 F2. $$$$$ 190 Orchard Boulevard. ☎ *6734 1110.* [FAX] *6733 0682.* [W] *www.fshr.com* This elegant hotel with an understated grandeur provides excellent service. The Sunday vodka brunch is remarkable. [24] ▦ 🍸 🍷 ♿ ***Rooms:*** *250*	●		●	■
GOODWOOD PARK Map 2 A3. $$$$$ 22 Scotts Road. ☎ *6737 7411.* [FAX] *6732 8558.* [W] *www.goodwoodparkhotel.com.sg* The second-oldest hotel (1929) in Singapore, set in spacious grounds, has been restored to its former colonial splendour *(see p89).* [24] ▦ 🍸 🍷 ***Rooms:*** *234*	●	■	●	■
SHERATON TOWERS Map 2 A2. $$$$$ 39 Scotts Road. ☎ *6737 6888.* [FAX] *6737 1072.* [W] *www.sheraton.com/towerssingapore* A business hotel with a dignified ambience, it provides the best of both worlds – convenience and serenity. [24] ▦ 🍸 🍷 ***Rooms:*** *413*	●	■	●	■

FURTHER AFIELD

COPTHORNE ORCHID $$$ 214 Dunearn Road. ☎ *6250 3322.* [FAX] *6250 9292.* [W] *www.millennium-hotels.com* A quiet garden hotel in a residential neighbourhood, just a 15-minute drive from Orchard Road. It houses a good Chinese restaurant. [24] ▦ 🍷 ♿ ***Rooms:*** *450*	●	■	●	■
LE MERIDIEN CHANGI $$$ 1 Netheravon Road. ☎ *6542 7700.* [FAX] *6542 5295.* @ *www.lemeridien-asiapacific.com* Set in Changi Village *(see pp106-7)*, this modern hotel is a relaxed hideaway from the city, and conveniently close to the airport. Under renovation until early 2004. [24] ▦ 🍸 🍷 ♿ ***Rooms:*** *275*	●	■	●	■
SHANGRI-LA'S RASA SENTOSA RESORT $$$ 101 Siloso Road, Sentosa. ☎ *6275 0100.* [FAX] *6275 0355.* [W] *www.shangri-la.com* This beach resort on Sentosa is immensely popular with local families. Most of its rooms are sea-facing. The spa is recommended. [24] ▦ 🍸 🍷 ***Rooms:*** *459*	●	■	●	■
BEAUFORT $$$$ 2 Bukit Manis Road, Sentosa. ☎ *6275 0331.* [FAX] *6275 0228.* [W] *www.beaufort.com.sg* On the leisure-orientated island of Sentosa, this beautiful hotel is set on the seashore amid lush greenery. Villas with private pools are available. Its large conference space attracts many business travellers. [24] ▦ 🍸 🍷 ***Rooms:*** *214*	●	■	●	
M-HOTEL $$$$ 81 Anson Road. ☎ *6224 1133.* [FAX] *6222 0749.* [W] *www.mhotel.com.sg* A well priced hotel with serviced office suites for business travellers. The rooms are slightly larger than those most other places offer. [24] 🍸 ♿ ***Rooms:*** *413*	●		●	
MERITUS NEGARA $$$$$ 10 Claymore Road. ☎ *6737 0811.* [FAX] *6737 9075.* [W] *www.meritus-hotels.com* This friendly and unpretentious hotel is located on the tranquil side of a prime shopping district. Rooms are comfortable. [24] ▦ 🍸 🍷 ♿ ***Rooms:*** *198*	●		●	■

For key to symbols see back flap

WHERE TO EAT

ONE OF THE THINGS for which Singapore is best known is the enormous choice of restaurants, and a visit would be incomplete without patronizing a few well-chosen dining rooms. Deciding where to eat is no easy task. There are many casual and fine-dining restaurants at which to sample authentic cuisine. Chinese food can be Cantonese, Hainanese, Sichuan or

Sign promoting a restaurant's fried rice

Shanghainese cuisines. Even restaurants that claim to serve "local" cuisine are no easier to pin down, as the populace includes Asians, Eurasians and Europeans. It is possible to find authentic cuisine styles or enjoy a mix of several cultures. New Asian cooking blends the best styles and seasonings from the region to produce food that tastes as good as traditional recipes.

TYPES OF RESTAURANT

LOCAL RESTAURANTS have embraced almost all the cuisines of the region and, indeed, the world. A myriad of cuisines are available and cater to most tastes. Diners can indulge in Irish, Turkish, Mediterranean, Brazilian, French, Korean, Thai, Vietnamese, Indian, Indonesian, Nepalese or New Asian cuisine. Sample also delicious seafood, which comes both from local shores and from countries overseas, such as Australia and Sri Lanka.

DINING HOURS

WHILE MANY CHAIN eateries, especially those in business districts, open all day, many restaurants keep a 12–2:30pm weekday lunch hour and a 6–10pm dinner time. Many restaurants in the financial district also close for Saturday lunch and often all day Sunday. Until recently, eating after midnight meant a

hawker stall or a 24-hour diner. Increasingly, more restaurants are staying open to cook a limited menu until midnight or later, but it is best to call ahead if dinner is planned for later than 10pm. For convenience, you could try Kopitiam *(see p141)*, a food court chain which has several branches in central areas and is open all hours. Places such as Newton Circus Hawker Centre also stay open after midnight.

RESERVATIONS

RESERVATIONS should be made for Friday or Saturday nights. As public and media attention quickly shifts from one area of town to another, it can be difficult to predict which restaurants will fill up, so calling ahead is advised. Some of the large hip eating spots refuse bookings on weekends, in which case arriving before 7:30pm should avoid the need to queue for a table.

Eating from banana leaves in an Indian restaurant

Make a reservation for any weekday lunch, as an executive crowd could quickly take up all the seating.

SET MEALS

UNLIMITED eat-all-you-can buffets are most often found in hotel outlets; the Sunday version often includes optional champagne, and many offer a theme such as seafood. One hangover from colonial times is high tea sessions. Taken between lunch and dinner, tea or coffee offerings accompany a buffet of western snacks or local food such as *dim sum (see p128)* and nonya *kueb (see p131)*.

VEGETARIANS

VEGETARIANS should ask what goes into the sauce and whether animal fats are used in preparing any part of the meal. Often "vegetarian" simply means there is no meat in the end product. Vegetarian Chinese restaurants serve "mock meat", such as realistic-looking steak or fish, which is, in fact, a soy or gluten substitute. Most food courts would have a vegetarian stall of this sort.

Imperial Herbal restaurant at Seah Street, which serves tonic food

Vegetarian dishes can be found in Indian restaurants. South Indian restaurants serve *dhosai* and *idli* (steamed rice cakes) with lentil curry, while North Indian restaurants serve *chapati, naan, dhals, palak paneer* and *raita* accompaniments *(see pp132–3).*

A good number of restaurants – McDonald's included – serve no pork, but still offer beef bacon and sausages. This helps them comply with *halal* requirements, meaning that the food prepared conforms to Islamic standards.

An Indonesian meal at Lagun Sari restaurant in Tanjong Pagar

DRINKING

ORDERING A BOTTLE of wine in Singapore is a relatively expensive procedure. As local restaurateurs have gradually become better educated in the art of wine, the quality of the wines on offer should be reliable.

The country's proximity to Australia and New Zealand means that New World wines often offer a better deal, compared with bottles from older, more expensive European houses.

Champagne and wine

Some restaurants encourage a "bring your own" (BYO) policy. Diners can bring in wine purchased outside and may be billed a small corkage charge for the privilege. But it should not be taken for granted that you can BYO wine. In addition, many restaurants also serve coffee and tea after meals.

PAYING THE BILL

IN MOST RESTAURANTS, a 10 per cent service charge is included, which means the service is paid for and there is no need to leave an additional tip. If the establishment does not include the service charge, leaving a 10 per cent tip is entirely at your discretion. In addition to service, a 5 per cent Goods and Services Tax (GST) is added to each bill. Most restaurants accept credit cards.

TABLE ETIQUETTE

THERE ARE A FEW customs worth following to avoid causing offence. The thin end of a pair of chopsticks should never be left pointed directly at anyone else, a gesture as rude as waving a fork in a dining companion's face.

Don't stick chopsticks upright in a bowl of food as it has connotations of death.

When not in use, chopsticks should be laid in the holder to the right of the main plate or resting across the edge of the main plate. In Indian and Muslim restaurants and food centres, however, there may be no utensils at all, and people often eat with their hands. To follow suit, only the right hand should be used to scoop rice and curry up with the tips of four cupped fingers; the fingers shouldn't

The chef at Angus Steak House, Ngee Ann City

come into contact with the lips as the food is pushed into the mouth with the thumb. The left hand can be used to lift the water jug to keep the handle clean. If all that sounds too much, just request a spoon and fork.

In Chinese, Indian, Malay and other Asian restaurants, several dishes should be ordered for the table to share. Each person is served with a small plate or bowl, which they should fill with food and then replenish as necessary. Serving spoons are usually provided to avoid anyone using their own cutlery in the communal dishes.

CHILDREN

SOME FAMILY STYLE restaurants cater to children specifically with high chairs and children's portions, but it is best to telephone in advance to confirm. There are plenty of chain restaurants serving burgers, pizza, chicken and tacos to satisfy young ones.

SMOKING

SMOKING is banned in all air-conditioned places where restaurant food is being served. Bars that allow smoking in air-conditioned spaces can only serve snacks, or "finger food", that does not require cutlery to eat. It is possible to smoke in some restaurants after the hours when food is served or in outdoor seating areas. Many of the fine-dining restaurants have terraces for coffee and smoking but without a full licence to serve dinner in these alfresco areas.

Chinese Cuisine

Shark's fin soup

THE MAJORITY OF ETHNIC CHINESE in Singapore originally came from the homelands of the Hokkiens and Teochews. Naturally there are many examples of dishes from these two areas. But you can also find Hainanese or Shanghainese cuisines, for example. Differences between the various regional foods are important; garlic is more prevalent in northern dishes, whereas chillies are used more heavily in fiery Sichuanese cuisine. Cantonese food is most noticeable in the popular *dim sum*, small parcels of steamed and fried food. Hokkien food is surprisingly not as prevalent but no visitor should leave without trying *popiah* (spring rolls) or *or luak* (oyster omelette).

Chee cheong fun *are long noodles with meat or prawn, eaten with a sweet sauce.*

Egg tart
Steamed pork dumpling
Steamed prawn dumpling
Fried pork dumpling
Pork pastry

Minced pork pastry
Char siew pau (minced pork bun)
Yam pastry
Carrot cake

Carrot cake *can also be fried with egg and seasoned with a sweet black sauce.*

Dim sum *are Cantonese-style parcels of food. The selection includes, besides those pictured, steamed chicken legs, fried prawn dumplings and pork ribs in light sauce.*

Popiah *are flour wrappers filled with turnip, lettuce, bean sprouts, egg and prawns.*

Oyster omelette *is a dish of oysters fried with egg, cornstarch and spring onion. It is dipped into chilli sauce.*

Peking duck *consists of the crispy skin of roasted duck served in a pancake with vegetables and a sweet sauce.*

Char kway teow *is fried flat rice noodles served with clams, Chinese sausage and egg in a sweet black sauce.*

Steamed chicken
Chilli sauce
Dark soya sauce
Chicken rice *consists of steamed chicken, cucumber and tomato slices served with fragrant rice.*
Rice

Diced red chillies
Flour fritters
Pork ribs
Steamed rice
Soya sauce

Bak kut teh *is pork rib soup with special herbs, served with rice and flour fritters for dipping.*

- Five spice powder
- Crackers
- Sliced raw salmon
- Lime
- Lemon wedge
- Plum sauce
- Shredded dried orange peel
- Pepper
- Dried winter melon
- Pickled yellow ginger
- Pickled red ginger
- Parsley
- Pickled onions
- Pickled melon
- Shredded carrots, sesame and peanuts

Yu sheng, *an auspicious Chinese New Year dish, includes raw salmon, carrots, radish, sweet ginger, grapefruit flesh, all of which are tossed together to make a sweet and sour treat. Each time someone lifts the mixture, saying the auspicious words, "lo hei" adds to the good fortune.*

Buddha jumps over the wall *is an expensive soup dish with abalone and sea cucumber.*

Black chicken herbal soup *is a nutritious tonic. Popular locally, it is said to improve health and well-being.*

Black pepper beef *is stir-fried to give that spicy peppery taste. It is like a Chinese version of peppered steak.*

Lemon chicken *is fried chicken flavoured with a lemon sauce which imparts a tangy taste.*

Chilli crab *is deep fried and cooked in a hot spicy gravy. A popular variation is black pepper crabs.*

Mango pudding *is a sweet, creamy dessert.*

Cheng teng *is a dessert of fruits, jelly, barley and beans.*

Ice kachang *is sweetened ice with corn, red beans and jelly.*

TROPICAL FRUIT

Southeast Asian fruits such as papaya, water melon, honeydew melon, pineapple, starfruit, pomelo, rambutan and jackfruit make a healthy dessert. Durian, a pungent favourite of many locals, and mangosteen are seasonal fruit.

Durian

Mangosteen

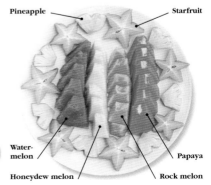

- Pineapple
- Starfruit
- Water-melon
- Papaya
- Honeydew melon
- Rock melon

Malay Cuisine

Otak-otak, fish paste wrapped in a coconut leaf

MALAY CUISINE SHARES recipes and ingredients with neighbouring Indonesia and employs many Thai cooking techniques and ingredients. It can mean traditional Muslim food or Peranakan cuisine. Both types of cuisine reflect the requirement for *halal* food (which contains no pork). Lemongrass and shrimp paste *(belacan)* are staple ingredients of Malay food, which also incorporates lots of coconut milk. Regional differences are noticeable, and so signature dishes such as *laksa* (spicy noodle soup) are as distinctive in Penang and Johor as they are in Singapore.

Roti John *is French bread fried with mutton and egg, and served with chilli sauce or ketchup.*

Mee siam *is vermicelli served in a spicy, sour and sweet gravy with eggs, grated peanuts and soya beans.*

Laksa *is rice flour noodles in a spicy coconut milk with beancurd and chunks of seafood, including cockles.*

Nasi lemak, *or rice cooked with coconut milk, is served with anchovies, peanuts, egg, cucumber and chilli.*

Mee rebus *is yellow noodles in a thick, sweet and spicy sauce served with egg and sliced green chillies.*

Sliced cucumber

Sliced onions

Mutton

Peanut sauce

Ketupat

Lontong *is rice cakes served in a spicy sauce with cabbage, french beans, beancurd and egg.*

Satay *is the Malay version of a kebab. Barbecued mutton, chicken or beef on skewers is served with a thick peanut sauce, onions, cucumbers and ketupat (rice cooked in cases woven from coconut leaves).*

Ayam panggang, *chicken barbecued with garlic and lime, is served with a hot sambal sauce.*

Rendang *is a spicy Malay/Indonesian-style dried curry. The meat can be mutton, chicken or beef.*

Sambal *prawn* *is a dish which combines prawns with the sambal sauce of chilli, onions and prawn paste.*

Sambal goreng *is long beans with beancurd and meat. It is cooked with coconut milk, tamarind and shallots.*

Nasi goreng *is Malay-style fried rice with prawns or meat and flavoured with coriander and cumin.*

Assam pedas *consists of fish cooked in a spicy, tamarind-based sauce combined with ladies' fingers (okra) or brinjal.*

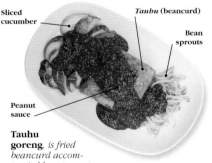

Sliced cucumber

Tauhu (beancurd)

Bean sprouts

Peanut sauce

Tauhu goreng, *is fried beancurd accompanied by a peanut sauce.*

Curry puff *is a pastry stuffed with either curried potatoes, chicken and egg or sardines.*

Lopez *is glutinous rice topped with grated coconut and sweet syrup.*

Bubur hitam *is black glutinous rice with coconut milk.*

Pulut seri kaya

Lempa haybi

Pulut durian

Bengka ubi

Bengka telur

Ondeh-ondeh

Kueh kosuree

Chendol *is iced coconut milk with palm sugar syrup and jelly. There is a version of chendol flavoured with durian.*

Pulut tatar with kaya

Pineapple tart

Kueh *are sweet rice cakes flavoured with coconut and palm sugar.*

Indian Cuisine

Vada, a lentil-based snack

IN GENERAL, INDIAN CUISINE is from either the North or the South and the two food varieties are distinctly different. Milder, creamier northern dishes contrast with the sharp spices of the south. Northern Indian cuisine is usually served with light *naans* to mop up the rich sauces; dishes from the south, on the other hand, feature thinner curry sauces, usually soaked up with rice. There is also a hybrid Singapore-Indian strain of cooking which incorporates Chinese elements such as noodles, or some new ingredients into old recipes such as the famous fish-head curry. The best way to experience Indian cuisine is to visit one of the "banana leaf" eateries in Little India.

Roti prata *("flipped bread") is a wafer-thin, flat bread, fried and served with curry. This is a breakfast favourite.*

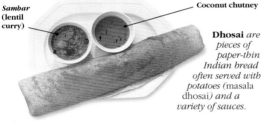

Sambar (lentil curry)

Coconut chutney

Dhosai *are pieces of paper-thin Indian bread often served with potatoes (*masala dhosai*) and a variety of sauces.*

Murtabak, *a variation of the prata, fried with egg, contains mutton, lamb or chicken. It is served with curry.*

Chapati *is roasted wholewheat bread. It has a crispy, slightly spicy flavour and goes well with other dishes.*

Mint **naan**

Plain **naan**

Naan, *a tandoori-style Indian bread, gets some of its flavour from ghee and onion seeds kneaded into the dough before baking.*

Garlic **naan**

Tandoori chicken *is marinated in spices such as turmeric and roasted in a clay tandoor (oven).*

Brinjal

Channa (gram curry)

Dhal

Cabbage

Kheer (rice and milk pudding)

Carrot and peas

Rasam (peppered water)

Rice

Cucumber **raita**

Puri (deep fried pancake)

Biryani

Yogurt

Pappadam

Fish-head curry *is a spicy dish best eaten with bread or rice. Fish head, often snapper, is cooked with ladies' fingers.*

Thali *is a tray on which a variety of food is served. Meat, condiments and pappadom (flour crackers) are part of the meal.*

Brinjal

Cabbage

Mutton *masala*

Biryani

Chicken *masala*

Pappadam

Prawn *masala*

Fish *masala*

Biryani *is seasoned rice cooked with vegetables, nuts and saffron. It is served on a banana leaf with meat and vegetables.*

Raita *is a side dish of yogurt, cucumber and mint.*

Mee goreng *is wheat noodles fried with chillies, minced meat, potatoes, bean sprouts and a light curry sauce.*

Mutton curry *is flavoured with shallots, garlic, ginger, star anise and cardamom.*

Chicken korma *is a milder version of the yogurt-based Indian chicken curry.*

Keema *is a spicy minced beef or mutton dish that is usually eaten with naan.*

Dhal, *made of lentil purée, is an essential part of any good set meal. The best dhal has been simmered slowly.*

Palak paneer *consists of spinach and cottage cheese, a mild and soothing dish to complement hot dishes.*

Alu gobi *is a palatable mixture of cauliflower and potatoes with mustard seeds, onions and turmeric.*

Mysore *pak* (gram flour fudge)

Milk *burfi* with dried fruit

Amriti (syrup-soaked pretzel)

Wheat *halwa* (fudge)

Milk *peda* (fudge)

Laddu (gram flour ball)

Chocolate *burfi*

Milk *burfi* (fudge)

Kesari (saffron *burfi*)

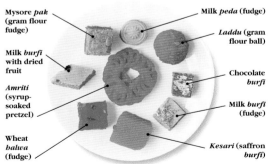

Kheer *is a pudding made of rice and milk.*

Gulab jamun *is syrup-soaked flour dumplings.*

Falooda

Indian desserts *are prepared in many different and radical ways but they all end up high in sugar. Try dipping sweets such as* gulab jamun *or desserts made of lentils such as* balushahi.

Lassi, *a yogurt-based drink, is available in salt, mint or fruit flavours.*

Kulfi *is an ice cream served with rose syrup, pistachios and* falooda *(vermicelli).*

Choosing a Restaurant

RESTAURANTS in this guide have been selected for their good value, excellent food and interesting location. They are listed area by area. Colour codes of each area are indicated on the thumb tabs. Map references refer to pages 185–9. Set menus, often available for weekday lunches, offer a comparatively economical way to sample food of good quality.

	CREDIT CARDS	AIR-CONDITIONING	OUTDOOR TABLES	GOOD WINE LIST	BOOKING RECOMMENDED

THE COLONIAL CORE AND FORT CANNING

ANNALAKSHMI Map 5 D2. $$
#02-10 Excelsior Hotel and Shopping Centre, 5 Coleman Street. 📞 6339 9993.
Top-quality vegetarian food is served either buffet-style or à la carte.
A favourite of certain politicians. ○ 11:30am–3pm, 6–9:30pm Mon–Sat. ♿

AE DC MC V	●			

BOBBY RUBINO'S Map 5 E1. $$
#B1-03 Fountain Court, Chijmes, 30 Victoria Street. 📞 6337 5477.
Ribs are the house speciality. Other American-style dishes, soups and
starters come up to the same high standard. ○ noon–10:30pm Mon, Tue, Thu,
Sun; noon–11pm Wed, Fri, Sat. ♿

AE DC JCB MC V	●	■	●	■

BUKHARA Map 4 C2. $$$
#01-40/44 The Cannery, Clarke Quay, 3C River Valley Road. 📞 6338 1411.
Here you can watch the chefs prepare creamy northwest Indian frontier
cuisine in the glass-fronted kitchen. ○ noon–2:30pm, 6:30–10:30pm daily. ♿

AE DC JCB MC V	●	■	●	■

CHINA JUMP BAR AND GRILL Map 5 E1. $$$
#B1-07/08 Fountain Court, Chijmes, 30 Victoria Street. 📞 6338 9388.
The standard American fare served goes well with the extensive cocktail
list. The place transforms into a dance floor at 10:30pm.
○ 5pm–1am Mon, Tue; 5pm–3am Wed, Thu, Fri; 11am–3am Sat, Sun. ♿

AE DC JCB MC V	●	■	●	■

EMPIRE CAFE Map 5 E1. $$$
Raffles Hotel, 1 Beach Road. 📞 6421 1101. Local specialities are served in a
coffee shop setting. This comfortable eatery is a far cry from a hot coffee
shop but the food is no less authentic. ○ 11am–10:45pm daily. ♿

AE DC JCB MC V	●	■	●	■

FATHER FLANAGAN'S Map 5 E1. $$$
#B1-06 Fountain Court, Chijmes, 30 Victoria Street. 📞 6333 1418.
Irish and English food is served in a traditional Irish-style setting; the
cottage pie, as well as beef and Guinness pie, is particularly worth trying.
○ 11am–midnight Sun–Mon, 11am–1am Tue–Thu, 11am–2am Fri–Sat. ♿

AE DC MC V	●	■		■

LEI GARDEN Map 5 E1. $$$
#01-24 Chijmes, 30 Victoria Street. 📞 6339 3822. Whether you are having
dim sum for lunch or a full banquet dinner in the main dining room or in
the private chambers, this Cantonese restaurant exudes class.
○ 11:30am–2:30pm, 6–10pm daily. ♿

AE DC JCB MC V	●			■

SENBAZURU Map 4 C2. $$$
Hotel New Otani, 177A River Valley Road. 📞 6433 8693. Truly a room with a
view – this restaurant enables diners to eat *sushi* and *sashimi* while
looking over the Singapore River and the financial district.
○ 11:30am–2:30pm, 6:30–10:30pm daily. ♿

AE DC JCB MC V	●	■		■

TUSCANY RISTORANTE Map 5 F2. $$$
Pan Pacific Hotel, Marina Square, 7 Raffles Boulevard. 📞 6826 8332.
A homey Italian restaurant, where you can pick starters and desserts from
the buffet table. ○ noon–2:30pm, 6:30–10:30pm daily. ● Sat–Sun L. ♿

AE DC JCB MC V	●	■	●	■

DOC CHENG'S Map 5 E1. $$$$
#02-20 Raffles Hotel Arcade, 1 Beach Road. 📞 6412 1261. In this fusion
restaurant serving East-West cuisine, staff in trendy attire serve a special
drink containing ginseng that should revitalize the weariest diner.
○ noon–2pm, 7–10pm daily. ● Sat–Sun L. ♿

AE DC JCB MC V	●	■	●	■

EMPRESS ROOM Map 5 E1. $$$$
Raffles Hotel, Storey 3, Raffles Hotel Arcade, 328 North Bridge Road.
📞 6412 1330. Fine Cantonese cuisine is served in a setting reminiscent of
old Shanghai of the 1930s (*see pp50–51*). ○ noon–2:30pm Mon–Sat,
11am–2:30pm Sun and public hols, 6:30–10:30pm daily. ♿

AE DC JCB MC V	●		●	■

<table>
<tr><td colspan="2">

Price categories for an evening meal for one including starter, main course, dessert and a non-alcoholic drink, inclusive of service charges and taxes:
$ under S$20
$$ S$20–30
$$$ S$30–50
$$$$ S$50–70
$$$$$ Over S$70

</td><td colspan="3">

CREDIT CARDS
This indicates which credit cards are accepted: *AE* American Express; *DC* Diners Club; *JCB* Japanese Credit Bureau; *MC* MasterCard; *V* Visa.
OUTDOOR TABLES
Some tables on a patio or terrace, often with a good view.
GOOD WINE LIST
A wide range of good quality wines is available.
BOOKING RECOMMENDED
Advance booking is strongly advised, especially on weekends and eves of holidays.

</td></tr>
</table>

	CREDIT CARDS	AIR-CONDITIONING	OUTDOOR TABLES	GOOD WINE LIST	BOOKING RECOMMENDED
EQUINOX THE RESTAURANT Map 5 E2. $$$$ Swissôtel the Stamford, 2 Stamford Road. **(** 6431 5669. Enjoy an all round view of the island while dining on fusion food from this restaurant's wide-ranging and imaginative menu. *noon–2:30pm, 7–11pm daily.*	AE DC JCB MC V	●		●	■
MARMALADE Map 5 E1. $$$$ #01-02 36 Purvis Street. **(** 6837 2123. The chic decor is all dark wood and subtle lighting; the food is modern European, meaning hearty portions and fresh seasonal ingredients. *noon–2:30pm, 7pm–midnight daily.*	AE JCB MC V	●		●	■
PREGO Map 5 E2. $$$$ Raffles the Plaza, 2 Stamford Road. **(** 6431 5156. The atmosphere in this Italian restaurant is always highly charged, with its lunching executives and theatre-going crowd. *11:30am–1am daily.*	AE DC JCB MC V	●		●	■
HAI TIEN LO Map 5 F2. $$$$$ Pan Pacific Hotel, Marina Square, 7 Raffles Boulevard. **(** 6826 8338. The height of this 37th floor restaurant reflects the price of the tremendous Cantonese food served. *noon–2:30pm, 6:30–10:30pm daily.*	AE DC JCB MC V	●		●	■
INDOCHINE WATERFRONT Map 5 D3. $$$$$ 1 Empress Place, Asian Civilisations Museum II. **(** 6339 1720. Nouvelle Vietnamese cuisine at a romantic riverside location. The outdoor dining area offers a sweeping view of Boat Quay, while the indoor dining room is resplendent with art and crystal chandeliers. More upscale than its sister restaurant at Club Street. *noon–2:30pm, 6–11pm daily.*	AE DC JCB MC V	●	■	●	■
KEYAKI Map 5 F2. $$$$$ Pan Pacific Hotel, Marina Square, 7 Raffles Boulevard. **(** 6826 8335. A walk through the Japanese garden will work up an appetite for the *sushi* served here. *noon–2:30pm, 6:30–10:30pm daily.* ● *Sun L.* certain levels.	AE DC JCB MC V	●		●	■
MORTON'S OF CHICAGO Map 5 F2. $$$$$ The Oriental Singapore, 5 Raffles Avenue. **(** 6339 3740. The steak is cut and weighed at your table and you pay for what you eat at this traditional steakhouse; you might like to share the potatoes and vegetables as servings here are absolutely huge. *5:30pm–11pm Mon–Sat, 5–10pm Sun.*	AE DC JCB MC V	●		●	■
RAFFLES GRILL Map 5 E1. $$$$$ Raffles Hotel, 1 Beach Road. **(** 6412 1185. This is the premier restaurant in the grand old hotel that played host to the likes of Somerset Maugham and Noel Coward *(see pp50–51).* Savour French cuisine at leisure in elegant surroundings. *noon–2pm, 7–10pm daily.* ● *Sat–Sun L.*	AE DC JCB MC V	●		●	■
RISTORANTE BOLOGNA Map 5 F2. $$$$$ Marina Mandarin Singapore, 6 Raffles Boulevard. **(** 6845 1118. This well-established restaurant has been in Singapore for over a decade. It serves excellent classic Italian food, with a favourably Italian wine list. *noon–3pm, Mon–Fri, 7–11pm Mon–Sat.*	AE DC JCB MC V	●		●	■

CHINATOWN AND THE FINANCIAL DISTRICT

	CREDIT CARDS	AIR-CONDITIONING	OUTDOOR TABLES	GOOD WINE LIST	BOOKING RECOMMENDED
GHORKA GRILL Map 4 C4. $ 21 Smith Street. **(** 6227 0806. This tiny Nepalese eatery in the heart of Chinatown serves food authentic enough to have diners looking for *sherpas* in the kitchen; the papaya prawns are a must. *11:30am–10:30pm daily.*	AE DC MC V	●	■		
IMPERIAL HOT WOK Map 5 D4. $ #01-01 Far East Square, 72 Telok Ayer Street. **(** 6438 8918. The restaurant serves a variety of Chinese cuisines, including Cantonese and Sichuanese dishes. Try its delicious Hakka rice, a house speciality which is made by tossing vegetables and nuts into specially cooked rice. *11am–2:30pm Mon–Fri,11:30am–2:30pm Sat–Sun, 6–10pm daily.*	AE DC MC V	●		●	■

Price categories for an evening meal for one including starter, main course, dessert and a non-alcoholic drink, inclusive of service charges and taxes:
$ under S$20
$$ S$20–30
$$$ S$30–50
$$$$ S$50–70
$$$$$ Over S$70

CREDIT CARDS
This indicates which credit cards are accepted: *AE* American Express; *DC* Diners Club; *JCB* Japanese Credit Bureau; *MC* MasterCard; *V* Visa.

OUTDOOR TABLES
Some tables on a patio or terrace, often with a good view.

GOOD WINE LIST
A wide range of good quality wines is available.

BOOKING RECOMMENDED
Advance booking is strongly advised, especially on weekends and eves of holidays.

BLUE GINGER Map 4 C5. $$
97 Tanjong Pagar Road. ☎ *6222 3928.* For traditional Peranakan food, this is unbeatable. The *ayam panggang* (fried chicken) is recommended.
○ *11:30am–3pm, 6:30–10:30pm daily.* ♿

BREWERKZ Map 4 C3. $$$
#01-05/06 Riverside Point, 30 Merchant Road. ☎ *6438 7438.* After eating chilli, a massive burger or tangy *quesadillos,* the only drink to order is one of the speciality brews made on the premises. ○ *noon–1am Mon–Thu, noon–3am Fri; noon–4pm, 11pm–3am Sat; noon–4pm, 11pm–1am Sun.* ♿

CAFÉ IGUANA Map 4 C3. $$$
#01-03 Riverside Point, 30 Merchant Road. ☎ *6236 1275.* Colourful Mexican fare in a fun and funky setting. Seats are bar stools and the tables communal; traditional Mexican art is set off against a sleek contemporary bar. Equally colourful is the tequila list, which boasts over 100 varieties.
○ *noon–3pm Mon–Fri, 11am–3pm Sat, Sun and public hols, 5pm-midnight daily.* ♿

INDOCHINE Map 4 C4. $$$
49 Club Street. ☎ *6323 0503.* After sampling the authentic Vietnamese and Lao food at this fashionable restaurant, diners often head downstairs to Bar Savanh for an after-dinner drink. ○ *11am–3pm, 6–11pm daily.* ♿

KINARA Map 5 D3. $$$
57 Boat Quay. ☎ *6533 0412.* In this tranquil little corner of busy Boat Quay, waiters serve delicious North Indian cuisine on brass and copper dishes. Set against a backdrop of antique furniture, the atmosphere is enchanting. ○ *11:30am–2:30pm, 6:30–10:30pm Sun–Thur, 6:30–11pm Fri–Sat.* ♿

MAMA AFRICA Map 5 D4. $$$
#01-01 Far East Square, 88 Telok Ayer Street. ☎ *6532 9339.* Call it modern African, but the food here, incorporating traditional ingredients in innovative dishes, is a lot more exciting than the kitsch decor might suggest. It serves African beers and has a good wine list.
○ *11:30am–2:30pm, Sun–Fri, 6:30–10:30pm daily.* ♿

THE MOOMBA Map 5 D3. $$$
52 Circular Road. ☎ *6438 0141.* Indulge in modern Australian fusion cuisine in a contemporary setting, not to mention an excellent wine list. The dessert selection is irresistibly good. ○ *11:30am–2:30pm, 6:30–10pm Mon–Fri, 6:30–10pm Sat.* ● *Sun and public hols.* ♿ *ground floor.*

PASTA BRAVA Map 4 C4. $$$$
11 Craig Road. ☎ *6227 7550.* Select the sauce to go into your pasta. Expect a delicious and traditional Italian feast – the pasta here is always cooked to *al dente* perfection. The service is personal and friendly.
○ *noon–2:30pm, 6:30–10:30pm Mon–Sat.* ● *Sun.* ♿

L'AIGLE D'OR Map 4 C4. $$$$$
Berjaya Duxton Hotel, 83 Duxton Road. ☎ *6227 7678.* This chic French restaurant in a beautifully restored boutique hotel is popular for expense-account lunches and romantic dinners. ○ *noon–2pm, 7–10pm daily.* ♿

SALUT Map 4 C5. $$$$$
25/27 Tanjong Pagar Road. ☎ *6225 7555.* Bright crisp colours give a contemporary touch to the elegant, romantic setting. The calamari here is excellent and should be ordered regardless of the menu of the day.
○ *11:30am–2:30pm, 6:30–10:30pm daily.* ● *Sun L.* ♿

SENSO RISTORANTE & BAR Map 4 C4. $$$$$
21 Club Street. ☎ *6224 3534.* Taste the different regional cuisines of Italy at this elegant yet warm and welcoming restaurant. The appetizers and pastas are rich and hearty, so save room for dessert. ○ *noon–2:30pm Mon–Fri, 6:30–10:15pm daily.* ♿

	CREDIT CARDS	AIR-CONDITIONING	OUTDOOR TABLES	GOOD WINE LIST	BOOKING RECOMMENDED
Blue Ginger	AE JCB MC V	●		●	■
Brewerkz	AE DC JCB MC V	●	■	●	■
Café Iguana	AE DC JCB MC V	●	■	●	■
Indochine	AE DC MC V	●	■	●	■
Kinara	AE DC MC V	●	■	●	■
Mama Africa	AE DC MC V	●	■	●	■
The Moomba	AE DC MC V	●		●	■
Pasta Brava	AE DC JCB MC V	●		●	■
L'Aigle d'Or	AE DC JCB MC V	●		●	■
Salut	AE DC JCB MC V	●		●	■
Senso Ristorante & Bar	AE DC JCB MC V	●		●	■

LITTLE INDIA AND KAMPONG GLAM

ANDHRA CURRY HOUSE Map 3 D3.
41 Kerbau Road. 6293 3935. This restaurant serves cuisine from the Indian state of Andra Pradesh, where India's hottest food purportedly comes from. The speciality of the house is *biryani* – saffron rice and meat cooked in a myriad of spices and served in the same pot that it was stewed in. Have a tall glass of cool lime juice at hand in case the food gets too spicy. ☐ *11:30am–3:30pm, 6:30–10:30pm daily.* ⓖ

Ⓢ	AE DC JCB MC V	● ▨

BANANA LEAF APOLLO Map 3 E2.
54/56/58 Race Course Road. 6293 8682. You will be greeted by friendly waiters who serve curries of mutton, fish and chicken as well as a variety of meat, seafood and vegetarian dishes in rich *masala* (blend of spices). Round off the meal with a mango ice cream. ☐ *10am–10pm daily.* ⓖ

Ⓢ	AE DC JCB MC V	● ▨

DELHI Map 3 E2.
48 & 60 Race Course Road. 6294 5276 & 6296 4585. For an initiation into north Indian food, there is a large selection of dishes here for you to choose from. You can savour your freshly made *naan* (bread) with spicy vegetables, chicken or prawn. ☐ *11:30am–11pm daily.*

Ⓢ	AE DC JCB MC V	● ▨ ▨

MUTHU'S CURRY Map 3 D2.
76-78 Race Course Road. 6293 2389. The service is swift at this South Indian restaurant, so you can count on a quick meal. Try Muthu's speciality, the fish head curry.
☐ *10am–10pm daily.* ● *Chinese New Year hols.* ⓖ

Ⓢ	AE DC MC V	●

YINGTHAI PALACE Map 3 E5.
#01-04, 36 Purvis Street. 6337 1161. At this no-frills eatery, the pineapple rice – a litmus test for any Thai restaurant – is as fragrant and fluffy as anyone could wish for. A place to stop by while you are strolling in the Arab Street/Kampong Glam area. ☐ *11:30am–2pm, 6–10pm daily.* ⓖ

ⓈⓈ	AE MC V	● ▨

ORCHARD ROAD

MUMTAZ MAHAL Map 2 A3.
#05-22/23 Far East Plaza, 14 Scotts Road. 6732 2754.
A popular North Indian restaurant. Specialities include *mumtaz kebab* (chicken on skewers), *raan aleshan* (lamb curry) and *jhinga masala* (prawn curry). Specify how hot you like your food, and the chef will cook accordingly. ☐ *noon–2:45pm, 6–10:30pm daily.*

Ⓢ	AE DC JCB MC V	● ▨ ● ▨

CAFÉ MODESTO'S Map 1 F2.
#01-09 Orchard Parade Hotel, 1 Tanglin Road. 6235 7808.
Seafood is the speciality at this casual Italian bistro, whether it comes on a pizza or in pasta. A good spot for late-night outdoor dining at the more tranquil end of Orchard Road.
☐ *noon–2am Sun–Thu, noon–3am Fri–Sat.* ⓖ

ⓈⓈ	AE DC MC V	● ▨ ▨

DAN RYAN'S CHICAGO GRILL Map 1 E2.
#B1-01 Tanglin Place, 91 Tanglin Road. 6738 2800. A toy train chugs around the top of the bar as the staff mix great Bloody Mary cocktails; the burger with chilli, Swiss cheese and bacon is unbeatable at this eatery serving Chicago/American cuisine. ☐ *11:30am–midnight daily.*

ⓈⓈ	AE DC JCB MC V	● ▨ ● ▨

HOUSE OF MAO Map 1 F2.
#01-09 Orchard Hotel Shopping Arcade, 442 Orchard Road. 6733 7667.
Hunan hotpot is this restaurant's main ofering. Succulent bite size pieces of vegetables and seafood which you cook at your table in steaming pots of broth – it's much like fondue.
☐ *noon–2:30pm, 6–10:30pm daily.*

ⓈⓈ	AE DC JCB MC V	● ▨ ● ▨

PATARA Map 1 E2.
#03-14 Tanglin Mall, 163 Tanglin Road. 6737 0818. A pleasant Thai restaurant with a good menu and courteous service. Try the pineapple rice, green curry and garlic-and-pepper spare ribs.
☐ *noon–3pm, 6–10pm daily.* ● *Chinese New Year hols.* ⓖ

ⓈⓈ	AE DC JCB MC V	● ▨

THE RICE TABLE Map 1 F2.
#02-09/10 International Building, 360 Orchard Road. 6835 3783.
This is one of the few places in town to offer the Dutch-Indonesian meal *rijstaffel*, which is a spicy rice, vegetable and meat combination.
☐ *noon–2:30pm, 6–9:30pm daily.* ⓖ

ⓈⓈ	AE DC MC V	● ▨

For key to symbols see back flap

	CREDIT CARDS	AIR-CONDITIONING	OUTDOOR TABLES	GOOD WINE LIST	BOOKING RECOMMENDED

Price categories for an evening meal for one including starter, main course, dessert and a non-alcoholic drink, inclusive of service charges and taxes:
$ under $20
$$ $20–30
$$$ $30–50
$$$$ $50–70
$$$$$ Over $70.

CREDIT CARDS
This indicates which credit cards are accepted: *AE* American Express; *DC* Diners Club; *JCB* Japanese Credit Bureau; *MC* MasterCard; *V* Visa.

OUTDOOR TABLES
Some tables on a patio or terrace, often with a good view.

GOOD WINE LIST
A wide range of good quality wines is available.

BOOKING RECOMMENDED
Advance booking is strongly advised, especially on weekends and eves of holidays.

CHATTERBOX Map 2 A4. $$$
Meritus Mandarin Hotel, 333 Orchard Road. 6831 6291. Among the many reasons why Chatterbox is well-known is the fact that this hotel coffee shop serves some of the best and most expensive chicken rice in town. Local delights such as chicken curry are available all day. *24 hours daily.*

CREDIT CARDS	AIR-CONDITIONING	OUTDOOR TABLES	GOOD WINE LIST	BOOKING RECOMMENDED
AE DC JCB MC V	●			

ESMIRADA Map 2 B4. $$$
#01-29 Orchard Hotel, 422 Orchard Road. 6735 3476. Waiters stride around clapping and yelling "Olé!" in this lively Mediterranean eatery serving generous salads, huge garlic bread and rich meat dishes. *11:30am–midnight daily.*

| AE DC JCB MC V | ● | | ● | ■ |

GRILL ON DEVONSHIRE Map 4 B1. $$$
6 Devonshire Road. 6733 9400. One of the most romantic city-centre locations, especially outside; the Grill serves Italian-influenced food in a candlelit atmosphere. *noon–2:30pm, 6–10:30pm daily. outside.*

| AE DC JCB MC V | ● | ■ | ● | ■ |

HARD ROCK CAFÉ Map 1 E2. $$$
#02-01 HPL House, 50 Cuscaden Road. 6235 5232. Offering exactly the same standards the whole world over, Hard Rocks are famous for burgers, brunches and beer; the house band is worth a listen for dessert, brownies are unbeatable. *11am–2am Sun–Thu, 11am–3am Fri–Sat.*

| AE DC | ● | ■ | ● | ■ |

STUART ANDERSON'S BLACK ANGUS Map 1 F2. $$$
#01-08 Orchard Parade Hotel, 1 Tanglin Road. 6734 1181. This is a steakhouse in the traditional sense, serving American cuisine in appropriately sized portions; it is worth leaving room for starters and desserts. *11am–11pm Sun–Thu, 11am–midnight Fri–Sat.*

| AE DC MC V | ● | ■ | ● | ■ |

CLUB CHINOIS Map 1 F2. $$$$
#02-18 Orchard Parade Hotel, 1 Tanglin Road. 6834 0660. As famous for the celebrity Canadian chef as for the exquisite Cantonese cuisine, Club Chinois serves pricy but excellent Peking duck with a sliver of mango and *foie gras.* *7–10am, noon–2:30pm, 6:30–10:30pm daily.*

| AE DC JCB MC V | ● | | ● | ■ |

GORDON GRILL Map 2 A3. $$$$
Goodwood Park Hotel, 22 Scotts Road. 6235 8637. It's Scottish and continental cuisine at this cosy upmarket restaurant where the staff weigh your choice of steak in front of you. For dessert, try the tasty and strong *suzuki* (Colombian) coffee. *noon–2:30pm, 7–10:30pm daily.*

| AE DC V | ● | | ● | ■ |

LA FORKETTA Map 2 A5. $$$$
#01-01 Valley Point, 491 River Valley Road. 6836 3373. The freshly baked bread and light pizza dough are two of the main reasons to visit this airy Italian eatery. They are made by the Italian chef before your eyes in its open kitchen. *noon–2:30pm, 6–10pm daily.*

| AE MC V | ● | ■ | ● | ■ |

MEZZA9 Map 2 A3. $$$$
Grand Hyatt Singapore, 10/12 Scotts Road. 6730 7189. In this open-concept restaurant, diners get a glimpse of kitchen activities. Different stations serve Chinese and Western food, *sushi*, seafood and dessert. *noon–2:30pm, 6–10:30pm daily.*

| AE DC JCB MC V | ● | | ● | ■ |

LES AMIS Map 1 F2. $$$$$
#02-14 Shaw Centre, 1 Scotts Road. 6733 2225. Fine French cuisine with prices to match; the slick service here is almost as legendary as its well-stocked wine cellar. *noon–2pm, 7:15–10pm Mon–Sat.*

| AE DC JC | ● | | ● | ■ |

SOL RESTAURANTE Map 1 F2. $$$$$
Goodwood Park Hotel, 22 Scotts Road. 6735 5322. Spanish fare that goes beyond just *tapas*. *Paella* is a speciality– choose between meat, seafood and vegetarian versions – as is *dorada* (oven baked snapper in a salt crust). *noon–2:30pm, 6:30–10:30pm daily.*

| AE DC JCB MC V | ● | ■ | ● | ■ |

TOP OF THE M Map 2 A4. $$$$$ | AE DC JCB MC V
Meritus Mandarin Hotel, 333 Orchard Road. █ *6831 6258.* The view from this revolving restaurant on the 39th floor is one reason to visit; the excellent and constantly varied continental cuisine is another. ◯ *noon–2:30pm, 6:30–10:30pm daily.* ♿

UNKAI Map 1 E2. $$$$$ | AE DC JCB MC V
ANA Hotel, 16 Nassim Hill. █ *6839 1574.*
The *teppanyaki* (stir-fry on a hotplate) at this Japanese restaurant is as good as the *sushi* and *sashimi.* ◯ *noon–2pm, 6:30–10pm daily.* ♿

FURTHER AFIELD

CASA BOM VENTO $$ | MC V
467 Joo Chiat Road. █ *6348 7786.* Where better to try real Peranakan cuisine than in the heart of the Peranakan quarter of Singapore. Go for *ayam buah keluak,* a stew comprising chicken or pork and an Indonesian nut. ◯ *11:30am–2pm, 6–9:30 pm Tues–Sun.* ♿

HUA ZHU $$ | AE DC JCB MC V
#02-101 Block 4, Queen's Road. █ *6479 4075.*
Great black pepper crab and other Cantonese and Sichuan favorites are offered in this friendly, family-run restaurant.
◯ *11:30am–2:30pm, 5:30–10:30pm daily.* ● *Chinese New Year hols.* ♿

BERNIE'S BFD $$$ | AE DC MC V
1000 East Coast Park. █ *6244 4434.* As famous for giant margaritas as southern barbecued food such as American-sized burgers, Bernie's by the beach also plays host to the odd rock group. ◯ *4pm–2am Mon–Thu, 4pm–3am Fri, noon–3am Sat, noon–2am Sun.* ♿

BRAZIL CHURRASCARIA $$$ | AE DC MC V
14 & 16 Sixth Avenue. █ *6463 1923.*
This Brazilian barbecue restaurant away from the city area has become very popular for meat lovers. Diners can sample several cuts of meat in addition to a well-stocked salad bar. ◯ *6:30–10:30pm daily.* ♿

JERRY'S BARBEQUE AND GRILL $$$ | AE MC V
277 Jalan Kayu. █ *6484 0151.* The ribs are marinated in Jerry's secret sauce, then charcoal grilled to perfection. Mouthwatering appetizers are spicy buffalo wings and deep-fried mushrooms. ◯ *noon–midnight Tue–Sun.* ♿

MICHELANGELO'S $$$ | AE MC V
#01-60 Chip Bee Gardens, 44 Jalan Merah Saga. █ *6475 9069.*
The portions of Australian-Italian cuisine that Angelo serves here are legendary in size, and few diners make it to the delicious desserts.
◯ *11:30am–3pm, 6:30–11pm daily.* ● *Sat L.* ♿ *outside.*

ORIGINAL SIN $$$ | AE MC V
#01-62 Chip Bee Gardens, 43 Jalan Merah Saga. █ *6475 5605.* The best Western vegetarian food in town is served in this casual, strictly no-meat eatery. The food is Mediterranean-Italian and always tastefully served.
◯ *11:30am–2:30pm Tue–Fri, 11:30am–3pm Sat–Sun; 6–10:30pm daily.* ● *Mon L.* ♿

EL PAPIO $$$ | AE DC JCB MC V
34 Lorong Mambong. █ *6468 1520.*
Mexican restaurant in the expatriate enclave of Holland Village with authentic food, and a small terrace. ◯ *11am–midnight daily.* ♿ *outside.*

PORTA PORTA $$$ | AE MC V
Changi Gardens, 971 Upper Changi Road North. █ *6545 3108.* Italian food, cooked home-style and served in a setting to match. ◯ *11:30am–2pm Mon–Fri, 6:30–9:15pm Mon–Sat.* ● *Sun L.* ♿

SISTINA GOURMET PIZZERIA $$$ | AE MC V
#01-58 Chip Bee Gardens, 44 Jalan Merah Saga. █ *6476 7782.* This homey Italian restaurant serves great pasta, fine Italian cuisine and delicious pies. ◯ *11:30am–2:30pm, 6–10:30pm daily.* ● *Mon–Tue L.* ♿

ALKAFF MANSION $$$$ | AE DC JCB MC V
10 Telok Blangah Green. █ *6278 6979.* This colonial mansion on a hill offers the most romantic meal and the most elegant outdoor dining in town. Order the *rijstaffel* dinner and a gong will announce the arrival of a procession of servers bearing one dish each. ◯ *7–10:30pm daily.*

For key to symbols see back flap

Hawker Food

Food court sign at Clarke Quay

HAWKER CENTRES are large hangar-like buildings crammed with stalls, each serving a different variety of cuisine. As eating out is the norm in Singapore, a huge variety of good-value food is on offer. Meal prices range from S$2–S$3.50 upwards. While the centres provide basic sustenance, they also offer an almost theatrical culinary experience to any visitor. Hawkers used to ply their trade on the streets, feeding people too busy to cook or without cooking facilities. Years ago, they were rounded up and then relocated in hawker centres; now most cuisine styles on offer in Singapore are available under these roofs.

Newton Circus hawker centre

HAWKER CENTRES AND FOOD COURTS

THE STANDARD hawker centre has some stalls selling variations of the same popular dish, such as fried noodles or chicken rice and stalls selling fruit, juices, beer, tea and coffee. The same kind of good-value local food can also be found at a *kopi tiam* (literally "coffee shop"), a smaller variation, which offers fewer stalls and at least one coffee outlet.

After a hot day sightseeing, a visit to one of the indoor, air-conditioned food courts might be more comfortable than sweating it out in the authentic setting. Given the greater degree of comfort, prices are marginally higher, but when a full meal can be had for under S$5, it hardly makes a great difference.

The real treat, however, can be found in the older, sometimes dilapidated warehouse-like hawker centres, open to the elements and cooled only by fans hung from the high ceilings. Compared to food courts, the food served by some veteran hawkers tends to taste more authentic.

HYGIENE

GENERALLY SPEAKING, it is safe to eat at hawker centres; after all, thousands of Singaporeans eat several meals a day at these places. Standards of cleanliness do, however, vary, and whole hawker centres or individual stalls can range from the slightly grubby to the downright uninviting. Some newer food courts and hawker centres boast gleaming tiles and bright new chopping surfaces; others are dark and less appetizing in appearance.

To boost consumer confidence, all stalls have been checked and graded A–D, according to levels of hygiene; A being the best and D being best avoided. These hygiene labels are displayed at the stalls. Serviettes are rarely provided for patrons.

VARIETIES OF FOOD

THE MOST COMMON food item is the humble noodle, whether served as a fine vermicelli or the thick, flat style found in *char kway teow* (see p128). But there are also many other kinds of Asian cuisine – most of the more upscale air-conditioned food centres even boast Japanese cuisine. Most hawker

centres also offer Indian, Malay, mainland Chinese and sometimes Western food. As far as local and Asian dishes are concerned, however, the food can be just as delicious as, and much cheaper than, the same dish served in a hotel restaurant. Dishes such as Hainanese chicken rice, *kway teow, mee goreng* and *dhosai masala* are very satisfying straight from the spitting griddle or *wok* of a hawker. Try also Western food done Singapore-style.

One disadvantage of hawker food and a *caveat* for visitors is the high usage of monosodium glutamate (MSG). This flavour enhancer is applied with a heavy hand and is prevalent in some soups and dishes containing oyster sauce, for example.

Old-style *kopi tiam* (coffee shop)

ORDERING YOUR FOOD

FIRST, FIND YOURSELF a table. Ignore the touts who offer you a table. You may sit anywhere you wish and order from any stall, not just those near your table. Remember your table number (if you are in a couple, you may have to share the large table with another small group) and walk around until you find the food you like. In some cases, you pay as you order; in others, the person delivering your food will take cash on delivery. In either case, when you place an order, tell the hawker your table number, then sit down and wait for the food to arrive. Occasionally,

A traditional *kopi tiam* breakfast

Picnic Scott, a food court

stalls prefer customers to wait in line to pay and collect food when the order is ready. Most stalls have food photographs and an English translation; if they don't, pointing usually helps convey the desired order. When ordering dishes that are to be shared, it is helpful to give the number of diners along with the order so the correct number of utensils is brought.

If the centre is crowded, eager diners without seats may hover near dining customers; no one should take this as a sign to hurry. Plates and utensils should be left behind for the cleaners to remove. They can be quick to clear half-eaten plates away, so remember to indicate that the food is still wanted. "Take-away" is an option, if there really are no seats.

DIRECTORY

Newton Circus Food Centre
Scotts Road.
🚇 *Newton*. 🚌 54, 124, 143, 162. ◐ 24 hours.

The city's most famous hawker centre is a must for visitors, even though prices may be a bit higher compared to other hawker centres. Expect a lively atmosphere even at midnight as people pour in for a late supper. **Recommended**: fishball noodles at Soon Wah; Fish Ball Kway Teow Mee stall 64; popiah at Bee Heng, Delicious Popiah and Satay stall 68; noodles with cockles and sausage at Tan Song Heng stall 79.

Lagoon Rendezvous
East Coast Park Service Road. Next to Europa Sailing Club. 🚌 401 (Sun and public hols). ◐ noon to late evening.

Aim for beachfront dining even though the limited number of tables here means that most diners will sit facing the busy inner courtyard. **Recommended**: satay at Harom stall 30; laksa noodle soup at Lemak Laksa stall 40; curry puffs at Lagoon Curry Puffs stall 12.

Maxwell Road Food Centre
Maxwell Road. 🚇 Tanjong Pagar. 🚌 80, 145, 608. ◐ mid morning till evening, daily.

This centrally located food centre always pulls a capacity crowd, of mostly office workers, at lunch time. When the crowd disperses, the older residents from the nearby housing estates come to buy local snacks, many of which are not sold elsewhere in Singapore. **Recommended**: chicken rice at Tian Tian Hainanese Chicken Rice stall 10; dim sum at Ho Kee Pau, stall 79/80; oyster omelette at Oyster Cake, stall 5.

Chomp Chomp Food Centre
Serangoon Garden Way. 🚌 73, 136, 315, 317. ◐ evening till late night.

Although not centrally located, this neighbourhood hawker centre is something of an institution and should give visitors with a little extra time and an adventurous streak a different view of the city and its food. **Recommended**: fried radish, egg and chilli at Carrot Cake #01-36; fishball at Teochew Fishball Mince Meat Noodle #01-16; soya bean milk at House of Soya Beans #01-20.

Chinatown Complex
Smith Street. 🚇 Chinatown. 🚌 2, 12, 33, 54, 62, 63, 81, 124, 961. ◐ afternoon to early evening.

Right in the heart of old Chinatown, this centre provides sustenance for anyone exploring the shophouses and temples in one of the more historic parts of town. Smith Street is also famous for its wet market. **Recommended**: glutinous rice balls at Hai Sin Ah Balling #02-90; fried noodles at Aisah Abdullah Stall #02-234; fish congee at Jiu Ji #02-157.

Lau Pa Sat
Junction of Robinson Road and Boon Tat Street. 🚇 Tanjong Pagar. 🚌 10, 75, 97, 196. ◐ 24 hours.

The renovated Victorian structure has a resident DJ and plays host to a mix of locals and visitors alike right in the centre of the hectic banking district. **Recommended**: seafood and rice dishes at MacPherson BBQ Seafood Branch 01-04/05; north Indian curries and naan at Khan's Tandoori #01-48; noodles at the oddly spelt Fantastic Hand Make Noodle #01-50.

Kopitiam
Le Meridien 100 Orchard Road. 🚇 Somerset. 🚌 7, 14, 16, 106, 111, 123, 124, 143. ◐ 24 hours.

First in a new generation of food courts; it recreates the atmosphere of the traditional hawker centre plus the comfort of air-conditioning. **Recommended**: claypot dishes at Lucky Claypot #24; fishballs at Fishing Ball #16; fish-head noodles at Hosanna Fishhead Beehoon #6.

Amoy Street Food Centre
Amoy Street. 🚇 Tanjong Pagar. 🚌 186, 608, 970.. ◐ early morning to mid-afternoon.

Near the temples and shophouses of Telok Ayer Street, this excellent food centre has a light airy feeling. **Recommended**: noodles with cockles and sausage at Fried Kway Teow #01-01, Hainanese chicken rice at Shenton Chicken Rice #02-104, fish porridge at Piao Ji Fish Porridge #02-100.

China Square
Telok Ayer Street. 🚇 Raffles Place. 🚌 10, 70, 75, 82, 97, 100, 107, 130, 162. ◐10am–10pm.

Three floors of stalls in air-conditioned comfort beckons. **Recommended**: claypot rice at Old Market Claypot Noodle.Rice, #B1-08; soup at Fried Fish Soup Blanco Court #01-10; Japanese cuisine at Hachi Tei, #B1-27.

Picnic Scotts
Scotts Shopping Centre, Scotts Road. 🚇 Orchard. 🚌 105, 124, 132, 143. ◐ 10am–10:30pm.

Filled with the evening cinema crowds and weekend shoppers, getting seats in this food court can be difficult. **Recommended**: tandoori and curry at North Indian #B1-19; Malay rice dishes at Nasi Padang #B1-17; rice dishes at Mixed Rice #B1-04.

SHOPPING IN SINGAPORE

SINGAPORE is a city dedicated to shopping, and Singaporeans are some of Asia's most sophisticated shoppers. There are more than 150 malls on the island. Many of the best-known are along Orchard Road *(see pp86–7);* some, Marina Square and Suntec City for example, are closer to the seafront. Other shopping options, such as shophouses and malls in Chinatown,

A locally designed *cheongsam*

Little India and Arab Street *(see pp144–5),* are also worth exploring, as are specialist stalls in shopping centres and daily, weekly or monthly fleamarkets. Singapore is no longer a cheap shopping destination, but it can still reward bargain hunters, particularly those whose currency is strong against the Singapore dollar. Electronics are bargained for.

The upmarket Tanglin Mall

DEPARTMENT STORES AND SHOPPING MALLS

NEARLY ALL shopping malls have information desks where shoppers can ask directions, consult a map of the centre, and enquire about shops or special events. Promotional events are often held on Saturdays at malls on the main shopping belt of Orchard Road *(see pp82-3).*

Most department stores are located in shopping centres, a notable exception being **C K Tang** on Orchard Road *(see p149).* **Robinsons** in Centrepoint is one of the oldest and it is known for its helpful staff. British retailer **Marks & Spencer** is here; **Isetan**, **Takashimaya**, and **Seiyu** are popular Japanese stores; and **Metro** is a local chain. Retailers in shopping malls near outlying MRT stations cater mostly for local people and the merchandise may be slightly cheaper than in the city centre.

MARKETS AND STALLS

SINGAPORE IS not a city famed for its second-hand markets, as many local people are very brand-conscious, and prefer to buy new goods.

Nevertheless, the weekly flea market at **Clarke Quay** draws curiosity seekers and bargain-hunters every Sunday from 9am to 5pm, with over 70 stalls selling junk and collectibles of all kinds. **Tanglin Mall** *(see p149)* holds an outdoor evening flea market on the third Saturday of every month (5pm–11pm), as well as a second-hand clothing market twice a month. In both these places, there are items of genuine interest among the junk, and they draw quite a crowd, made up of both locals and tourists.

Every day from around 11am till 9pm, souvenirs, batik clothing and low-priced accessories can be purchased from the many stalls at **Bugis Village**. Even more appealing are the pushcarts at **Clarke Quay** where vendors sell attractive, handmade jewellery, woodcarvings and other handicrafts every evening from 5pm.

SHOPPING HOURS

SHOPPING CENTRES, department stores and most shops are open seven days a week, from around 9.30–10:30am to 8:30–9pm. On Friday and Saturday evenings, many stay open until 9.30pm. Only retailers in the downtown business district tend to close earlier, at 7pm, as their office-worker customers will have dispersed by then. Popular book and music retailers such as **Borders** and **Tower Records** regularly stay open until 11pm, and up to midnight on Fridays and Saturdays. **HMV Music** closes nightly at 11pm *(see p149).* With more than 90 outlets all over the island, **7-Eleven** convenience stores stay open 24 hours.

METHODS OF PAYMENT

CASH AND MAJOR credit cards (Visa, Mastercard, Diners Club and American Express) are accepted almost everywhere. Surcharges are not supposed to be added to credit card transactions; but

The Alessi Shop, a home furnishing store in Park Mall

because the commissions charged to the retailer by the credit card companies vary, some shop owners may express a preference for one credit card over another.

Cash is useful for bargaining because it can help knock extra dollars off the final price. Travellers' cheques in major currencies are accepted by big department stores (a passport will be needed for identification).

Visitors will see signs saying "NETS accepted here" in shops all over Singapore. Used by most Singaporeans, NETS is a debit card system linked to local savings or current accounts. The system is quite separate from international credit cards.

SALES TAX

Goods and services tax paid for goods purchased, usually added only at the till, can sometimes be claimed back on departure from Singapore (see p173).

An Oriental curio store

BARGAINING

Bargaining is standard practice throughout Southeast Asia, and Singapore is no exception. Prices are fixed in department stores and in shops displaying "Fixed Price" signs, but smaller retailers are often prepared to negotiate (even if the goods they sell display price tags). A good opening ploy is to indicate an item and ask with a friendly smile, "What is your best price?" This sets the stage for amicable negotiation. When the seller replies, make a counter offer or ask, "Any more discount?" Eventually, there should be mutual agreement – but once a price is agreed upon, it is inappro-

The flea market at Clarke Quay, held on Sundays

priate to refuse to make the purchase. To get a fair idea in advance of what a particular item ought to cost, visit several shops first and check out the prices. The variation can be surprising. Also, knowing what similar items would cost back home helps in determining whether a price in Singapore represents good value.

GUARANTEES

Always check that the warranty card on any electrical item purchased is correctly completed, that the serial numbers on the card and product match, and that the card entitles you to an international guarantee.

THE GREAT SINGAPORE SALE

This aggressive sale event takes place every June, when most big retailers offer major reductions. Throughout the year, however, keen shoppers can usually find a sale on somewhere as department stores and other retailers cut their prices and sell off unwanted stock. Look at the announcements in *The Straits Times*.

Tower Records, where customers listen to new releases

CONSUMER RIGHTS

The rights of consumers are heavily protected in Singapore. Shops which display the "Gold Circle" sign in their windows have the Singapore Tourism Board's (STB) seal of approval for the quality of their goods, prices and services. Look for a list of these retailers in STB's free guidebook, *An Insider's Guide* to Singapore, available at most hotels, tourist offices and at Changi Airport.

Shoppers who encounter problems with their purchases can call the **Retail Promotions Centre** for advice or assistance. Those who feel they have been duped by a retailer should contact the **Small Claims Tribunal**. Tourists' grievances are heard instantly and a judgment given immediately.

IMITATIONS

Everything from pirated software to imitation designer clothes, video CDs, and watches can be found in Singapore. These are usually sold at illegal makeshift stalls throughout the island. The government clamps down on their production and sale regularly. Quality is poor – buy strictly at your own risk.

> ### CONSUMER RIGHTS
>
> **Retail Promotions Centre**
> 6458 6377
>
> **Small Claims Tribunal**
> 6435 5937

Singapore's Best: Shopping Centres and Markets

S INGAPORE'S BEST shopping areas can be found in Orchard Road and its vicinity as well as in suburban locations. While Orchard Road offers most Western-type items the tourist would ever want, Dempsey Road and some older shopping centres, as well as the traditional shophouses of Chinatown and Little India, stock imports from the region and mainland China or India, generally well-priced.

Ngee Ann City
Packed with luxury goods shops such as Cartier, Bulgari and Tiffany & Co., Ngee Ann City is Singapore's premier shopping mall.

Tanglin Shopping Centre
This is the best shopping centre for antiques, books, maps, carpets and art from around the region and beyond.

HOLLAND ROAD
COMMONWEALTH AVENUE
COMMONWEALTH DR
QUEENSWAY
TYER SALL AVE
CLUNY ROAD
NASSIM ROAD
STEVENS ROAD
NAPIER ROAD
TANGLIN ROAD
ORCHARD BOULEVARD
GRANGE ROAD
PATERSON ROAD
ZION RD

| 0 metres | 750 |
| 0 yards | 750 |

Holland Village
Popular with expatriates, Holland Village not only has a wet market, restaurants and pubs, but also some good shops selling handicrafts and other regional products.

Dempsey Road warehouses
Dempsey Road's warehouses are full of rice carriers, Chinese wedding chests, Indian dowry boxes, Persian carpets, and other artifacts.

Tekka Centre
Fronted by shops selling gold, Tekka Centre contains a hawker centre (selling mostly Muslim food), a wet market (above) and many clothing stores (second floor).

Sim Lim Square
This is a shopping complex dedicated to electronic goods – the latest video gear, computer software and audio components.

Arab Street
Baskets, textiles, mats, carpets and dry goods can be found here in abundance.

Funan the IT Mall
This is Singapore's best computer mall. It has a Challenger superstore and a Mac Shop, and dealers for virtually all other brands.

Yue Hwa Chinese Products Store
This Chinese department store has an excellent range of goods from mainland China, such as medicinal products, silk shirts and even blackwood opium beds.

What to buy in Singapore

**Risis orchid
jewellery**

SINGAPORE WAS the first city in Southeast Asia to boast Western labels, franchises and products, and as such, attracted a great many tourists from within the region in search of prestige goods at accessible prices. With increasing industrialization in countries such as Indonesia, Malaysia and Thailand and the recent devaluation of Southeast Asian currencies, the picture has changed. Singapore is no longer the region's bargain basement – but to Western pockets, there are still cheap deals to be found and some good-value purchases that are particular to Singapore.

Antiques and crafts
Regional and Oriental antiques and crafts can be found at Tanglin Shopping Centre, Holland Road Shopping Centre, Chinatown Point and nearby shophouses, and Arab Street (see p148).

Gold
Little India and Chinatown are the best locations for cheap gold (see p148). Gold is sold by weight, workmanship adding relatively little to the price.

Watches
Brands such as Seiko, Rolex and Tag Heuer are readily available, and can be bargained for (see p150).

Electronic goods
Singapore is a treasure trove of gizmos and gadgets (see p150). Be sure to check whether the voltage of the item you are buying will work at home (see p169). Plugs will usually be changed on request to suit your country's standard usage.

Jade
Chinatown and Tanglin Shopping Centre offer a wide selection of sculptures, amulets, bracelets and rings in auspicious jade.

DVD/Video CD/CD player

Video camera

Decorative fan

Souvenirs
Singapore is an excellent place to buy souvenirs, whether inexpensive but attractive items made in the region, or more expensive art and craft pieces.

**Souvenirs from
Raffles Hotel**

**Chinese
seals**

Pewterware

Sports goods
Discount sporting goods shops offer significant bargains in branded sportswear (see p150).

Suits
There are many excellent tailors who will make a made-to-measure suit from fine textiles in the latest style. Two days is the normal turnaround time.

Textiles
The Jim Thompson shops have the best Thai silk; Little India sells sari material at reasonable prices; Arab Street has very good batik; and People's Park Complex is notable for the sheer variety of textiles on offer (see p148).

Oriental outfits
Different versions of the Oriental outfit are available. A happy coat (left) is great for lounging at home.

Carpets
Among the dealers in antiques and craft items at Dempsey Road (see p144) are several specializing in carpets. The prices are very competitive by international standards.

Chinese medicines
Chinese medicated oil alleviates aches and dizziness. Tiger Balm soothes mosquito bites and aches.

Food
Try Chinese delicacies such as ginseng with bird's nest essence and barbecued sweet meat. The ingredients for your favourite Singapore dish are readily available and make good presents.

Chinese tea

Barbecued sweet meat

Oyster sauce

Sambal prawn rolls

***Sambal* chilli sauce**

Ginseng with bird's nest essence

Essence of chicken

Sesame oil

Where to shop

Lady's bag

SINGAPORE PRESENTS plenty of shopping opportunities for the tourist. Orchard Road still retains its magnetism, and here one finds the biggest crowds, especially on weekends. Most of the leading department stores are here, along with Western and local designer brands. Those looking for computers or electronic goods should head for the downtown malls which specialize in them. A search for exotic fabrics, antiques or Chinese medicines can lead further afield. The suburban housing estates offer clothing and everyday necessities at bargain prices.

CLOTHING

BIG FASHION NAMES, such as **Calvin Klein**, **Gucci**, **Hugo Boss**, **Armani**, **Burberrys**, **Kenzo**, **Chanel** and many more, maintain stylish boutiques in Singapore. Local Asian designers, like **Allan Chai**, **Daniel Yam** and **Vera Wang** sometimes create contemporary fashion based on the classic *cheongsam* (a tight-fitting dress with a Mandarin collar and high-slit skirt) or the *samfoo* (Chinese-style pyjamas). Women's sizes tend to be small, to cater for the petite Asian frame. Basic no-label clothes such as shorts, jeans and T-shirts are very good value here.

Latest footwear from On Pedder

SHOES

A WIDE SELECTION of footwear is available. Try **Charles & Keith**, **Substance**, **On Pedder**, or **C K Tang** department store. The large sizes are hard to find; most shops do not stock anything larger than women's European size 6/US size 8 or men's European size 10/US size 10½.

A wide selection of textiles is used in locally designed fashion

TEXTILES

THERE IS a plentiful and varied range of textiles in Singapore. Arab Street offers a wide array of Middle Eastern, Indonesian, Malaysian and Thai fabrics: two shops here are **Poppy Fabric** and **Aljunied Brothers' House of Batik**. For Indonesian handmade one-off batik of good quality, visit **Bin House** in Ngee Ann City *(see p89)*. In Little India, there is exquisite material for *saris* and cotton for *dhotis*. The **People's Park Complex** in Chinatown has printed fabrics, including silks, from all over the world.

JEWELLERY, GEMS AND GOLD

JEWELLERY SET WITH precious stones is a good purchase in Singapore. The variety available is dazzling, and quality of craftsmanship high. Besides trusted local jewellers such as **Lee Hwa** and **Larry**, world-renowned **Bulgari** and **Tiffany** are also here. Gold used for settings is mostly 18K; but 22K or 24K gold pieces (verified and stamped by the Singapore Assay Office) are also available at prevailing market rates per gramme – these generally represent good value. Little India houses many goldsmiths and other jewellers. Bargaining at local jewellers is acceptable.

ANTIQUES AND CRAFTS

FURNITURE, sculpture, terracotta, lacquerwork, paintings and ceramics from China and Southeast Asia are available. Ask if wood in furniture is seasoned; if not, it may crack in a temperate climate.
A carbon-dating certificate for old terracotta proves authenticity. Good places to browse are **Dempsey Road**, **Tanglin Shopping Centre**, **Tomlinson Antique House** and **Lim's Arts & Crafts**.
Carpets are another favourite purchase; but there are import bans for American citizens on carpets from some Middle Eastern countries.

Handmade mask

Antique shop on Trengganu Street, Chinatown

DIRECTORY

DEPARTMENT STORES

Isetan
Shaw House,
350 Orchard Road.
6733 1111.

Wisma Atria,
435 Orchard Road.
6733 7777.

John Little
Specialist Shopping
Centre, 277 Orchard Road.
6737 2222.

Marks & Spencer
Wheelock Place,
501 Orchard Road.
6733 8122.

Centrepoint,
176 Orchard Road.
6734 1800.

Raffles City,
252 North Bridge Road.
6339 9013.

Metro
Paragon,
290 Orchard Road.
6835 3322.

Marina Square,
6 Raffles Boulevard.
6333 3322.

Robinsons
Centrepoint,
176 Orchard Road.
6733 0888.

Raffles City,
252 North Bridge Road.
6216 8388.

Seiyu
Parco Bugis Junction,
230 Victoria Street.
6223 2222.

Takashimaya
Ngee Ann City,
391 Orchard Road.
6738 1111.

C K Tang
310/320 Orchard Road.
6737 5500.

CLOTHING

Allan Chai
#01-18
Capitol Building,
11 Stamford Road.
6338 0293.

Anna Sui
Level 2
Isetan Wisma Atria,
435 Orchard Road.
6733 7777.

Asiatropics
#01-19/20
Scotts Shopping Centre,
6 Scotts Road.
6235 6686.

Bossini
#01-30
Centrepoint,
176 Orchard Road.
6738 0120.

#B1-45/48 Wisma Atria,
435 Orchard Road.
6733 7167.

British India
#B1-31 Ngee Ann City,
391 Orchard Road.
6834 1172.

Burberrys
#03-00 Isetan Scotts,
350 Orchard Road.
6734 7510.

Calvin Klein
#02-26/27 Hilton
Shopping Gallery, Hilton
Hotel, 581 Orchard Road.
6735 5790.

Chanel
#01-25 Ngee Ann City
391B Orchard Road.
6733 5120.

Daniel Yam
#01-32/33 Wisma Atria,
435 Orchard Road.
6733 7220.

Emporio Armani
#01-01 Forum Galleria,
508 Orchard Road.
6734 5766.

Giordano
#B1-07/08 Lucky Plaza,
304 Orchard Road.
6736 4302.

Gucci
#01-01/04 Paragon,
290 Orchard Road.
6734 2528.

Hugo Boss
#01-03 Ngee Ann City,
391B Orchard Road.
6735 0233.

Kenzo
#02-30 Raffles Hotel,
328 North Bridge Road.
6334 2520.

People of Asia
#04-51/52 Far East Plaza,
Scotts Road.
6736 0411.

#B1-11 Wisma Atria,
435 Orchard Road.
6834 1703.

Vera Wang
#03-03 Palais Renaissance,
390 Orchard Road.
6235 4648.

SHOES

Charles & Keith
#01-214 Liang Court,
177 River Valley Road.
6338 1217.

On Pedder
#02-12P/Q Ngee Ann City,
391B Orchard Road.
6835 1307.

Substance
#02-12 Wheelock Place,
501 Orchard Road.
6836 0111.

TEXTILES

**Aljunied Brothers
House of Batik**
95 Arab Street.
6294 6897.

Bin House
#02-12F Ngee Ann City,
391B Orchard Road.
6733 6789.

**People's Park
Complex**
Eu Tong Sen Street.
Various shops.

Poppy Fabric
111 Arab Street.
6296 6352.

JEWELLERY

Bulgari
#01-01 Ngee Ann City,
391B Orchard Road.
6735 6689.

#01-08 Hilton Hotel,
581 Orchard Road.
6737 1652.

Larry Jewellery
#01-10 Paragon,
290 Orchard Road.
6732 3222.

#02-12A Ngee Ann City,
391B Orchard Road.
6235 5848.

Lee Hwa
#01-23 Bugis Junction,
200 Victoria Street.
6334 2838.

Tiffany & Co.
#01-05 Ngee Ann City,
391B Orchard Road.
6735 8823.

#01-05 Raffles Hotel,
328 North Bridge Road.
6334 0168.

MARKETS AND STALLS

Bugis Village
Queen Street/Victoria
Street/ Rochor Road.
6876 0088.

Clarke Quay
3E River Valley Road.
6337 3292.

Tanglin Mall
163 Tanglin Road.
6736 4922.

ANTIQUES AND CRAFTS

Dempsey Road
*Off Tanglin Road. A
collection of warehouses*

Lim's Arts & Crafts
#02-01 Holland Road
Shopping Centre,
211 Holland Avenue.
6467 1300.

**Tanglin Shopping
Centre**
19 Tanglin Road
6737 0849.

**Tomlinson Antique
House**
460 Sims Avenue.
6744 3551.

CDs AND VIDEO

Borders
#01-00 Wheelock Place,
501 Orchard Road.
6235 7146.

HMV
#01-11 The Heeren,
260 Orchard Road.
6733 1822.

Tower Records
#02-63 Suntec City,
3 Temasek Boulevard.
6338 5755.

WATCHES

AN EXPENSIVE WATCH is the standard badge of success in Singapore, as in much of Asia (even your taxi driver may wear a Rolex). There is an exceptional range of genuine brands for sale. In outlets other than the **Rolex** shop on Orchard Road and dedicated **Swatch** shops, it is acceptable to bargain *(see p143)*. **Lucky Plaza**, among the major shopping malls, has numerous watch shops, **Peng Kwee** sells second-hand Rolexes, and **The Hour Glass** (there are several branches) offers many brands. Always ask for a good discount if buying two or more.

A shop specializing in watches

ELECTRONICS

BECAUSE ASIAN consumers demand the most recent innovations in television, home cinema and the like, visiting shoppers enjoy access to the latest models of everything at specialist retailers such as **Electric City** and **V-8 Movies**.

Singapore is a good place to buy audio products. **Lucky Plaza**, **Sim Lim Square** and **Mustafa Centre** have a good array of mid-range equipment. Aficionados of high-end hi-fi will find **The Adelphi** shopping centre an essential destination. Here, one can usually arrange a listening test just by walking into any "audio boutique" such as **Precision Audio** or **Tat Chuan**, and making a request. The staff are well informed. In Plaza Singapura, try **Atlas Hi-Fi**.

The absence of import duties keeps prices, even of western products, reasonable. It's always worth bargaining.

A display of high-end audio equipment

CAMERAS

FOR THE LATEST digital cameras, try **John 3:16**. **Ruby Photo** stocks equipment for professionals. **Cathay Photo Store** offers cameras and video equipment. Second-hand camera bodies and lenses, including top industry brands such as Nikon and Canon and some collectors' models, can be found at dealers such as **The Camera Workshop** and **Prime Camera Centre**.

COMPUTERS

A GOOD RANGE is available, but prices are really only marginally lower in Singapore than elsewhere. The best computer mall in Singapore is **Funan the IT Mall** *(see p145)*, the shops include **Challenger** and one **Mac Shop**. It is worth visiting also **Sim Lim Tower** and **Sim Lim Square**; and **Best Denki** in Ngee Ann City.

Laptop computers on sale at Funan Centre

FLOWERS

INNOVATIVE FLOWER SHOPS such as **Greeting Cuts**, **The Flower People** and **Good-wood Florist** provide very creative arrangements. The best value for money is offered by small stallholders.

SPORTS GOODS

MANY MAJOR brands are manufactured in nearby countries, so prices are often lower in Singapore than elsewhere. Leading retailers include **Why Pay More?**, **Pan West Golf Shop** and **Royal Sporting House**. Almost every shopping mall has one or more good sports retailers.

Sports shoes on display

FOOD

IN ADDITION to large super-markets such as **Cold Storage**, **Carrefour**, and the pricier **Tierney's Gourmet** and **Jasons**, specialist outlets such as **Brown Rice Paradise**, **The Tea Chapter**, and **Yue Hwa Chinese Products** are worth investigating for foodstuffs.

BOOKS

THE BEST specialist stock on South-east Asian subjects is at **Select Books**; the best children's department is at **Borders**; and the best new fiction selection is at Japan-ese bookstore giant **Kinokuniya**. **Times** and **MPH** are also worth visiting.

Browsing a Borders

DIRECTORY

WATCHES

The Hour Glass
#01-11 Scotts Shopping
Centre, 6 Scotts Road.
6235 7198.

#01-02 Ngee Ann City,
391 Orchard Road.
6734 2420.

Lucky Plaza
Various shops.
304 Orchard Road.
6235 3294 (enquiries).

Peng Kwee
(second-hand Rolex)
#01-45A Peninsula Plaza,
111 North Bridge Road.
6334 0155.

Sincere Watch
#01-12 Ngee Ann City,
391B Orchard Road.
6733 0618.

Swatch Stores
#B1-27 Plaza Singapura,
68 Orchard Road.
6334 8042.

#01-08/09 The Heeren,
260 Orchard Road.
6737 1917.

#01-41 Raffles City,
250 North Bridge Road.
6334 5951.

ELECTRONIC PRODUCTS

Boon Hi-Tech Superstore
#03-29 Raffles City,
252 North Bridge Road.
6339 3421.

Electric City
#02-01 Suntec City Mall,
3 Temasek Boulevard.
6332 3460.

Lucky Plaza
Various shops.
304 Orchard Road.
6235 4568.

Mustafa Centre
145 Syed Alwi Road.
6298 2967.

V-8 Movies
#03-14/22
Bugis Junction,
200 Victoria Street.
6338 8878.

HI-FI

The Adelphi Shopping Centre
Various shops.
1 Coleman Street.
6339 9179.

Atlas Hi-Fi
#03-19 Plaza Singapura,
68 Orchard Road.
6339 0966.

Precision Audio
#01-01 The Adelphi
Shopping Centre,
6334 4611.

Tat Chuan Audio
#01-17 The Adelphi
Shopping Centre,
6334 5566.

CAMERAS

Camera Workshop
#01-31 Peninsula
Shopping Centre,
3 Coleman Street
6336 1956.

Cathay Photo
#01-11
Peninsula Plaza,
111 North Bridge Road.
6338 0451.

#02-219
Marina Square,
6 Raffles Boulevard.
6339 6188.

John 3:16 Photo Supplies
#03-37 Funan the IT Mall,
109 North Bridge Road.
6337 1897.

Prime Camera Centre
#01-15 Peninsula Plaza
111 North Bridge Road.
6334 7581.

Ruby Photo
#01-01 Peninsula Hotel,
1 Coleman Street.
6338 0236.

COMPUTERS

Best Denki
#05-05 Tower A,
Ngee Ann City,
391 Orchard Road.
6835 2855.

Challenger SuperStore
#06-00 Funan the IT Mall.
6336 7747.

#02-02
DBS Tampines Centre,
12 Tampines Central.
6426 9123.

Funan the IT Mall
Various shops.
109 North Bridge Road.
6336 8327.

The Mac Shop
#04-11 Funan the IT Mall.
6334 1633.

Sim Lim Square
Various shops.
1 Rochor Canal Road.
6332 5839.

Sim Lim Tower
Various shops.
10 Jalan Besar
(junction of Sungei Road).
6294 0590.

FLOWERS

The Flower People
#01-01, 3 Seah Street.
6337 3477.

Goodwood Florist
565 Thomson Road.
6255 2266.

Greeting Cuts
19 Jalan Pisang.
6296 6838.

SPORTS GOODS

Pan West Golf Shop
#02-035 Suntec City Mall,
3 Temasek Boulevard.
6337 5133.

Royal Sporting House
#01-157 Suntec City Mall,
3 Temasek Boulevard.
6332 1495.

#B2-15/23
Ngee Ann City,
391A Orchard Road.
6538 8888.

Why Pay More?
#02-57/59/61,
Suntec City Mall,
3 Temasek Boulevard.
6336 7568.

FOOD

Brown Rice Paradise
#03-15 Tanglin Mall,
163 Tanglin Road.
6738 1121.

Carrefour
#01-199
Suntec City Mall,
3 Temasek Boulevard.
6333 6868.

Cold Storage
#B1-14 Centrepoint,
176 Orchard Road.
6737 4222.

#01-05 Holland Road
Shopping Centre.
6468 5566.

Jasons
#01-01 Orchard Towers,
1 Claymore Drive.
6235 4355.

The Tea Chapter
9A-11A Neil Road.
6226 1175.

Tierney's Gourmet
#02-01/04 Serene Centre,
10 Jalan Serene.
6466 7469.

Yue Hwa Chinese Products
70 Eu Tong Sen Street.
6538 4222.

BOOKS

Borders
#01-00 Wheelock Place,
501 Orchard Road.
6235 7146.

Kinokuniya
#03-10/15
Ngee Ann City, 391B
Orchard Road.
6737 5021.

#03-09
Parco Bugis Junction,
200 Victoria Street.
6339 1790.

MPH
#02-24/25 Raffles City,
252 North Bridge Road.
6336 4232.

Select Books
#03-15 Tanglin Shopping
Centre, 19 Tanglin Road.
6732 1515.

Times the Bookstore
#06-01A/B/C Centrepoint,
176 Orchard Road
6734 9022.

#06-11/14
Plaza Singapura,
68 Orchard Road.
6837 0552.

ENTERTAINMENT IN SINGAPORE

NTERTAINMENT in Singapore comes in the same forms – theatre, dance, film, pubs, clubs and sports – as entertainment in any other big city. However, Singapore is a young country and some of these entertainment forms, particularly film, have been imported *en masse* from the USA for years, thereby stifling local initiatives. In recent years, Singaporeans have worked hard to redress the balance, and

A Chinese dancer performing a pugilistic stance

now, for the first time since the 1950s, Singaporean films are being produced. Other entertainment has developed locally also, and Singapore can now lay claim to a thriving theatre and club scene. The club world has encompassed all musical tastes at a wide variety of venues. Theatre can be found in small and medium-sized performance spaces, presented by both fledgling and long-established local companies.

INFORMATION SOURCES

THERE ARE several widely available free publications with entertainment listings. The best are *I-S* (Inside-Singapore) and *Where Singapore*. *I-S*, which comes out twice a month, has a central pull-out section giving current showing details and short reviews. *Where* is published monthly. These magazines can be picked up in bars, cafés and hotels. *The Straits Times* and *The New Paper* have listings of movies and arts events.

BOOKING TICKETS

YOU CAN book tickets for many arts events (except movies) from **SISTIC** or **Ticketcharge** outlets which are at many locations across the island. You may also book through their websites, by telephone or by fax. Tickets can sometimes be bought at the venues themselves.

INTERNATIONAL SHOWS

SINGAPORE has become a regular stopover for international touring companies presenting major theatrical, musical and dance productions. These are usually staged during festivals and in medium-sized and larger venues such as the **Victoria Theatre**, **Kallang Theatre**, **Singapore Indoor Stadium** or the **University Cultural**

Centre. Another venue, **Esplanade–Theatres on the Bay**, features a spacious 2,000-seat theatre as well as an 1,800-seat concert hall. The Singapore Festival of Arts, which takes place every June in even-numbered years, attracts talented performers from all over the world, with street shows as an added bonus. The Festival of Asian Performing Arts, held in June in odd-numbered years, concentrates on Asian works.

Ah Kong's Birthday Party, a dinner play performed in a restaurant

LOCAL THEATRE

AS WELL AS traditional Chinese opera, Singapore supports a growing number of drama groups, mostly formed in recent years. These young companies are attempting to create a uniquely Singaporean voice in theatre – one that reflects Western influence (performance is usually in English) but takes inspiration from Asian theatre forms and music *(see pp34–5)*. Venues change depending on the anticipated size of the

audience. The quality and scope of these productions vary, but local companies such as **Action Theatre**, **Theatreworks**, **Toy Factory** and **The Necessary Stage** are among those offering consistently high-quality work *(see p34)*. The **Singapore Repertory Theatre** performs a repertoire of English-language classic dramas and original plays, with Asian casts. The **Singapore Stage Club**, an amateur troupe with an international cast, puts on a pantomime at Christmas.

MUSICALS

WHEN FAMOUS pop stars such as Michael Jackson and Robbie Williams perform for one night in Singapore, they attract audiences big enough to fill the National Stadium. Performances by Western a cappella groups, chamber orchestras and opera troupes are also a frequent occurrence, and Asian pop idols have their own avid followings. Touring musical productions such as *Cats* and *Miss Saigon* are consistently popular, but in the late 1990s a local musical, *Chang & Eng*, about the lives of

Local musical *Chang & Eng*

the famous Siamese twins, ran to sell-out audiences at home and abroad. This has stimulated the production of more local musicals, such as *Nagraland*, an Asian pop

musical by resident singer-composer Dick Lee. The music in these shows is Western-inspired and the dialogue is in English, but the themes and presentation styles are Singaporean.

Local performing artist

OPEN-AIR ENTERTAINMENT

FORT CANNING PARK is the venue for regular "Ballet under the Stars" performances by the **Singapore Dance Theatre**, as well as the four-day WOMAD (World of Music, Arts, Dance) Festival each year. Latin and jazz concerts are regularly held at the Chijmes Lawn and

Fountain Court on Sunday evenings. Buskers from many countries perform by the Singapore River during the annual Buskers' Festival, usually held in November.

DANCE

TOURING PRODUCTIONS from companies as illustrious as the Paris Opera Ballet come

Teochew street *wayang* (Chinese opera) (*see pp34–5*)

to Singapore but the local **Singapore Dance Theatre** is well worth seeing for its Asian and Western ballet interpretations (*see p35*). Performances of Indian

classical dance are organized by associations such as the **Nrityalaya Aesthetics Society**, thus helping to keep the art alive.

CHINESE OPERA

CHINESE OPERA takes place on makeshift stages erected in Housing Board estates, especially during the

Hungry Ghosts Festival (*see p24*). There are no publicized listings. Opera excerpts for visitors are staged by the **Chinese Opera Institute** and **Chinese Theatre Circle**.

DIRECTORY

TICKET OUTLETS

SISTIC
6348 5555.
FAX 6440 6784.
W www.sistic.com.sg
SISTIC outlets are located at Alliance Française; Bhaskars Arts; Junction 8; Chinese Opera Teahouse; Cold Storage Jelita; DBS Arts Centre; Downtown East; Lot 1; Millenia Walk; Parco Bugis Junction; Raffles City; Scotts; Singapore Conference Hall; Singapore Indoor Stadium; Specialists'; Suntec City Mall; Tampines Mall; Victoria Concert Hall; and Wisma Atria.

Ticketcharge
6296 2929.
FAX 6296 9897. W www.ticketcharge.com.sg
Ticketcharge outlets are located at Centrepoint; Century Square; Chijmes; Downtown East; Forum

the Shopping Mall; Great World City; Jurong Point; Marina Square; Tanglin Mall; and West Mall.

VENUES

Chijmes Hall
30 Victoria Street.
Map 5 E1. 6336 1818.

DBS Arts Centre
20 Merbau Road.
Map 4 C2. 6733 8166.

Esplanade–Theatres on the Bay
60 Raffles Avenue.
Map 5 F2. 6828 8222.
W www.esplanade.com

Jubilee Hall
3rd Storey, Raffles Hotel, 328 North Bridge Road.
Map 5 E1. 6412 1312.

Kallang Theatre
Stadium Walk.
6345 8488.

Shaw Foundation Stage
Botanic Gardens, Cluny Road. **Map** 1 D1.
6471 9943.

Singapore Indoor Stadium
2 Stadium Walk.
6344 2660.

Substation
45 Armenian Street.
Map 3 D5.
6337 7535.

Telok Ayer Performing Arts Centre
#01-01, 182 Cecil Street.
Map 5 D4.
6221 4726

The Room Upstairs
42 Waterloo Street.
Map 3 D4.
6837 0842.
W www.action.org.sg

University Cultural Centre
10 Kent Ridge Crescent.
6874 1224.

Victoria Theatre and Concert Hall
9 Empress Place.
Map 5 D3.
6339 6120.

PERFORMING GROUPS

Action Theatre
6837 0842.

Chinese Opera Institute
6339 1292.

Chinese Theatre Circle
6324 1098.

Nrityalaya Aesthetics Society
6336 6537.

Singapore Dance Theatre
6338 0611.

Singapore Repertory Theatre
6221 5585.

Theatreworks
6338 6735.

The Necessary Stage
6440 8115.

Toy Factory
6222 1526.

Music

THERE IS A WIDE VARIETY of music playing in Singapore: from concerts by the Singapore Symphony Orchestra to performances by traditional Chinese, Malay and Indonesian orchestras, open-air jazz concerts and contemporary music in red-hot night spots for the dedicated clubber. Western pop acts stop off in Singapore, but less regularly than in Tokyo or Hong Kong. Indeed, the most rapidly changing aspect of the musical scene can be found in the nightclubs and bars that now line Boat Quay, and others springing up in restored shophouses in Chinatown and Mohamad Sultan Road.

Local entertainer

CLASSICAL MUSIC

THE SINGAPORE SYMPHONY Orchestra (SSO), founded in 1978 to bring classical music into Singaporeans' lives, has its home at the Victoria Concert Hall *(see p153)*. It splits its concert year into halves with the first season running from January to June, and the second from July to December. Western classics are the staple of the SSO's performances. Western guest composers and soloists are a regular feature and new Asian composers are occasionally showcased. The SSO also gives outdoor performances.

ORCHESTRAL MUSIC

THE **PEOPLE'S ASSOCIATION** supports the teaching and performance of ethnic music in the form of the Chinese Orchestra, Orkestra Melayu (the Malay orchestra) and the Indian Orchestra. Call the association for performance times if you are interested in these aspects of music.

The **Singapore Chinese Orchestra** (SCO) has a good reputation for spirited performances of both traditional Chinese music and works by modern Chinese composers *(see p35)*. The orchestra performs regularly at the Victoria Concert Hall. Check *The Straits Times* for listings or contact the box office *(see p153)*.

Chinese pipa player

OPEN-AIR CONCERTS

OPEN-AIR CONCERTS are frequently held at either the Shaw Foundation Stage in the Botanic Gardens *(see p99)* or at Fort Canning Park. These free concerts, performed by the Singapore Symphony Orchestra and various other ensembles, are attended enthusiastically by picnicking families. *The*

Straits Times has listings. WOMAD (World of Music, Arts, Dance), a four-day world music carnival, takes place in Fort Canning Park every year.

Aaron Kwok, a Cantopop artiste

POP CONCERTS

FOREIGN POP BANDS regularly play in Singapore (check *The Straits Times* for details). International stars commanding big audiences play at large venues such as Esplanades–Theatres on the Bay and the Indoor Stadium. It is now legal for audience members to stand up in their seats and dance at a pop concert (the law was changed in 1998). Besides Western acts, Cantopop stars such as Aaron Kwok and Andy Lau have given successful concerts in Singapore.

CONTEMPORARY MUSIC

THE CONTEMPORARY music scene in Singapore is fairly sedate compared with Europe and North America. There are no large gatherings in disused warehouses for raves on a massive scale and there are no vacant fields given over to pop music festivals like Glastonbury or Woodstock. But knowledge of Western music culture is high among young people and so is the desire to change the club scene to reflect a dynamic and culturally-up-to-date Southeast Asia.

Every kind of dance music can be found here from hard house to techno, hip-hop, garage, future fusion and

Singapore Symphony Orchestra performing at the Botanic Gardens

ambient, in clubs designed to rival their counterparts in Europe and America (although there's nothing on the scale of a venue such as London's Ministry of Sound). See *Juice* magazine for up-to-the-minute listings and details of special themed nights and promotions. Be prepared to pay a price for all this cutting-edge sound technology though – cover charges in clubs are standard and range from S$20 upwards.

Every hotel lounge in Singapore seems to have its own Filipino band doing cover versions of current and "oldie" pop songs. For live music at a local level, pubs and bars are the best venues, with many featuring different types of music every night of the week, open-mike and open-jam sessions once a week, and guest bands from overseas. No. 5 in Emerald Hill Road *(see p161)* is a well-established example of the way many bars operate: on Mondays this wine bar features acoustic pop; on Tuesdays and Wednesdays, contemporary pop; on Thursdays saxophone; on Fridays, reggae and pop alternately; and on Sundays, an open blues jam session.

For those interested in open jam sessions, Crazy Elephant *(see pp158–9)* on Clarke Quay holds the most regular ones (rock n roll, blues). On the last Friday of every month, Robertson Quay is host to jazz jam sessions played from 8–10pm.

Muddy Murphy's *(see p159)*, supports traditional Irish music (direct from Ireland). For information about performances call individual bars for details *(see p159)* or refer to *I-S* magazine for listings of traditional music.

Local musicians playing at the Crazy Elephant

World of Music, Arts and Dance (WOMAD) held at Fort Canning Park

WORLD MUSIC

APART FROM bars, pubs and clubs with particular themes or themed nights, there is not much world music in Singapore (apart of course from Chinese, Indian and Malay classical groups). But Singaporeans' interest in world music is increasing and so, with market demand, are the number and variety of acts that are being brought in by concert promoters – everything from Spanish flamenco guitar soloists to "classical mambo rock" can be found throughout the year.

Apart from these, the Coco Carib at Clarke Quay is one place where lovers of Caribbean rhythms and Latino sounds can go to rumba, reggae, soca and merengue the night away.

LOCAL BANDS AND PERFORMING ARTISTS

LOCAL BANDS are a relatively new part of Singapore's music scene. Most of them have sprung up in the 1990s. The greatest number of albums released by Singaporean bands ever, was seen in 1997–8. Unfortunately they were issued by small labels and so did not achieve the promotion, distribution or following which they deserved. In addition to these teething problems, local radio continues to be driven by requests for Western pop music so local groups do not receive as much play time as they need. The best-known local bands are Stomping Ground, Concave Scream and Humpback Oak; but several new groups have recently released albums, among them the Flying Pills, the Lilac Saints, Plain Sunset and vARnish. Check *The Straits Times* for concert listings.

Singapore bands often play for free on Saturdays at the Youth Park on Orchard Boulevard (behind Orchard Cineleisure) between 6:30 and 9:30pm. It is possible to hear

A local band performing at the Youth Park

resident singer-songwriters performing solo or in jamming sessions at certain pubs and bars. Check *I-S* or *Pop Out* for listings. *BigO*, a local magazine, provides good coverage of local bands and promotes their CDs.

ORCHESTRAL MUSIC

People's Association
☎ *6344 8222.*

Singapore Chinese Orchestra
☎ *6440 3839.*

Cinema

The Picturehouse logo

Aᴄᴄᴏʀᴅɪɴɢ ᴛᴏ a recent survey, Singapore has the highest cinema-going population in the world per head – this is a major leisure activity. Many people, especially young people, go to the cinema as often as two or three times a week, and popular shows can be busy, particularly at the weekend. Films Singaporeans watch are mainly Hollywood blockbusters, interspersed with a smattering of mainstream and art-house European films, Indian "Bollywood" releases and Hong Kong action flicks.

The deluxe Grand Cinema, in opulent style

MAINSTREAM AND ART-HOUSE MOVIES

Mᴏsᴛ ᴏꜰ ᴛʜᴇ ꜰɪʟᴍs shown in Singapore's major cinemas are American. These are screened in English, often with Chinese subtitles. When a film in another European language or Japanese is shown, it will usually have both English and Chinese subtitles. Even Chinese-language films may carry Chinese subtitles because the dialogue may not be fully understood by speakers of a different dialect.

Many cinemas cater to weekend demand with midnight shows on Friday and Saturday. Sometimes there are midnight movies on Wednesdays and Thursdays as well, when a film has been widely advertised and is expected to be popular.

Special screenings of French and German films (usually art films) are organized by the Alliance Française and the Goethe Institute. Film festivals featuring critically acclaimed films are put on every year by the British Council, the Alliance Française and the organizers of the Singapore International Film Festival.

Lido Theatre at Shaw Centre

VENUES AND PRICES

Mᴏsᴛ sɪɴɢᴀᴘᴏʀᴇ movie-houses belong to a large chain such as Shaw Brothers, which is Singapore-owned; or Golden Village, which belongs to a Hong Kong company. Many are located within shopping centres and operate as "cineplexes", offering several films simultaneously. Generally, cinemas are scrupulously clean and air-conditioned, and boast state-of-the-art sound and projection equipment. The Golden Village Grand cinema (located in the Great World City shopping complex) is a "Gold Class" movie theatre with the largest screen in Singapore, thick carpets, subtle lighting, surround sound and special seats. There are individual and paired reclining armchairs complete with footrests and tables, waiter service, and a decent menu. The price for all this pampering – S$20 to S$30 per person, depending on the programme – is three to four times higher than a standard cinema ticket.

Weekend filmgoers catching a movie in town are advised to book or buy their tickets in advance (two days to 40 minutes before screening, by telephone or in person).

FILM CENSORS' RATINGS

G (General): wholesome viewing suitable for everyone.
PG (Parental Guidance advised): parents may wish to check the content of a PG film before watching it with their children or allowing them to view the film on their own. There may be some scenes with violence, some innocuous forms of nudity, and moderate sex scenes and swear words.
NC-16 (No Children below 16): unsuitable viewing for children below the age of 16. This rating is hardly ever used (*Saving Private Ryan* was a notable exception).
R(A) (Restricted (Artistic)): admission to R(A) films is restricted to those above 21. Films rated R(A) have an adult theme and contain graphic scenes of sex and/or violence. R(A) films are not allowed to be screened at cinemas located in HDB estates.

A Japanese film rated R(A)

CENSORSHIP

Since July 1991 all films and videos in Singapore have had to go through a revised rating procedure administered by the Singapore Board of Film Censors. The ratings determine who is allowed to view the film or video. While it is intended to be objective, the rating system reflects cultural biases characteristic of Singapore – violence seems to be tolerated more readily than nudity.

SINGAPORE INTERNATIONAL FILM FESTIVAL

The Singapore International Film Festival is held annually in April or May and lasts for two weeks. The festival features movies, documentaries, animation and shorts from 250 countries. Films screen across the island. Tickets can be obtained from Ticketcharge outlets. Popular films sell out quickly.

MADE-IN-SINGAPORE MOVIES

The first Singaporean film, *Majnun Laila*, was made in 1933 by Indian filmmakers. Films continued to be produced here until the Japanese Occupation (1942–45) when production was turned over to the creation of propaganda. After World War II, the 1950s emerged as the "Golden Age" of Singapore film. The multi-talented P Ramlee sang, danced, wrote, acted and directed his way across the screen in various guises and delighted audiences throughout Singapore and Malaysia. But a huge influx of American films and the arrival of television in the 1970s virtually killed the local film industry.

Only in the 1990s did Singaporean cinema tentatively find a voice via films such as *Army Daze* (a comedy which evolved out of a Singapore stage production), *12 Storeys* (the first Singaporean film to be acclaimed at the Cannes Film Festival), *Money No Enough* (a top-grossing comedy with takings of $5.8 million) and *Forever Fever* (a dance movie picked up by Miramax, and regarded as Singapore's most international film).

A scene from *Forever Fever*

DIRECTORY

THE COLONIAL CORE

Alliance Française de Singapour
1 Sarkies Road.
6737 8422.

Eng Wah
Suntec City Mall
6836 9074. www.ewcinemas.com.sg

Golden Village Marina
3rd level Marina LeisurePlex.
1900 912 1234. www.gv.com.sg

CHINATOWN

Shaw Oriental Duplex
Oriental Plaza, New Bridge Road.
6323 2809.

Yangtze
3 & 4 Pearl's Centre, 100 Eu Tong Sen Road.
6223 7529.

ORCHARD ROAD

Orchard Cineplex
#05-01 Cineleisure Orchard.
6235 1155.

Goethe Institute
#05-01 Winsland House 2
163 Penang Road.
6735 4555.

Golden Village Plaza
7th Level Plaza Singapura.
1900 912 1234.

Shaw Lido Cineplex
Level 5 Shaw House.
6738 0555. www.shaw.com.sg

LITTLE INDIA & KAMPONG GLAM

Shaw Prince/Jade
100 Beach Road, Shaw Towers.
6738 0555

United Artists Bugis Junction
4th Level Parco Bugis Junction, 200 Victoria Street.
6337 9655.

FURTHER AFIELD

Cathay Causeway Point
Level 7 Woodlands Square. 6235 1155.

Golden Village Bishan
#04-03 Junction 8 Shopping Centre, 9 Bishan Place.
1900 912 1234.

Golden Village Eastpoint
#06-01 Eastpoint Shopping Centre, 3 Simei Street.
1900 912 1234.

Golden Village Grand
3rd level Great World City.
1900 912 1234.

Golden Village Tiong Bahru
4th level Tiong Bahru Plaza.
1900 912 1234.

Golden Village Yishun
51 Yishun Central 1.
1900 912 1234.

Overseas Movie, Golden
Golden Nite Tower, Beach Road.
6298 5466. www.oegroup.com.sg

Shaw Balestier
Shaw Plaza
360 Balestier Road.
6738 0555.

Shaw Choa Chu Kang
Lot 1 Shoppers' Mall Choa Chu Kang Ave 4.
6738 0555.

Shaw Jurong
Jurong 4 Cineplex Jurong East St 13.
6569 3463.

FILM ASSOCIATIONS

Singapore Film Society
www.sfs.org.sg

Singapore International Film Festival
(at cinemas island-wide)
www.filmfest.org.sg

Pubs and Bars

SINGAPORE IS well-provided with pubs and bars, most of them located near obvious tourist stretches such as Orchard Road, Boat Quay and Clarke Quay. There is a good range of styles and types of atmosphere. Alcohol tends to be expensive but most pubs have Happy Hours (usually until 9pm) so you can spare some expense if you start drinking early.

A celebrity's guitar at Hard Rock Cafe

Bar & Billiard Room at Raffles Hotel

THE COLONIAL CORE

AT RAFFLES HOTEL, the **Long Bar** and the **Bar & Billiard Room** are essential visits. Dig into bowls of peanuts in the Long Bar while you sip away at a Singapore Sling. The Bar & Billiard Room serves an excellent selection of coffees, whiskies and cigars. In **Father Flanagan's**, an "Irish pub", your Guinness arrives with the shape of a shamrock impressed into the head and free snacks are served at 7pm every day. **Bar Opiume** at Empress Place offers a beautiful riverside setting. **Somerset's** has the longest bar in Singapore. Several bars have opened next to the new Esplanade – Theatres on the Bay, including **Fabulous**

Fizz, a champagne bar, and jazz bar **Harry's @ The Esplanade** which has a popular sister bar on Boat Quay. **Balaclava** at Suntec City is a chic, modern and spacious bar with plush armchairs to sink into. **The Lobby Terrace** has comfortable seats and a good-value happy hour (5–8pm). **Paulaner Brauhaus** is a microbrewery dominated by working brewery machinery. For a Latin feel head to **Maracas Concina Latina.**

CHINATOWN

FOR AN AUTHENTICALLY Irish pub, try **Molly Malone's**, shipped out from Ireland in pieces and reconstructed in Singapore. **The Flag & Whistle**, an "English" pub, is a quiet place to drink. **J J Mahoney's** has three floors and 50 different beers. In the popular and reverent **Elvis Pub** there is a blissfully endless round of Elvis songs on the turntable. **Bar Sá Vanh** has a sophisticated Asian feel with low tables and Thai

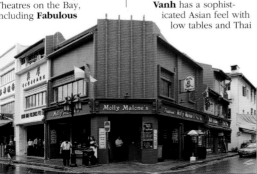

Molly Malone's, for Irish drinks, grub and music

cushion-seats for sitting on the floor. **Tong Heritage Bar** is set in a traditional Chinese medical hall, after which the bar is named. Wall to wall chinois decor and a courtyard pool create an historical feel. On Boat Quay the **Penny Black** is a "London pub" with good food and British beer. **Harry's Bar** was voted the World's Best Bar in 1995 and lives up to this reputation with live jazz and good service. **Pierspoint Pub** is very popular with the young executive crowd from the nearby business district. On Clarke Quay, **Crazy Elephant** has an outdoor drinking area and live blues or rock and roll.

ORCHARD ROAD

THE SINGAPORE branch of the **Hard Rock Café** offers exactly the same successful formula as its other outlets around the world. **Muddy Murphy's** is a lively "Irish pub" which serves Sunday lunch and a wide range of beers. The clientele of **Anywhere** is usually a very lively young crowd. **Ice Cold Beer** is located in a pleasant converted shophouse. **The Dubliner** Irish Bar has an elegantly colonial atmosphere. On Emerald Hill an alley behind some shophouses has been imaginatively converted into **The Alley Bar.**

FURTHER AFIELD

ACROSS THE RIVER from Clarke Quay, **Brewerkz** is a North American-style brewery with an extensive, quality beer list and a menu with many innovative dishes. In the Robertson Walk area, **Bar** is the best place to go for stylish cocktails. River Valley Road offers a "British pub" in the form of **The Yard**, and a rather more "local" type of experience in the form of the **Blue Cow**. On Mohamad Sultan Road, **Wong San's** offers a good selection of retro music, a pool table and a lively Extreme Sports Nite every Thursday. **The Next Page** is a Chinese-theme pub.

Nearby **Wala Wala's** alfresco seating and bar snacks are always popular. The **Stop-Over Pub** on Bukit Timah Road is an Australian watering-hole with a friendly atmosphere. In Sentosa, the Maholo Hawaiian Beach bar serves coktails in a South Pacific setting, and the **Sunset Bay Beach Bar** is a beach-front bar with a good weekend BBQ.

Father Flanagan's at Chijmes

DIRECTORY

THE COLONIAL CORE

Balaclava
#01-01B Suntec City, 1 Raffles Boulevard.
Map 5 F1.
6339 1600.

The Bar and Billiard Room
Raffles Hotel,
1 Beach Road.
Map 5 E1.
6412 1194.

Bar Opiume
1 Empress Place, Asian Civilisations Museum II.
Map 5 D3.
6339 2876.

Fabulous Fizz
#01-09 Esplanade Mall, Esplanade – Theatres on the Bay, 8 Raffles Avenue.
Map 5 E2.
6336 9918.

Father Flanagan's
#B1-06 Chijmes,
30 Victoria Street.
Map 5 E1. 6333 1418.

Kalture Pub
26 Purvis Street.
Map 5 E1. 6339 6970.

The Long Bar
Raffles Hotel,
1 Beach Road.
Map 5 E1.
6337 1886.

Maracas Concina Latina
#01-15/15A CHIJMES,
30 Victoria Street.
Map 5 E1.
6336 9151.

Paulaner Braühaus (microbrewery)
#01/01 Millenia Walk.
Map 5 F2.
6883 2572.

Post Bar
Ground Floor, The Grand Fullerton Hotel, 1 Fullerton Square. **Map** 5 E3.
6733 8388.

Somerset's Bar
3rd Floor, Raffles the Plaza Hotel. **Map** 5 E2.
6431 5331.

The Lobby Terrace
2 Temasek Boulevard, Conrad International Centennial. **Map** 3 F2.
6432 7483.

CHINATOWN AND THE FINANCIAL DISTRICT

Alley Bar
2 Emerald Hill.
Map 2 B4.
6738 8818.

Bar Sá Vanh
49 Club Street.
Map 4 C4.
6323 0145.

Crazy Elephant
#01-07, 3E Clarke Quay, River Valley Road.
Map 4 C2.
6337 1990.

Elvis Pub
1A Duxton Hill. **Map** 4 C4.
6220 1268.

Harry's Bar
28 Boat Quay.
Map 5 D3.
6538 3029.

J J Mahoney's
58 Duxton Road.
Map 4 C4.
6225 6225.

Molly Malone's Irish Pub and Grill
42 Circular Road (round the back of Boat Quay). **Map** 5 D3.
6536 2029.

The Penny Black
26/27 Boat Quay.
Map 5 D3.
6538 2300.

Pierspoint Pub
36A Boat Quay. **Map** 5 D3
6438 8884.

Tong Heritage Bar
50 Eu Tong Sen Street.
Map 4 C3.
6532 6006.

ORCHARD ROAD

Anywhere
#04-08/09 Tanglin Shopping Centre, 19 Tanglin Road.
Map 1 E2.
6734 8233.

The Dubliner
165 Penang Road, Winsland House. **Map** 4 C1
6835 1110.

Hard Rock Café
50 Cuscaden Road,
#02-01 HPL House.
Map 1 E2.
6235 5232.

Ice Cold Beer
9 Emerald Hill Road.
Map 2 B4.
6735 9929.

Muddy Murphy's Irish Pub
#B1-01, Orchard Hotel Shopping Arcade,

442 Orchard Road.
Map 1 F2.
6735 0400.

FURTHER AFIELD

Bar
#01-23/24 Robertson Walk, 11 Unity Street.
Map 4 C2
6738 1318.

Brewerkz
#01-05 Riverside Point,
30 Merchant Road.
Map 4 C3.
6438 7438.

Blue Cow
397 River Valley Road.
Map 4 B1.
6735 3774.

Maholo Hawaiian Beach Bar
10 Siloso Beach Walk, Sentosa.
6274 2378.

Sunset Bay Beach Bar
60 Siloso Beach Walk, Sentosa. 6275 1053.

The Next Page
17 Mohamad Sultan Road,
Map 4 C2.
6835 1693.

The Yard
294 River Valley Road.
Map 4 B1. 6733 9594.

Wala Wala
31 Lorong Mambong, Holland Village.
6462 4288.

Wong San's
12 Mohamad Sultan Road.
Map 4 C2.
6738 3787.

Wine Bars, Clubs and Karaoke

Sign at a club

Many of Singapore's wine bars are housed in beautifully converted shophouses that offer candlelit tables and friendly service. For those who would prefer a more lively night, then the city has some of the best clubs in the region. Karaoke (KTV) is endemic in pub and club life in Singapore – even the most modest pub usually has a wall-mounted KTV set displaying the words to English-language and Chinese pop songs.

No. 5 Emerald Hill

WINE BARS

No. 5 was Singapore's first wine bar and is probably still its most popular one. No 5's next door neighbour on Emerald Hill, **Que Pasa** ("what's happening?" in Spanish), is a Spanish wine bar which serves tapas and Havana cigars alongside the drinks. **BarCelona** also serves tapas in quasi-Mediterranean surroundings. **Beaujolais** has comfortable armchairs (upstairs) and a cosy ground floor which extends onto the bar's five-foot way. There's a

regular Wine of the Month promotion and an extensive standard wine list. **Bisous** is frequented by all sorts of trendy media professionals as it sits right in the middle of "Media Chinatown", the home of many independent production houses. **Tango**'s Japanese-inspired interior decoration is calm and quiet but the bar itself still makes a considerable contribution to the bustle of Holland Village. **J P Bastiani Wine Bar** serves French, Italian, Spanish, Californian, Chilean, South African and Australian wines against a background of live music. **Les Amis Wine Bar** stocks old vintages and is one of the most expensive wine bars in town – definitely the place for a celebration.

CLUBS

Singapore has a great many music clubs but only one of them, **Zouk**, has managed to achieve an international reputation. Zouk is really an amalgamation of three clubs – Zouk, **Velvet Underground** and **Phuture** – in three converted warehouses down by the Singapore River. Zouk's resident DJs, Andrew Chow

and Tony Tay, have high standards and the club regularly brings in well-known DJs from London, Paris, Tokyo and Germany, including John Digweed, Norman Cook, Sven Vath, Satoshi Tomiie and Adam Freeland. Queues for Zouk start to form early so make sure you allow for extra time.

China Black sports some great interior design, beautiful people and formidable but tame bouncers. One Fullerton is the latest club location with two hot venues: **Centro** and **Embargo**. Centro was voted Nightspot of the Year 2002 by the Singapore Tourism Board and boasts both resident and guest DJs to rival Zouk's. Embargo is the place to chill

Retro chic at China Jump

out to down tempo drum 'n' bass and acid jazz tunes. **Insomnia @ CHIJMES** is open 24/7 and is for hardcore party animals only.

China Jump Bar & Grill is not for the faint-hearted as the music is loud, the clientele determined to enjoy themselves, and the cocktail list long (over 100 to choose from). **Bar None** plays host to local rock band Energy. Led by the ever-energetic Douglas O, their slick cover versions of 80s and 90s pop and rock hits keep the 20–30 something crowd entertained.

On Mohamad Sultan Road, both **Madame Wong's** and **Urbane** attract radio and TV personalities to their unique environments (Madame Wong's has a retro Oriental terrace bar and Urbane features some very good

Zouk, a popular club housed in a refurbished warehouse

music and some very strong cocktails). **The Liquid Room** admits only the trendiest and super cool.

Lox takes a step back in time with medieval decor, but the music is nothing but contemporary. **Georgio's** has a quiet bar as well as a disco which plays Chinese pop music (mainly in Cantonese and Mandarin).

Sultan of Swing is an intimate pub complete with cigar room and band stage (live acts do perform) while a connecting lobby leads to a club area at the back of the venue. **Shanghai Sally's** has something for everyone: from top 40 hits to house, acid jazz and R&B.

KARAOKE

Due to the all-pervasive nature of karaoke (KTV), the listing in the directory only scratches the surface of the venues that are available. Some karaoke lounges have hostesses whose job it is to make you buy as many drinks as possible.

Some KTV rooms are decorated along themes, such as in **Vogue** where the KTV room is decked out as a "soundproof rain forest room". **The Joy Luck Club** is the most upmarket KTV pub on our list and is combined with a wine and cigar bar.

A karaoke session at The Joy Luck Club

Violet Karaoke has reasonable rates and good private rooms. **Ming's Cafe and Pub** has mostly classic English-language songs in its stock and well-priced beer. The decor at **My Place Entertainment** is less-than-tasteful and invites customers to leave their inhibitions at the door.

DIRECTORY

WINE BARS

BarCelona
#01-30/31
Robertson Walk,
11 Unity Street.
Map 4 C2. ☎ 6235 3456.

Beaujolais Wine Bar
1 Ann Siang Hill.
Map 4 C4. ☎ 6224 2227.

Bisous
#01-01 Capital Square 3,
25 Church Street.
Map 5 D3. ☎ 6226 5505.

J P Bastiani Wine Bar
#01-12 Clarke Quay,
3A River Valley Road.
Map 4 C2. ☎ 6433 0156.

Les Amis Wine Bar
#02-16 Shaw Centre,
1 Scotts Road. Map 1 F2.
☎ 6733 2225.

Mag's Wine Kitchen
86 Circular Road.
Map 5 D3. ☎ 6438 3836.

No. 5
5 Emerald Hill Road.
Map 2 B4. ☎ 6732 0818.

Que Pasa
7 Emerald Hill Road.
Map 2 B4. ☎ 6235 6626.

Tango
35 Lorong Mambong,
Holland Village.
☎ 6463 7365.

CLUBS

Bar None
#B/1 Singapore Marriott,
320 Orchard Road.
Map 1 F2. ☎ 6222 8117.

Brix
Grand Hyatt Hotel,
10-12 Scotts Road.
Map 2 A3. ☎ 6416 7108.

Centro
#02-02 One Fullerton,
1 Fullerton Road.
Map 5 E3. ☎ 6220 2288.

China Black
Level 12, Pacific Plaza,
9 Scotts Road.
Map 1 F2. ☎ 6734 7677.

China Jump Bar & Grill
B1-07 Fountain Court,
Chijmes,
30 Victoria Street.
Map 5 E1. ☎ 6338 9388.

Dbl O
#01-24 Robertson Walk,
11 Unity Street.
Map 4 C2. ☎ 6735 2008.

Embargo
#01-06 One Fullerton,
1 Fullerton Road.
Map 5 E3. ☎ 6220 6556.

Giorgio's
B1-01/16
The Riverwalk Galleria.
Map 5 D3.
☎ 6533 1055.

Insomnia@CHIJMES
#01-21 Chijmes,
30 Victoria Street.
Map 5 E1. ☎ 6338 6883.

The Liquid Room
#01-05
The Gallery Hotel,
76 Robertson Quay.
Map 4 B2. ☎ 6333 8117

Lox
#02-04 Block 3C,
Clarke Quay,
River Valley Road.
Map 4 C2. ☎ 6334 4942.

Lush
#01-75 UE Square.,
205 River Valley Road
Map 2 A5. ☎ 6733 6388.

Madame Wong's
28/29 Mohamad Sultan
Road. Map 4 C2.
☎ 6834 0100–7.

Milieu
Level 2 Peranakan Place,
180 Orchard Road.
Map 2 B4. ☎ 6738 1000.

Nox
11 Mohamad Sultan
Road. Map 4 C2.
☎ 6835 2823.

Phuture
17, 19, 21 Jiak Kim Street.
Map 4 A2. ☎ 6738 2988.

Shanghai Sally's
#01-01 Central Mall,
5 Magazine Road.
Map 4 C3.
☎ 6557 0828.

Sultan of Swing
#01-02/03 Central Mall,
5 Magazine Road.
Map 4 C3. ☎ 6557 0828.

Urbane
12 Mohamad Sultan Road.
Map 4 C3. ☎ 6735 6613.

Velvet Underground
17, 19, 21 Jiak Kim Street.
Map 4 A2. ☎ 6738 2988.

Zouk
17, 19, 21 Jiak Kim Street.
Map 4 A2. ☎ 6738 2988.

KARAOKES

Joy Luck Club
65 Tanjong Pagar Road.
Map 4 C5. ☎ 6324 3037.

Kwan Sisters
42 Prinsep Street.
Map 5 D1. ☎ 6333 4482.

Ming's Cafe & Pub
195 Upper Thomson Road.
☎ 6251 3187.

My Place Entertainment
4 Lorong Telok. Map 5 D3.
☎ 6536 4859.

Nashville
446 Joo Chiat Road.
☎ 6344 2103.

Prince KTV
67 Beach Road.
☎ 6339 2668.

Violet Karaoke
9 Maju Avenue.
☎ 6283 8422.

OUTDOOR ACTIVITIES AND SPECIAL INTERESTS

SINGAPORE DOES NOT HAVE mountains to climb or rivers to raft but it makes the most of what it has. You can join Singaporeans relaxing at the East Coast Park and Sentosa, in Bukit Timah Nature Reserve, on bikes, and at tennis courts and fishing spots across the island. Watersports are popular all year round, thanks to the maritime setting and tropical climate. You can play golf, take scuba-diving or archery lessons or learn *tai chi*. It is often cheaper to learn a new sport or skill as a group than to do it individually, so it may be worth finding like-minded people to join you.

Windsurfing off the East Coast

ADVENTURE SPORTS CLUBS

SINGAPORE **Adventure Club** lives up to its name by organizing a variety of trips around the islands in canoes for sporty individuals and groups (fees include canoe hire, life jackets and expert advice from guides). Intensive courses in kayaking, sailing, and, for the even more gung-ho and ruggedly robust types, abseiling, are offered all-year-round by **Outward Bound Singapore**.

Archery practice at the Archery Training Centre

ARCHERY

THE GENTLEMANLY SPORT of archery is taught by enthusiasts at the **Archery Club of Singapore**, a non-profit organization. The cost of a two-hour lesson is reasonable, and you can buy four-lesson courses, which include the costs of the hire of equipment, relatively cheaply. This activity is for people of all ages, and is not taxing for the conditions.

DIVING

SINGAPORE IS ONE of the cheapest places in the world to learn to dive, from as little as S$350–S$560 for a PADI (Professional Association of Diving Instructors) sport diver qualification course. You can learn to dive here in a few days, and then head for the clearer waters of Malaysia's east coast, Thailand, or Indonesia's Riau Archipelago. Basic PADI training involves classroom sessions, pool sessions and four dives in open water.

There are number of reputable dive schools, and the **Big Bubble Centre** and **Blue Wave Sports** both come highly recommended. **Waikiki Dive Centre**, **Scuba Connection**, **Scuba Corner**, **Seadive Adventures** and also **Sentosa Water Sports Centre** are others. **Marsden Brothers** (probably the best) have the only custom-made dive boat in Singapore (a catamaran), and offer live-aboard packages (a two-day cruise to the Riau Archipelago includes five dives).

WATER-SKIING AND WAKEBOARDING

CALL INDIVIDUAL OPERATORS for hourly rates to hire a speedboat and equipment. Tuition is extra. Two such operators are **Cowabunga Ski Centre** and **Friendly Water Seaports Services**. **William Water Sports Centre** offers water-skiing every day and wakeboarding clinics every Thursday.

SWIMMING

IF YOU ARE FRUSTRATED with the size of your hotel pool, try the excellent public pools such as the **Delta** or **Bishan Swimming Complex**, or the rather older one at **River Valley**. Other public pools are located at **Buona Vista**, **Bedok** and **Katong**, but these are slightly further afield. Alternatively you could visit a water theme park such as the **Big Splash**, where there are enormous, seven- storey slides to speed down. Although more expensive than public pools, it has more to offer.

Big Splash water theme park

SAILING AND WINDSURFING

Take to the waves at the **National Sailing Centre**, **Keppel Marina**, **Seasports Centre**, **Raffles Marina**, **Singapore Yacht Club** or the **Changi Sailing Centre** (weekdays only). Some, such as the **National Sailing Club**, conduct lessons; call in advance for details. Besides sailing and windsurfing, the

SAFRA Seasports Centre also offers kayaking and jet-skiing. Remember, you are in the tropics; the sun will burn even if there is some cloud around, so you will need to take some kind of protective hat, sunglasses, sunscreen and drinking water.

FISHING

Visit a fishing shop to ask about tides and

"bumboat" hire. **Sea Tackle** has friendly and knowledgeable staff and operates a Ladies' Fishing Club. Or just approach any group of fishermen and ask for their advice about the best spots for a good catch. March to September offer the best fishing – and many locals think it is best to avoid Singapore's rainy season (Nov–Jan).

An angler's catch

DIRECTORY

ADVENTURE SPORTS CLUBS

Outward Bound Singapore
Pulau Ubin.
(6545 9008.

Singapore Adventure Club
74B Lorong 27, Geylang.
(6749 0557.

ARCHERY

Archery Club of Singapore
9 Lantana Avenue.
(6468 1813.

DIVING

Big Bubble Centre
57 Cantonment Road.
(6222 6862.
w www.bigbubble.com

Blue Wave Sports
#02–9 Riverside Point,
30 Merchant Road.
(6557 2702.
w www.asiandiver.com

Marsden Brothers Dive School
113 Holland Road.
(6475 0050.

Scuba Connection
104A Tanjong Pagar Road.
(6372 0200. w www.
scubaconnection.com

Scuba Corner
#04-162 Kitchener Complex, 809 French Road
(6338 6563.

Seadive Adventures
#01-03 Singapore Yacht Club, 52 West Coast Road
(6774 0105.
w www.seadiveadventures.com

Sentosa Water Sports Centre
Ferry Terminal Building, 1 Garden Avenue, Sentosa.

Singapore Underwater Federation
River Valley Swimming Complex
1 River Valley Road
(6334 5519.
w www.asian-diver.com/suf.html

Waikiki Dive Centre
#01–35 The Concourse, 298 Beach Road
(6291 1290.

WATERSKIING

Cowabunga Ski Centre
10 Stadium Lane.
(6344 8813.

Friendly Water Seasports Services
#01-22 The Riverwalk, 20 Upper Circular Road.
(6557 0016.

William Water Sports Centre
35 Punggol, 24 Avenue.
(6257 5859.

SWIMMING

Bedok Swimming Complex
901 New Upper Changi Rd.
(6443 5511.

Big Splash
902 East Coast, Parkway.
(6345 6762.

Bishan Swimming Complex
Bishan Street 14.
(6353 6117.

Buona Vista Swimming Complex
76 Holland Drive.
(6778 0244.

Delta Swimming Complex
900 Tiong Bahru Road.
(6474 7573.

Katong Swimming Complex
111 Wilkinson Road
(6344 9609.

SAILING AND WINDSURFING

Changi Sailing Club
32 Netheravon Road.
(6545 2876.

Keppel Marina
Bukit Chermin Road.
(6270 6665.

National Sailing Centre
1500 East Coast Parkway.
(6444 4555.
w www.sailing.org.sg

Raffles Marina
10 Tuas West Drive.
(6861 8000.
w www.rafflesmarina.com.sg

SAFRA Seasports Centre
10 Changi Coast Walk.
(6546 5880.

Seasports Centre
East Coast Lagoon,
1212 East Coast Parkway.
(6449 5118.

Singapore Sailing Federation
1500 East Coast Parkway.
(6444 4555.
w www.sailing.org.sg

Singapore Yacht Club
52 West Coast Ferry Road
(6768 9288.
w www.rsyc.org.sg

FISHING

Bedok Jetty
🚌 10, 12, 14 to Bayshore Park and follow underpass to East Coast Park.

Kallang Park
(this is a popular location for fishing, along the coast from the Seasports Centre, East Coast Lagoon)
1210 East Coast Parkway.

Sea Tackle
6 Lorong 1 Geylang.
(6741 5988.

Seletar Reservoir
Mandai Lake Road
(look for the fishing jetty).
🚌 137, 171.

IN-LINE SKATING

Rollerblade hockey

SENTOSA is a good location for in-line skating (visitors rent skates from **Sport Entertainment**), as is East Coast Parkway. However, you have to be alert on weekends, as the routes are crowded (slightly less so on Saturday mornings). The **Sunsport Centre** (East Coast Parkway) also rents skates at a fairly reasonable price.

FLYING

THERE IS NOT MUCH air space above Singapore (the Singapore Air Force trains in Australia) so flights for enthusiasts tend to be short. You can take a trial flight in a light aircraft (with instructor) at the **Republic of Singapore Flying Club**.

Cycling on the bike track at the Bukit Timah Nature Reserve

CYCLING

CYCLING BY THE SEA is pleasant at East Coast Parkway, where **Sunsport Centre**, and **SDK Recreation** rent bikes for a few dollars. An excellent place for a bike ride is Pulau Ubin (see p107). Bikes can be rented near the ferry point. **Bukit Timah Nature Reserve** has a good 7-km (4 mile) mountain-bike track but you need to bring your own bike. The surfaces are good and the landscape varied (from rainforest to quarry). **Ulu Pandan Boy's Brigade Mountain Bike Track** is

shorter than the Bukit Timah trail at 2.4 miles (4 km) but the terrain is more adventurous. Bikes are available here for hire.

Singapore Tennis Centre

TENNIS

COURTS CAN BE RENTED every day between 7am and 10pm at various centres, such as the **Kallang Squash and Tennis Centre**, and **Farrer Park Tennis Courts**. The **Singapore Tennis Centre** offers one-on-one coaching, and you can put your name on a partner list and hire a court. An "Instant Tennis" course for beginners is available at a very reasonable fee.

GOLF

THERE ARE 18 golf courses in Singapore, all beautifully kept, brilliantly green and sensitively landscaped. Although golf club membership is prohibitively expensive, tourists are permitted to play at most clubs on weekdays (not weekends). The popular golf clubs include **Laguna National Golf & Country Club**, **Raffles Country Club** and the **Superbowl Golf & Country Club**. The **Seletar Country Club** is open to non-Singaporeans and non-members on weekends only. Remember to present your passport to gain entry to the air base. The golf course at **Sentosa Golf Club** boasts a

Golf driving range at East Coast Park

spectacular view of the South China Sea. For those who would simply like to hit a few balls, about 40 balls can be rented cheaply at driving ranges around the island.

RUNNING TRACKS

SINGAPORE HAS ALL manner of tracks and running surfaces to choose from and the least polluted urban air in Southeast Asia to breathe. The **Botanic Gardens** is a favourite jogging spot and very central. **Marina Promenade** is a 2-km (1.2-mile) paved track running next to the sea and swaying palm trees. **MacRitchie Reservoir** has fitness parks, where you can punish yourself with chin-ups and sit-ups, as well as shaded running tracks from 10 km (6 miles) to 12 km (7 miles) in length, depending on the route you take. Along the way you are likely to see families of monkeys.

ART AND CRAFTS

THERE ARE courses at the **Substation** in tapestry, Chinese calligraphy, batik painting and photography throughout the year, and **Nanyang Academy of Fine Arts** and **LaSalle-SIA College of the Arts** run graphic design and fine arts courses. You can learn how to make your own jewellery or can attend seminars on diamonds, gems and pearls at **JusTanja** on Emerald Hill.

DANCING

JITTERBUGS SWINGAPORE offers one-off classes and six-week courses in lindy hop, salsa, hip hop and swing. The **YMCA** offers courses in line dancing, ballroom, salsa, disco-rock, rock and roll and waltz, both one-off and ten-week. Classical ballet courses are available at **Singapore Ballet Academy** and **Singapore Dance Theatre**.

Classical Asian dance forms, such as

Thai and Balinese dance, tend to be taught at one-off workshops at the **LaSalle-SIA College of the Arts** and the **Substation**. Check *The Straits Times* for daily listings.

COOKING

THE MOST FAMOUS culinary classes in Singapore are held at Raffles Hotel by the **Raffles Culinary Academy**. Classes are given daily by Raffles' chefs in a custom-built studio. Classes cover Asian cuisines and some of the hotel's own "culinary secrets". **Academy at-sunrise** offers hands-on cooking classes preceded by a tour of their spice garden. Menus vary and change every three months.

NATURE WATCH

Bird outings to interesting locations, for those who like to meet like-minded people, are organized by the **Nature Society of Singapore** twice each month. The

Sungei Buloh Wetland Reserve is a good place to go on your own to see migratory birds and mangrove swamp dwellers (*see p92*). Otherwise any of Singapore's many nature reserves is well worth a visit.

Class in progress at Raffles Culinary Academy

| DIRECTORY | **Kallang Squash & Tennis Centre** | **Superbowl Golf and Country Club** | **Singapore Ballet Academy** |

IN-LINE SKATING

Sport Entertainment
Sentosa 6272 8676.

Sunsport Centre
East Coast Parkway.
6440 9827.

FLYING

Republic of Singapore Flying Club
140B East Camp, Seletar Airbase. 6481 0200.

CYCLING

Pulau Ubin
Take your pick from a number of bike hire shops on the island.

SDK Recreation
East Coast Recreation Centre, 1000 East Coast Parkway. 6445 2969.

Ulu Pandan Boys' Brigade Mountain Bike Track
Dover Road.

TENNIS

Farrer Park Tennis Courts
Rutland Road.
6299 4166.

Kallang Squash & Tennis Centre
Stadium Road.
6440 6839.

Singapore Tennis Centre
1020 East Coast Parkway.
6442 5966.

GOLF

Jurong Country Club
9 Science Centre Road.
6560 5655,
6568 5188.

Laguna National Golf & Country Club
11 Laguna Golf Green.
6542 6888,
6541 0200.

Orchid Country Club
Yishun Avenue 1.
6755 9811.

Raffles Country Club
450 Jalan Ahmad Ibrahim.
6861 7649/7655.

Seletar Country Club
101 Seletar Club Road,
Seletar Airbase.
6481 4812.

Sentosa Golf Club
27 Bukit Manis Road.
6275 0022/0657.

Superbowl Golf and Country Club
6 Marina Green.
6221 2811.

RUNNING TRACKS

MacRitchie Reservoir
Lornie Road.

Marina Promenade
15 min from City Hall MRT.

Singapore Botanic Gardens
Cluny Road.

ARTS AND CRAFTS

JusTanja
20 Emerald Hill Road.
6221 5253.

LaSalle-SIA College of the Arts
90 Goodman Road.
6344 4300.

The Substation
45 Armenian Street.
6337 7535.

Nanyang Academy of Fine Arts
111 Middle Road.
6337 6636.

DANCING

Jitterbugs Swingapore
78 Tras Street.
6223 5323.

Singapore Ballet Academy
Level 2 Fort Canning Centre, Cox Terrace.
6237 9125.

Singapore Dance Theatre
Level 2 Fort Canning Centre, Cox Terrace.
6338 0611.

YMCA
1 Orchard Road.
6336 6000.

COOKING

Academy at-sunrise
Fort Canning Centre, Fort Canning Park.
6336 3307.
www.at-sunrise.com

Raffles Culinary Academy
Raffles Hotel, 1 Beach Road. 6412 1256.

NATURE WATCH

Nature Society
#02-05 The Sunflower, 510 Geylang Road.
6741 2036.
www.nss.org.sg

Sungei Buloh Wetland Reserve
301 Neo Tiew Crescent
6794 1401.
www.sbwr.org.sg

SURVIVAL GUIDE

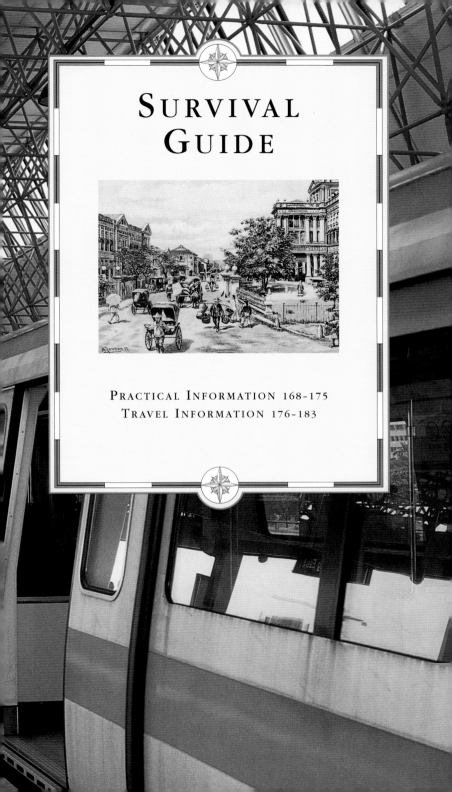

PRACTICAL INFORMATION 168-175
TRAVEL INFORMATION 176-183

PRACTICAL INFORMATION

SINGAPORE IS one of the most visitor-friendly countries in the world. It is an easy place in which to change money and to call, fax or e-mail home; it has a good public transport system running along well-marked roads and it is largely free of violent crimes, dirt and most tropical diseases. While there are four official languages (Malay,

Singapore Tourism Board logo

Tamil, Mandarin Chinese and English), English is dominant, making communication relatively easy. There is, however, a Singapore variant of English commonly known as "Singlish". Interspersed with phrases from other local languages, and spoken in a rhythm similar to Chinese, Singlish can sound a little strange to Western ears.

WHEN TO GO

SINGAPORE is renowned for having two climates - warm and sunny or warm and rainy. The rainy season is mild and lasts from October to around the end of January. At all times the temperature rarely drops below 24˚C or rises much above 34˚C, day or night, so you can visit all year round without any fear of hitting a cold spell.

WHAT TO TAKE

LIGHT CLOTHING, such as short-sleeved shirts, shorts and T-shirts, is essential. An umbrella is useful, sunglasses and suntan lotion advisable, as is a cotton jumper, a shawl or a light jacket for air-conditioned restaurants, malls and museums.

TOURIST INFORMATION

YOU WILL FIND free leaflets distributed by the **Singapore Tourism Board** (STB) on just about all of

Singapore's tourist attractions and these can be obtained in the airport, hotels, convention centres, shopping malls and even restaurants.

There is a **Tourist Information Centre** in the main STB office at the Tanglin Mall end of Orchard Road, and STB also operates **Singapore Visitors Centres** in Suntec City Mall, a shopping and convention centre which opens daily and keeps the longest and most convenient opening hours. This is also an ideal place to make bookings and purchase tickets to events, attractions and local tours.

ADMISSION CHARGES

YOU CAN PICK and choose attractions to suit your budget. There are lower rates for children. Entry to museums starts at S$3 for adults while an attraction such as the Night Safari is comparatively expensive, with prices close to S$20 per adult and above S$10 per child.

OPENING HOURS

OFFICE HOURS are generally 9am to 5:30pm. Some offices open on Saturdays; these usually close at 12:30pm. Shops in the heart of town are open seven days a week, from around 10am till 8-9pm; but shops close earlier in outlying areas and many are closed on Sundays. Normal museum hours are 9am to 5pm. Museums and some sightseeing attractions are closed on Mondays.

FACILITIES FOR CHILDREN

LARGE DEPARTMENT STORES have feeding and changing facilities for mothers and babies. All tourist attractions in Singapore are child-friendly and children are welcomed in restaurants, shops and cinemas, day and night.

ETIQUETTE

SINGAPOREANS are very accommodating towards people from other cultures but can sometimes seem rude to outsiders. Some may jump queues, chat during theatre performances and movies, spit on the street and behave pushily in shops. The government has been discouraging anti-social behaviour since the 1970s with an undying annual courtesy campaign.

A Courtesy Campaign poster

Singapore Visitors Centre at Suntec City Mall

PLACES OF WORSHIP

Most places of worship in Singapore welcome visitors as long as their behaviour is circumspect. Always remove your shoes before entering a Hindu, Muslim or Buddhist religious building and do not take photographs without permission. Do not wear clothes that may be deemed offensive, such as very short shorts or skimpy T-shirts. Do not show the soles of your feet to a Buddhist. Never point at a Muslim.

World clock at Changi Airport

BUSINESS CARDS

There are lots of "do's and don'ts" regarding the use of business cards in Singapore, as in the rest of the Southeast Asian region. It is essential to have one (displaying the most impressive title you can give yourself) if you want to do business here.

Give your card with both hands, with your name facing the recipient. Accept a card with both hands and look at the name on it as an indication of your sincerity. Do not put the card away in the presence of the person who gave it to you. Place it in front of you on the table to show your acknowledgement. If you are eating when introduced to someone, stand up to receive his or her card as a sign of respect.

TIPPING

Tipping is not usual in Singapore (it is explicitly banned at Changi Airport, for instance) and is not encouraged in taxis, restaurants and hotels. You may, however, leave the change as a tip if you wish. However, you do pay for service in a more formal way – when you see "+++" on your menu or accommodation bill, it means that the following extras will

be added on top of the listed price:
- 10% service charge
- 1% government tax
- 5% Goods and Services Tax (GST)

SINGAPORE TIME

Singapore is eight hours ahead of Greenwich Mean Time (GMT). Sydney Standard Time (SST) is two hours ahead of Singapore time.

Singapore clocks do not go forward by one hour (as they do in the US, UK and Australia) in March and April.

ELECTRICITY

Singapore supplies 220–240 volts AC at 50 cycles, as does Australia, the United Kingdom and Hong Kong; Canada, Japan and the United States use 110–120 volts at 60 cycles. Most hotels are installed with both three-pin plugs (with flat pins similar to those used in the UK) and two-pin fittings for power sockets.

Standard three-pin plug

CONVERSION CHART

The metric system is generally used in Singapore.

Imperial to metric
1 inch = 2.5 centimetres
1 foot = 30 centimetres
1 mile = 1.6 kilometres
1 ounce = 28 grams
1 pound = 454 grams
1 pint = 0.6 litre

Metric to imperial
1 centimetre = 0.4 inch
1 metre = 3 feet 3 inches
1 kilometre = 0.6 mile
1 gram = 0.04 ounce
1 kilogram = 2.2 pounds

Personal Security and Health

No smoking sign

ALL THE BASIC conditions essential to personal safety and good health exist in Singapore. The streets are free from crime. The environment is almost spotless. Good doctors are plentiful, both of Western training and oriental traditions. And unlike most Southeast Asian and many Western countries, tap water is drinkable.

A traditional Chinese medical hall

LAW AND PENALTIES

SINGAPORE LAW is based on the British legal system, a colonial legacy. Although it can seem harsh in Western eyes, the fine of S$2,000 imposed on anyone found guilty of selling chewing gum is perhaps the most widely known example of the stringency of Singaporean law. The death penalty is enforced for armed robbery,

Tanglin neighbourhood police post, for making a report

murder and drug-dealing; caning is imposed for other crimes such as rape, pickpocketing and vandalism.

Smoking is not allowed in air-conditioned public spaces, restaurants or queues of more than five people (even outdoors). If you are caught, you will have to pay a minimum fine of S$1,000. However, you can smoke in bars, pubs and clubs. In addition, one can be liable for heavy fines for jaywalking, spitting, littering and not flushing public toilets.

PERSONAL SECURITY

IN SINGAPORE "no-go" areas are virtually non-existent, and visitors of both sexes can walk around freely at night without fear. Common sense is all that is required. Although thefts are rare, it nevertheless makes sense to use the safe-deposit facilities provided in hotels. Petty theft is the only real hazard to look out for. Pickpockets do frequent crowded places and they tend to target tourists, so look after your passport and your wallet. In the event of any problems, there are many police posts and police stations all over the island.

MEDICAL ATTENTION

SINGAPORE DOES NOT have any reciprocal healthcare agreement with other countries, so if you are ill or injured you have to pay for treatment on the spot. It is a strong argument for arranging travel insurance before you arrive in Singapore.

You will notice immediately that the streets of Singapore are clean compared to some Southeast Asian capitals. This nation-wide cleanliness has a consequential effect on health – Singapore is safe from most tropical diseases found in the region (except for occasional

outbreaks of dengue fever), so no inoculation is required prior to your visit.

The Singapore customs and immigration authorities require proof of vaccination (within the last ten years) against yellow fever if you come from a country where this disease is endemic. It is sensible to check that your polio, hepatitis A, tetanus and typhoid vaccinations are active prior to departure. Inoculations can be updated at the **Travellers' Health and Vaccination Centre**. If you are leaving Singapore for other parts of Southeast Asia, it is a good idea to make sure that you are fully vaccinated.

COMMON AILMENTS

TRAVELLERS may suffer from the following when in Singapore: sunstroke, dehydration headaches, prickly heat, fungal infections, stomach aches, and lingering cuts – cuts take longer to heal in the tropics. Common-sense health care can prevent or ease most of these problems. Preventative steps are useful.

Do not go out into the sun without sufficient sunscreen protection and headgear. Dehydration is deceptively rapid in the tropics, so carry water with you, drink it constantly, and take plenty of refuelling stops. Buy prickly heat powder (easily available in supermarkets and pharmacies) and apply it before you think you need it.

Policeman with a patrol car

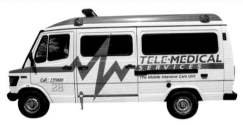

Ambulance

Fire engine

Always wash your hands before eating. If you sustain a cut, clean it immediately and continue to do so regularly.

Western medicine in Singapore is of as high a standard as in the West, with hospitals employing state-of-the-art equipment, medical staff trained to high standards and well-stocked pharmacies in most shopping centres.

Oriental medicine, reflexology, homeopathy, aromatherapy, acupuncture and Chinese herbal medicine are also widely available. Go to **Chinatown** (*see pp60–1*) to visit a traditional Chinese medical hall, or walk through **People's Park Complex** (*see pp62–3*) or other shopping malls if you wish to find foot reflexology and acupuncture shops. You may like to try a consultation with Chinese *sinseb* (physicians) for a variety of common ailments.

A private hospital

TOILETS

THERE ARE clean public toilets, of both Western and squatting type, at most MRT stations, food centres, shopping centres, cinemas and restaurants. There are some variations in the standard of hygiene from place to place but in general they are well run. Most public toilets are free, but some will collect 10 or 20 cents per entry and may provide a small pack of tissues.

Toilet sign

DISABLED TRAVELLERS

MOST OF the shopping centres, public buildings and cinemas in Singapore are designed with disabled visitors in mind, and are provided with ramps, lifts and toilet facilities. The only taxis that are specially fitted for wheelchairs are London cabs operated by TIBS.

Singapore's **National Council of Social Services** (NCSS) publishes a free guide, *Access Singapore: Physically Disabled Person's Guide to Accessible Places*, which provides access information covering hotels, concert venues, educational institutions, government departments, immigration checkpoints, libraries, hospitals, tourist attractions and shopping centres.

DIRECTORY

IN AN EMERGENCY

Police
[999 *(toll-free)*.

Fire and Ambulance
[995 *(toll-free)*.

Samaritans (SOS)
[1800 221 4444 *(toll-free)*.

LOST CREDIT CARDS

Tanglin Police Station
17 Napier Road. [6391 0000.

American Express
[1800 732 2244 *(toll-free)*.

Diners Club
[6294 4222.

MasterCard
[800 1100 113 *(toll-free)*.

Visa
[800 448 1250 *(toll-free)*.

MAJOR HOSPITALS AND CLINICS

Gleneagles Hospital
6A Napier Road. **Map** 1 D2.
[6470 5688 *(24-hour A&E)*.

Mount Elizabeth Hospital
3 Mount Elizabeth. **Map** 2 A3.
[6731 2218 *(24-hour A&E)*.

Raffles Hospital
585 North Bridge Road.
[6311 1555 *(24-hour A&E)*.

Travellers' Health and Vaccination Centre
Tan Tock Seng Hospital, Sinaran Drive (off Moulmein Road). [6357 2222.

DENTIST

Embrace Dental Surgery
#01-14 International Building, 360 Orchard Road. **Map** 1 F2.
[6235 6325.

DISABLED TRAVELLERS

National Council of Social Services
11 Penang Lane. **Map** 4 C1.
[6336 1544. FAX 6336 7729.
W www.ncss.org.sg

Currency and Banking

GST cash refund sign at Changi Airport

Dᴜʀɪɴɢ ᴛʜᴇ Aꜱɪᴀɴ currency meltdown of 1997, Singapore's currency retained a greater percentage of its previous value than any other Southeast Asian currency and bounced back to almost total health in the shortest time. Part of the credit for this relative resilience must go to Singapore's banking industry, a shining example of uncorrupt practices and conscientiously policed regulations. Visitors from countries with strong currencies in relation to the Singapore dollar will find that their money goes a long way here – due partly to their currencies' relative strength and partly to Singapore's low goods and services tax.

Bᴀɴᴋꜱ ᴀɴᴅ Bᴀɴᴋɪɴɢ Hᴏᴜʀꜱ

Aʟʟ ᴛʜᴇ ᴍᴀᴊᴏʀ ʙᴀɴᴋꜱ are represented in Singapore though some may not have high street branches. Indeed the island is a major banking centre. Singapore is the regional base for many merchant and consumer banks. International consumer banks with a major presence on the island include **Bank of America, Citibank** and the **Hongkong and Shanghai Bank.** Among the largest local banks are **Oversea Chinese Banking Corporation** (OCBC), the **Development Bank of Singapore** (DBS), **Overseas Union Bank** (OUB) and the **United Overseas Bank Group** (UOB).

Most banks in Singapore are open from 9:30am to 3pm, Monday to Friday and 9:30am to 12:30pm on Saturday. Banks are closed on public holidays.

International bank in Singapore

Differences in the exchange rates offered by banks are negligible (daily rates are published in the *The Straits Times*). However, the amount of commission taken by them is significantly less than that charged by hotels.

A moneychanger

Mᴏɴᴇʏᴄʜᴀɴɢᴇʀꜱ

Mᴏɴᴇʏᴄʜᴀɴɢᴇʀꜱ can be found in shopping centres, MRT stations, convenience stores and food centres, just about everywhere in Singapore. They usually offer better exchange rates than banks as they do not charge a fee, but may have limited quantities of some currencies. Rates vary, so you might want to check with several moneychangers before buying or selling.

At Changi Airport *(see pp178–9)*, you will find moneychanging outlets situated near your baggage collection point, just before you proceed through customs. More moneychangers can be found in the arrival hall. There are no restrictions on the quantity of money you can bring into Singapore. This applies to all currencies.

Cʀᴇᴅɪᴛ Cᴀʀᴅꜱ

Aʟʟ ᴍᴀᴊᴏʀ credit cards are accepted in Singapore and credit cards can be used in most of the island's ATM machines. Some taxis accept credit-card payments (it is best to check when you board), but will impose a 10 per cent surcharge. If you lose your credit card, report the loss to Tanglin Police Station *(see p171)* and call your credit card company.

Tʀᴀᴠᴇʟʟᴇʀꜱ' Cʜᴇǫᴜᴇꜱ

Aʟʟ ʙᴀɴᴋꜱ change travellers' cheques, but **United Overseas Bank** (UOB) usually offers the best rates. Remember to carry your passport with you when you want to cash travellers' cheques. **American Express** has a corporate office and a currency exchange which will cash Singapore-dollar American Express travellers' cheques free of charge.

ATMs

Aᴜᴛᴏᴍᴀᴛᴇᴅ ᴛᴇʟʟᴇʀ machines (ATMs) can be found everywhere in Singapore. They facilitate most aspects of consumer banking, so share dealings, fund transfers between accounts and banks, and bill payments can all be conducted from terminals located in car parks, housing estates, banks and shopping malls. ATMs are well-marked

Automated teller machine (ATM)

and easy to use. Most of them accept major credit cards, Plus and Cirrus. The minimum amount ATMs will issue is S$20. One can normally obtain up to S$2,000 a day from an ATM machine (in two withdrawals of S$1,000). For larger amounts, you will have to join the queue in a bank.

GST

AGOODS AND SERVICES tax (GST) of 5 per cent is added to the price of most goods and services in Singapore. Tourists can claim a tax refund for goods purchased if they have a receipt from one retailer totalling S$300 or more. For purchases made in shops which display a Tax Free Shopping Sticker, individual receipts of S$100 or more can be pooled to total S$300. Ask for a blue-and-white Global Refund Cheque to accompany the receipts.

Before your departure from Singapore, go to a **GST Refund Counter (Global Refund Singapore)** at Changi Airport *(see pp178–9)*, and present your purchases, and Global Refund Cheque. As refund you can make a choice between a cash refund, a bank cheque (sent by mail), or a refund to your credit card account.

(see pp178–9)

DIRECTORY

BANKS

Bank of America
#17-00 Republic Plaza Tower,
9 Raffles Place.
📞 6239 3888.

Citibank
#01-00 Yen San Building,
268 Orchard Road.
📞 1800 225 5221.

Development Bank of Singapore
#01-11 Raffles City
252 North Bridge Road.
📞 1800 111 1111.

Hongkong and Shanghai Banking Corporation
#01-00 MacDonald House,
40A Orchard Road.
📞 1800 227 8888.

Oversea Chinese Banking Corporation
#01-01
Specialists Shopping Centre,
277 Orchard Road.
📞 1800 438 3333.

United Overseas Bank
UOB Plaza, 80 Raffles Place.
📞 6533 9898.

TRAVELLERS' CHEQUES

American Express International
#18-01/07 The Concourse,
300 Beach Road. 📞 6880 1111.

GST REFUND

Global Refund Singapore
📞 6225 6238.

$2 note

$5 note

$10 note

$50 note

$100 note

BANK NOTES

Singapore's bank notes come in denominations of $2, $5, $10, $20 (rare), $50, $100, $500, $1,000, and $10,000. You may occasionally receive a $1 note but this is rare as they are being phased out. Do not worry if you receive Bruneian dollars while in Singapore – bank notes of Brunei Darussalam are acceptable in Singapore.

COINS

Coins come in denominations of 1, 5, 10 and 20 cents, and a dollar.

1-cent coin

5-cent coin

10-cent coin

20-cent coin

50-cent coin

one-dollar coin

Communications

Singapore is a country obsessed with communication technology. Singaporeans routinely carry both pagers and mobile phones and hardly ever switch them off as they pride themselves on being contactable round-the-clock. Cybercafés aren't very common, although many Singaporeans own the latest computers so they are constantly wired up to the Internet. Even "snail mail" is swift in Singapore – if you post a letter to a local address before 2pm, it will be delivered by 5pm the next working day.

PUBLIC TELEPHONES

All public telephones are operated by Singapore's national telephone company, SingTel. Clean public phone boxes in good working order can be found everywhere.

In addition to very sophisticated phones that accept cash, phonecards and credit cards and are capable of international direct dialling (IDD) calls, you will also find small navy blue or orange phones placed in many food centres, outside shops, on street corners and in pubs. These phones will only accept 10-cent, 20-cent, 50-cent and $1 coins.

Telephones offer very good value for local calls in Singapore – talk time costs 10 cents for about three minutes. Slot in more coins if you want to continue talking.

A public telephone booth

The most convenient way to make a call is with a phonecard. Phonecards can be bought from post offices, most moneychangers, newsagents, supermarkets and convenience stores for values of S$2, S$5, S$10, S$20 and S$50.

IDD CALLS

International Direct Dialling (IDD) calls can be made from any public phone that accepts credit cards or phonecards. If you make an IDD call from your hotel, there will be a surcharge of

---

REACHING THE RIGHT NUMBER

- Dial **104** for collect calls, operator-assisted calls and international directory information.
- Dial **100** to request local directory information.
- For an IDD call, dial **001** then country, city or area code, then telephone number.
- Dial **001 013** for an International Budget Call (save up to 40 per cent on IDD).
- Dial **1900 777 7777** for telephone yellow pages, 7am–11pm.
- Dial **800 011 1111** with an AT&T calling card to access AT&T's global system.
- Singapore Phone Book on-line
  w www.phonebook.com.sg

USING A PHONECARD/CREDIT CARD-OPERATED PHONE

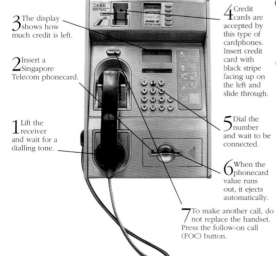

3 The display shows how much credit is left.

2 Insert a Singapore Telecom phonecard.

1 Lift the receiver and wait for a dialling tone.

4 Credit cards are accepted by this type of cardphones. Insert credit card with black stripe facing up on the left and slide through.

5 Dial the number and wait to be connected.

6 When the phonecard value runs out, it ejects automatically.

7 To make another call, do not replace the handset. Press the follow-on call (FOC) button.

A coin-operated telephone

Singapore Telecom phonecards

around 25 per cent. A comprehensive list of IDD codes is posted inside public phone booths, in phone books or in SingTel's *International Telephone Service Handbook* (found in most hotel rooms).

MOBILE PHONES

THREE TELECOMMUNICATIONS companies, SingTel, M1 and StarHub run mobile phone networks in Singapore. Other operators are entering the scene. If you have a GSM digital mobile phone, you can dial out from Singapore as it will just tune into one of the local networks. Mobile phone rental can usually be arranged at the airport.

POSTAL SERVICES

IN ADDITION TO post offices, there are post boxes at every MRT station, at Changi Airport, and on all main streets. Most hotels will post your letters for you if you leave them with the front desk. You will require a 50-cent stamp to send a postcard and one dollar postage to

send an airmail letter to Europe or America. You can buy booklets of stamps suitable for local postage from newsagents and convenience stores, as well as post offices.

A local post box

To send parcels by surface mail to countries outside Southeast Asia (except for the USA) costs between S$14 and S$19 for the first kilogram (2.2 lb) and between S$25 and S$30 for up to 5 kg (11 lb). It costs twice as much to send to the USA.

INTERNET ACCESS

SENDING OR RECEIVING e-mail messages is easy in Singapore. **Cyberstar Comcentre** is a 24-hour Internet café. Other Internet cafés are **Cyberarena** and **Chills Café** on Stamford Road, **Cyberia** on Orchard Road and

Cybercafé at Boat Quay

Cyberbyte at Parco Bugis. Chills Cafe also rents out books. For people who are unsure of the technology, some Internet cafés even offer tutorial sessions for about S$15 an hour.

The business centres in most hotels also offer their guests access to e-mail facilities and the Web at around the same hourly rates as the Internet cafés.

NEWSPAPERS

BESIDES FOUR DAILY Chinese-language newspapers, two Tamil-language papers, and one Malay-language daily, Singapore supports the English-language *The Straits Times*, *The Business Times* (broadsheets) and *The New Paper* (tabloid).

These newspapers are available all over the city: at newsagents, mini-marts, bookshops and from vendors outside MRT stations. Buzz booths, which are small newsagents along Orchard Road, sell maps, drinks, phonecards, cigarettes, candies as well as newspapers.

To keep up with the news from back home, try **Borders**, **Times the Bookstore**, **Kinokuniya**, **MPH**, and the news stand outside Holland Road Shopping Centre for a wide range of foreign newspapers and magazines *(see p97)*.

Local English-language newspapers

TRAVEL INFORMATION

THE EASIEST WAY to get to Singapore is by air. The island nation is surrounded by sea, but much of Singapore's waterfront is given over to its function as a commercial port, rather than as a leisure travel destination. Most of the visitors who arrive in Singapore by sea are passengers on large cruise ships, stopping off for a few days. Making your way into Singapore by road (car or bus) can be

Singapore Airlines' aeroplanes at Changi Airport

a crowded and chaotic experience. Large numbers of Malaysian workers commute to the island every day, and the roads become very congested during peak periods. Rail travel to Singapore from the Malay Peninsula offers a civilized, air-conditioned alternative, with sightseeing along the way. For the passenger who has the time to spare, getting to Singapore by rail is recommended.

Meeting area in Changi Airport's terminal building

ARRIVING BY AIR

MOST PEOPLE TRAVEL TO Singapore by air. Changi Airport *(see pp178–9)* is the largest airport in the region and many flights stop off at Changi or use it as a gateway to the rest of Southeast Asia. Direct flights from European cities such as Paris and London take an average of 13 hours; from Sydney or Melbourne, an average of eight hours; and from New York, about 23 hours (including one stopover).

Taxis from the airport into town are plentiful (besides the metered fare, there is a surcharge). A six-seater Maxicab Shuttle service also operates every 15–30 minutes to most hotels (7am–11pm).

ARRIVING BY RAIL

ARRIVING BY TRAIN from Bangkok, Kuala Lumpur or any of the stations inbetween, you will disembark at Tanjong Pagar Railway

Station, one of only two stations in Singapore, owned and run by Malayan Railway. The station is a little piece of Malaysia stranded in Singapore – the general feel is relaxed (even for a busy railway station): the tiled murals high up on the walls hark back to the golden age of rail travel. Call **Malayan Railway** for details of train departure times and fares.

If you are looking for luxury (US$1,300 per person is the cheapest fare), the **Eastern & Oriental Express** runs between Singapore and Bangkok. It is a sister train to

Tanjong Pagar railway station

the more famous Venice-Simplon Orient Express. The journey takes three days, stops off in Penang and crosses the River Kwai.

ARRIVING BY SEA

CRUISE SHIPS and liners arrive at the HarbourFront Centre's Singapore Cruise Centre *(see p103)*, while ferries to various regional destinations arrive and depart regularly from the Tanah Merah Ferry Terminal.

Checkpoint sign for vehicles at the Woodlands causeway

ARRIVING BY ROAD

THE LAND ROUTE to Singapore from Malaysia is either via the Woodlands Causeway in the north or through a second link at Tuas in the west. Drivers entering Singapore at Tuas must pay a toll charge. Vehicles leaving Singapore either via either Tuas or Woodlands are also subject to tolls; these charges are paid by CashCards purchased at banks, petrol stations, and 7-Eleven stores. ERP cash cards *(see p180)* can also be used. Drivers of

Malaysian-registered cars must display a Vehicle Entry Permit (VEP) for the duration of their stay in Singapore. A VEP can be bought at the Land Transport Authority booths at the checkpoint, or at the Changi Ferry Terminal (where car ferries arrive from Malaysia). Drivers who stay longer than anticipated can extend the validity of their VEP at any post office. VEPs are free for entry and travel from 7pm to 2am Monday to Friday; after 3pm on Saturday; and all day on Sundays and during public holidays.

Travelling into or out of Singapore by bus at Woodlands involves an elaborate sequence of immigration and customs checks, and means getting off and on to the bus once at each end of the causeway. The queues are huge and noisy, especially in the mornings and evenings, and also on weekends and public holidays. There is usually a scramble to get back on the bus and tempers are short. Traffic at the Second Link is considerably lighter by comparison, and the crossing through the immigration point is generally a great deal quicker.

Singapore Immigration building

VISAS

IF YOU ARE entering Singapore from the USA, EU or a Commonwealth country, you do not at present require a visa. Anyone entering Singapore requires a passport valid for six months from the date of entry. In any case, before travelling check with the Singapore Embassy in your country of origin, a good travel agent, or the **Singapore Immigration Department**. Permission for a 30-day stay is often stamped in international air travellers' passports, but people entering by sea or road usually get two weeks. If you need to extend your stay, visit the Immigration Department (proof of funds or your air ticket may be requested).

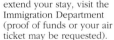

Vehicle entry permit

CUSTOMS ALLOWANCE

Certain items are not allowed into Singapore – weapons of any kind, drugs, pornographic videos or publications, and pirated software or recordings. If you are carrying videos with you, a customs official may ask to inspect or view your tapes. If you enter Singapore via Changi Airport the duty-free allowance is one litre (2.1 pt) of liquor, one litre of wine and one litre of beer per person. There is no duty-free tobacco and cigarette allowance.

To qualify for duty-free allowance, you need to be over the age of 18. There are duty-free shops very conveniently located for travellers arriving at Changi airport along the way to the baggage hall. In Singapore you will find that a great many items are duty-free, so there is not a great deal to be saved by shopping at the airport on your departure. It is very easy to spend money in Singapore so keep an eye on your home country's duty-free allowance limit.

Duty-free shop at Changi Airport

Travelling by Air

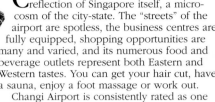

CHANGI AIRPORT is, in many ways, a reflection of Singapore itself, a microcosm of the city-state. The "streets" of the airport are spotless, the business centres are fully equipped, shopping opportunities are many and varied, and its numerous food and beverage outlets represent both Eastern and Western tastes. You can get your hair cut, have a sauna, enjoy a foot massage or work out. Changi Airport is consistently rated as one of the most efficient and welcoming airports in the world.

Control tower

Free Singapore tour counter

SERVICE COUNTERS

KNOWLEDGEABLE AND helpful staff attend to your needs at the many service counters situated around the airport. For those with more than four hours to spend, go to any Free Singapore Tour Counter to register for a two-hour sightseeing bus tour. Hotel reservations can be made through the Singapore Hotel Association at the counters.

Visitors who have spent more than S$300 on goods can claim tax back at the numerous GST Refund Counters *(see p173)* at the airport.

Hotel Reservations
Terminal 1 **☎** 6542 6955/6966.
Terminal 2 **☎** 6545 9789/ 0318.

Flight Information Counter
☎ 1800 542 4422 (toll-free).

Left Baggage Facilities
Terminal 1 **☎** 6546 2738.
Terminal 2 **☎** 6542 2061.

Receipts must be presented and goods inspected by customs. 24-hour left luggage facilities can be found in both terminals. Terminal 1 also has electronic luggage lockers.

Taxi boarding area

GETTING TO AND FROM THE AIRPORT

A TAXI TRIP into the city (a 25-minute journey) costs S$15 to S$22, including a S$3–S$5 surcharge for trips from the airport. Bus no. 36 gets you to Changi Airport within an hour from almost every bus stop on Orchard Road. The east-west MRT line stops at Terminal 2 of the airport.

HEALTH AND FITNESS

CLINICS ARE OPEN from 8am to midnight in both Departure Transit Lounges. Raffles Medical Centre in the basement of Terminal 2 opens

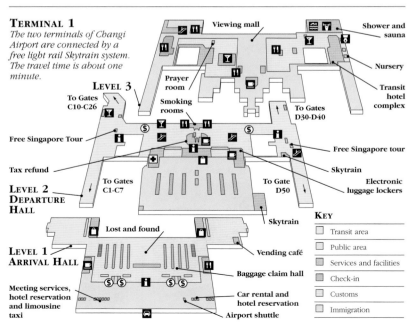

TERMINAL 1
The two terminals of Changi Airport are connected by a free light rail Skytrain system. The travel time is about one minute.

LEVEL 3

To Gates C10-C26

Free Singapore Tour

Tax refund

LEVEL 2 DEPARTURE HALL

To Gates C1-C7

Viewing mall

Prayer room

Smoking rooms

To Gates D30-D40

To Gate D50

Shower and sauna

Nursery

Transit hotel complex

Free Singapore tour

Skytrain

Electronic luggage lockers

Skytrain

LEVEL 1 ARRIVAL HALL

Lost and found

Meeting services, hotel reservation and limousine taxi

Vending café

Baggage claim hall

Car rental and hotel reservation

Airport shuttle

KEY
☐	Transit area
☐	Public area
☐	Services and facilities
☐	Check-in
☐	Customs
☐	Immigration

24 hours. The fitness centres in both terminals offer excellent value at around S$15 per person – including equipment use, shower and towels. Alternatively, you can have a shower, a sauna or a swim for a small fee. Except for designated smoking rooms in each terminal, smoking is banned in Changi Airport.

The Entertainment Centre, which provides a variety of games

Gymnasium in the fitness centre

LEISURE

THE AIRPORT IS packed with shopping opportunities. You will find shops selling books, electronic and sporting goods and souvenirs as well as the usual duty-free alcohol and cigarettes. In Terminal 2, children can be kept amused at the Science Discovery Corner or in the nursery, while you spend your time on line at the Internet Centre or Entertainment Centre.

If you are looking for something to eat in Terminal 1, you can choose between Cantonese cuisine, speciality ice cream, gourmet coffee, a French cafe and fast food. Terminal 2 offers refreshments and meals in the form of snacks, ice cream, noodles, Indian, Chinese and Japanese food, and fast food. There is also an internet café.

BUSINESS

THE BUSINESS CENTRES in both terminals provide work-stations, internet hook-ups, photocopiers, facsimile machines and meeting rooms

for travellers. Translation and secretarial services are available on request. Roaming service subscribers with an internet account may plug into any of the personal computer and internet connection points installed on telephone panels and writing tops around the airport terminals.

Computer terminal at the business centre

TERMINAL 2

Singapore Airlines has a 24-hour automated check-in facility at this terminal. Public bus services are located in the basements of both terminals.

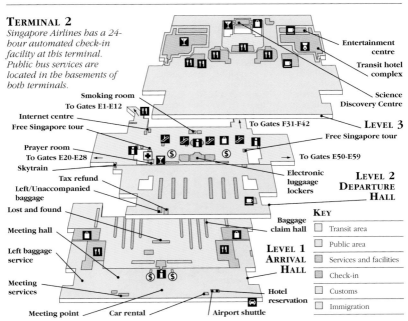

Entertainment centre

Transit hotel complex

Science Discovery Centre

Smoking room
To Gates E1-E12
Internet centre
Free Singapore tour
Prayer room
To Gates E20-E28
Skytrain
Tax refund
Left/Unaccompanied baggage
Lost and found
Meeting hall
Left baggage service
Meeting services
Meeting point   Car rental

To Gates F31-F42   **LEVEL 3**
                          Free Singapore tour
To Gates E50-E59
                          Electronic
                          luggaage   **LEVEL 2**
                          lockers   **DEPARTURE**
                                        HALL

Baggage
claim hall

LEVEL 1
ARRIVAL
HALL

Hotel
reservation
Airport shuttle

KEY

☐	Transit area
☐	Public area
☐	Services and facilities
☐	Check-in
☐	Customs
☐	Immigration

Travelling Around Singapore

In-Vehicle Unit, a road pricing device

THE CITY AREA of Singapore is very easy to navigate. There are free tourist maps available in most hotels, at the airport and at tourist information offices; these focus on those parts of town most frequented by visitors. In the outlying housing estates, however, it can be extremely difficult to find one's way around, as these "new towns" often consist of rows and rows of almost identical-looking housing blocks unrelieved by distinctive landmarks. The bus and the Mass Rapid Transport (MRT) systems are straightforward and easy to use. Taxis are cheap, but even a taxi driver may sometimes have trouble locating the place where a passenger wants to go, simply because Singapore's environment is never static – maps and guidebooks quickly fall out of date in the face of the country's constant and rapid development.

Car rental company

CAR HIRE

IN SINGAPORE car rental is very expensive by many visitors' standards: charges of S$200 or more per day are not unusual. **Avis, Hertz, Budget** and **Thrifty** are well-established and reliable car hire companies. Useful to drivers unfamiliar to Singapore is the *Singapore Street Directory*, available at most bookshops. It covers every area and helps to identify one-way streets.

Driving across to Malaysia is not recommended, as the surcharges on the Singapore bill will be heavy. It is more worthwhile hiring a car at Malaysian rates in Johor Bahru.

Foreigners can drive in Singapore on their own licence for six months. Singapore follows mostly British road conventions, with driving on the left and overtaking on the right. Singaporean drivers are more orderly than their counterparts elsewhere in the region, but they are sometimes criticized for rudeness and less-than-accomplished driving skills. Roads are well lit and signposted in English, and they only become congested in peak hours.

To hire a car with a driver, enquire at your hotel front desk. Car-and-driver companies such as **San's Tours and Car Rentals** and **Friendly Transport Services** provide chauffeur-driven Mercedes. **CityCab** and **TIBS** also offer this service for slightly lower charges.

TRAFFIC AND PARKING

IN A BID to ease downtown traffic, an Electronic Road Pricing (ERP) scheme requires motorists to pay a fee to enter the "Restricted Zone", comprising the Central Business District, Orchard Road and Chinatown, between 7.30am and 6.30pm from Monday to Friday. (Similar fees apply during peak hours to some expressways.) A small gadget, an In-Vehicle Unit (IU), is fixed between the dashboard and the windscreen. A prepaid Cash Card is inserted, and when the car passes beneath an ERP gantry spanning the road at Restricted Zone entry points, the required fee is deducted from the card automatically. Whenever the card's monetary value falls below $5, the IU alerts the driver to the necessity of "topping up".

To park in public carparks drivers display parking coupons in their front car windows. Books of ten coupons can be purchased from post offices, carpark booths and service stations.

TAXIS

SINGAPORE IS SERVED by three main taxi firms – **CityCab, Comfort** and **TIBS**. You will also see white Mercedes taxis and Black-and-Yellow-Top cabs, both of which are owned by Comfort. CityCabs are yellow, Comfort cabs are blue, and TIBS taxis are white. Several independent firms offer car-and-driver services. In addition to standard taxis, you can order station wagon taxis if you have a great deal of luggage, mini vans to transport large groups, and London taxis (in tropical white as opposed to London black), which are the only taxis in Singapore licensed to carry five adults.

An Electronic Road Pricing gantry

CityCab taxi

Comfort taxi

London taxi

They cost an extra eight dollars on average, including an advance booking charge.

CATCHING A TAXI

Taxis in Singapore are plentiful and with over 15,000 of them servicing the area it is seldom difficult to flag one down. They are also surprisingly cheap. However, taxis are scarcer on the streets when it rains, during the peak hours of 8 to 9am and 5 to 7pm, and 15 minutes before midnight. (Because a 50 per cent surcharge is added to all fares between midnight and 6am, taxi drivers tend to take a coffee break until it strikes twelve.) A sign displayed next to the windscreen specifying the name of an area means that the driver is changing shift and will only accept customers heading that way.

BOOKING A TAXI

To avoid frustration, book a cab. It is worth noting that for calling half an hour in advance, the booking charge is about 70 per cent higher than if the cab is requested immediately. Booking immediately is called a "current booking"; the reason it costs less than booking ahead is taxi companies use a satellite system that lets them locate an available taxi within minutes. Normally, a Mercedes taxi booked in advance costs about four times more than an ordinary taxi (one can also book an airport drop-off service a day ahead.) But people who flag down an empty Mercedes taxi on the street can ride to their destination in style at no extra cost because Mercedes taxis operate at the standard taxi rate for casual passengers.

It's not unheard of for some taxi companies to run special promotions where bookings after certain times are free - this is always worth checking out in advance.

TAXI FARES

When you get into a taxi in Singapore, it helps to have small notes of S$10 or less to pay the fare. Very often drivers come on shift without change and have difficulty changing S$50 notes. Singaporean taxi drivers can be extremely taciturn or incredibly friendly. A friendly and talkative driver is often an entertaining source of information about the local scene. Taxi drivers here are honest; you need never worry about being overcharged or short-changed.

All taxis price their journeys the same way, with the use of an electronic meter – a liberating experience if you have braved the taxi drivers of Bangkok or Jakarta. The meter starts at S$2.40, and remains so for the first kilometre (0.6 mile). Ten cents will be added for every 225 m (247 yd) that follow. A surcharge of S$1 is added to your fare when you travel during morning and evening peak hours from Monday to Saturday. A variable surcharge applies for

Taxi sign

travel into the Central Business District during the periods when Electronic Road Pricing is in operation. A surcharge on trips from the airport applies; depending on one's destination amounting to 20 or 30 per cent of the fare.

Mercedes taxi

DIRECTORY

CAR HIRE

Avis
Concorde Hotel, Outram Road.
(6737 1668.
Airport Terminal 2. (6542 8855.

Budget
#26-01A Clifford Centre, 24
Raffles Place. (6532 4442.

Hertz
#01-01 Thong Teck Building, 15
Scotts Road
(1800 839 3388 (toll free).
Airport Terminal 2. (6542 5300.

Thrifty
Level 1 Marina Mandarin, 6
Raffles Boulevard. (6338 7900.

CAR-AND-DRIVER

**Friendly Transport
Services**
(6736 0477.

**San's Tours and Car
Rentals**
(6734 9922.

TAXI BOOKINGS

CityCab
(6552 2222 (cash bookings),
6553 8888 (credit card bookings)
and 6454 2222 (bookings more
than 15 minutes in advance)

Comfort
(6552 1111 (cash bookings)

TIBS
(6555 8888 (cash bookings)

Public Transport

AT INDEPENDENCE, the Singapore government realized that it had to create an extensive transport infrastructure capable of moving workers out of housing estates and into work environments quickly and efficiently. The Mass Rapid Transit System (MRT) and the bus networks are the products of this forward planning, and between them they criss-cross the island in a comprehensive network of lines and routes. Singapore's public transport system provides an essential service – especially in the light of the fact that the government's high-taxation car policies mean that many people cannot afford a car.

Bus sign at Bugis Junction

Fully air-conditioned MRT train travelling on elevated track

THE MRT

SINGAPOREANS are very proud of the MRT, with good reason. The MRT trains are modern, quiet, cool and quick. They run underground in the downtown, Orchard Road and Newton areas, and above ground everywhere else. Daily train times are 6am to around 11:30pm. There are three main routes. The Boon Lay–Pasir Ris line runs east-west; on the MRT map this route is coloured green. The line coloured red runs in a loop between Jurong East and Marina Bay. These two lines intersect at the Raffles Place, City Hall and Jurong East interchanges. The third line runs north-east from HarbourFront to Punggol. There are MRT maps in every station and every carriage. A small Light Rapid Transit System (LRT) linked to the MRT serves some suburban housing estates, but is not of importance to the visitor. MRT tickets can be bought

Transport logo

individually in every station, but better value is the ez-link card which can be used on buses as well. It is sold at Transitlink ticket offices, MRT stations and bus interchanges. Visitors here for a week who intend to go every-where by MRT or bus are advised to buy an ez-link card. It can be "topped up" easily for $15 at any MRT ticket office, and the $5 deposit plus any unused ticket value can be refunded before you leave. Having an ez-link card also saves the trouble of hunting for change to buy a ticket, and having to figure out the fare each time you travel.

Downtown bus stop

USING THE BUSES

BUSES ARE THE CHEAPEST way to travel around Singapore. Non-air-conditioned buses cost slightly less in fare than air-conditioned buses. Fares range from 58 cents to S$1.70, depending on whether you use cash or an ez-link card. When you board the bus, hold the card flat against the blue oval panel of the card reader located near the entrance. The value of the card will appear on the screen. Wait for a beep before removing the card. When you alight, repeat the same process with the card reader at the exit. Your bus fare will be automatically calculated and deducted, and the remaining value of the card shown on the

Double-decker SBS bus

Air-conditioned TIBS bus

screen. Payment by ez-link costs 5–10 cents less than payment by cash. This serves as an incentive to encourage its use. There are also rebates for transferring between buses, or from bus to MRT, or vice versa.

An ez-link card and a visitor's card.

VISITOR'S CARD

THE VISITOR'S CARD is an ez-link cum incentive card for tourists only. It costs S$45 and includes an encoded S$10 value for travel on public transportation, a Singapore guide booklet, and benefits at selected outlets. It can be purchased at MRT stations around the Orchard Road area and at Changi Airport. Present your passport upon purchase.

TRANSITLINK GUIDE

PEOPLE WHO PLAN to spend a lot of time on buses should invest in a *Bus Guide*, a pocket book on Singapore's bus and MRT services. It contains details on all bus routes, fares and timings, together with maps of the areas around all MRT stations.

Bus guide and travel map

MAKING A JOURNEY BY MRT

1 Entrances to MRT stations are marked by beacons bearing its yellow logo on main roads and walkways. Some stations are linked directly to shopping centres and can be entered through the underground passageway. Many stations have several entrances.

2 To buy a single-trip ticket, refer to the MRT map located above the general ticketing machines (GTM). The fare is shown in a circle below your destination station.

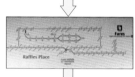

3 Proceed to any GTM and on the touch-screen, choose the language you are most familiar with, then select the option "Buy Standard Ticket".

4 Press on the system map the station you are going to and your fare will be shown on the touch-screen. This amount includes a S$1 deposit which is refundable at the end of your journey at any GTM. You have up to 30 days after the date of purchase to get your refund.

5 Insert coins or notes in the slots located at the top, right hand corner of the machine. Wait for the ticket to be issued and collect it from the return cup below the touch-screen.

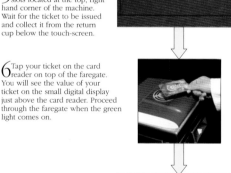

6 Tap your ticket on the card reader on top of the faregate. You will see the value of your ticket on the small digital display just above the card reader. Proceed through the faregate when the green light comes on.

7 Check the schematic map to see which platform you should board the train from, and if you need to transfer to another train along the way.

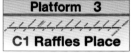

STREET FINDER

THE PAGE GRID superimposed on the *Area by Area* map below shows which parts of Singapore are covered in this *Street Finder*. Map references given for sights and shopping and entertainment venues described in this guide refer to the maps in this section. Map references are also given in the listings for hotels *(see pp122–5)* and restaurants *(see pp134–9)*. Major sights are clearly marked so they are easy to locate. A complete index of street names and places of interest shown on the maps follows on pages 190–93. The key, below, indicates the scale of the maps and shows what other features are marked on them, including post offices and tourist information centres.

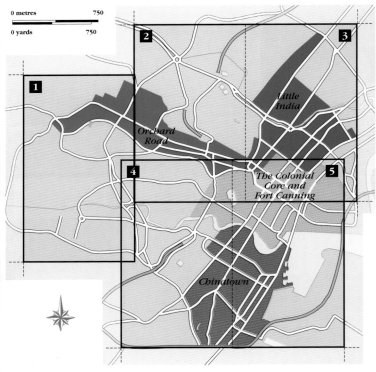

| 0 metres | 750 |
| 0 yards | 750 |

1

2

3

Little India

Orchard Road

4

The Colonial Core and Fort Canning

5

Chinatown

KEY TO STREET FINDER

Major sight		P Parking		Railway line
Place of interest		Police station		Expressway
Other buildings		Tourist information		One-way street
M MRT station		Indian temple		Pedestrianized street
Railway station		Church		
Bus station		Chinese temple		**SCALE OF MAP PAGES**
⊠ Post office		C Mosque		0 metres 250
Hospital		Synagogue		0 yards 250

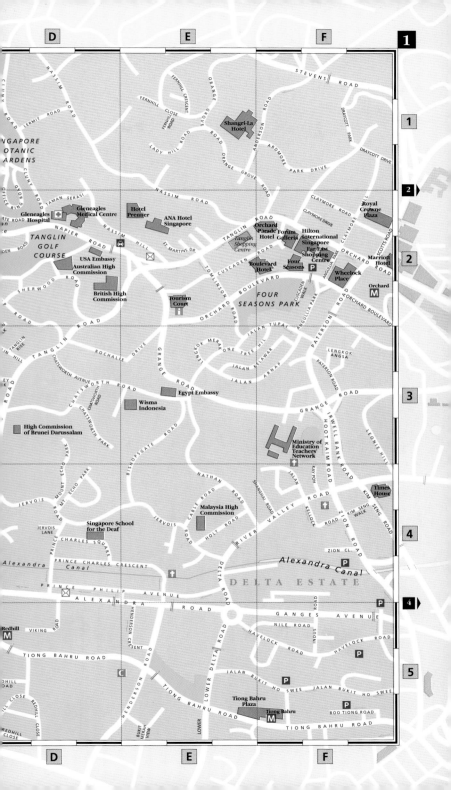

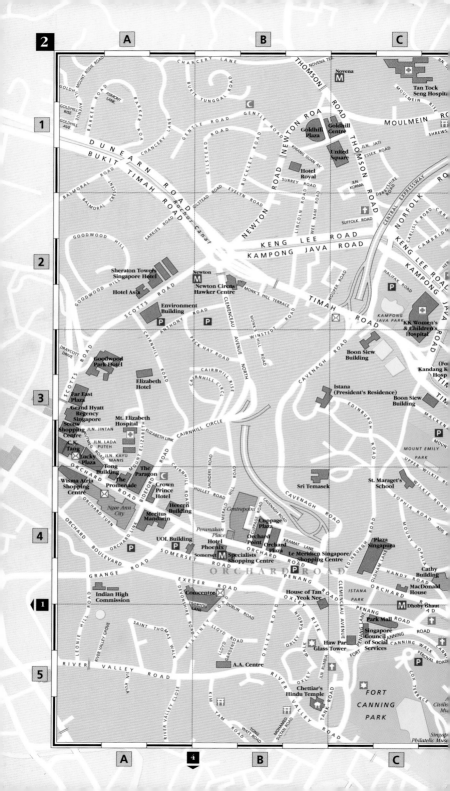

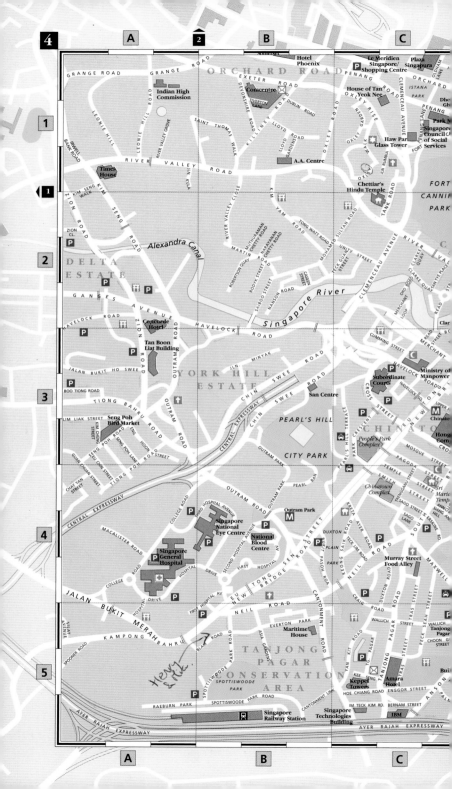

Street Finder Index

A

A.A. Centre   **2 B5** & **4 B1**
Adis Road   **2 C4**
Al-Abrar Mosque   **5 D4**
Albert Street   **3 D4** & **3 E4**
Alexandra Canal   **1 D4**
  continues   **4 A2**
Alexandra Road   **1 D4**
Amara Hotel   **4 C5**
Amoy Street   **5 D4**
ANA Hotel Singapore **1 E2**
Anderson Road   **1 E1**
Angullia Park **1 F2** & **1 F3**
Ann Siang Hill   **4 C4**
Ann Siang Road   **4 C4**
Anson Road   **4 C5** & **5 D5**
Anthony Road   **2 A2**
Arab Street   **3 E4**
Ardmore Park   **1 F1**
Armenian Church   **3 D5**
  continues   **5 D2**
Armenian Street   **3 D5**
  continues   **5 D2**
Asia Gardens   **4 B5**
Asian Civilisations
  Museum I   **2 C5** & **5 D2**
Asian Civilisations
  Museum II   **5 D3**
Asimont Lane   **2 A1**
Australian High
  Commission   **1 D2**
Ayer Rajah
  Expressway   **4 A5**

B

Baboo Lane   **3 D3**
Bain Street   **3 D5** & **5 E1**
Balestier Road   **3 E1**
Balmoral Crescent   **2 A2**
Balmoral Road   **2 A1**
Barker Road   **2 A1**
Battery Road   **5 E3**
Beach Road   **3 F4** & **5 E1**
Beatty Road   **3 E2**
Bencoolen Street   **3 D4**
  continues   **5 D1**
Bendemeer Road   **3 F2**
Benjamin Sheares
  Bridge   **5 F3**
Bernam Street   **4 C5**
Bideford Road   **2 A4**
Birch Road   **3 D2**
Bishopsgate   **1 E4**
Blair Road   **4 B5**
Boat Quay   **5 D3**
Boon Keng Road   **3 F1**
Boon Siew Building **2 C3**
Boon Tat Street   **5 D4**
Boon Tiong Road   **1 F5**
  continues   **4 A3**

Boulevard Hotel   **1 F2**
Bras Basah Park   **3 D5**
  continues   **5 D1**
Bras Basah Road   **3 D5**
  continues   **5 D1**
British High
  Commission   **1 D2**
Buckley Road   **2 B1**
Bugis Junction   **3 E4**
  continues   **5 E1**
Bugis Station **3 E4** & **5 E1**
Bugis Street   **3 E4** & **5 E1**
Bukit Merah View   **1 E5**
Bukit Pasoh Road   **4 B4**
Bukit Timah Road   **2 A1**
  continues   **2 B2** & **3 D3**
Bukit Tunggal Road   **2 A1**
  continues   **2 B1**
Burmah Road   **3 E2**

C

Cable Road   **1 E4**
Cairnhill Circle   **2 A3**
Cairnhill Rise   **2 B3**
Cairnhill Road   **2 A3**
Cambridge Road   **2 C2**
  continues   **3 D1**
Camp Road   **1 D2**
Canning Lane   **4 C2**
Canning Rise **2 C5** & **5 D1**
Canning Road   **4 C1**
Canning Walk   **2 C5**
Cantonment Link   **4 B5**
Cantonment Road   **4 B4**
Carlisle Road **2 C2** & **3 D2**
Carlton Hotel **3 D5** & **5 E1**
Carpenter Street   **5 D3**
Caseen Street   **4 B2**
Cashin Street **3 D5** & **5 E1**
Cathay Building   **2 C4**
  continues   **5 D1**
Cathedral of the Good
  Shepherd **3 D5** & **5 D1**
Cavan Road   **3 F2**
Cavenagh Road   **2 B3**
Cecil Street   **5 D4**
Centennial Tower   **3 F5**
  continues   **5 F2**
Central Expressway   **2 C2**
  continues **3 D1** & **4 A4**
Central Sikh Temple **3 F1**
Centre Tourism
  Court   **1 E2**
Centrepoint   **2 B4**
Chancery Lane   **2 A1**
Chander Road   **3 D3**
Chatsworth Avenue   **1 D3**
Chatsworth Park   **1 D3**
Chatsworth Road   **1 D3**
Chay Yan Street   **4 A4**

Chettiar's Hindu
  Temple   **2 B5** & **4 C2**
Chijmes   **3 D5** & **5 E1**
Chin Chew St.   **5 D3**
Chin Swee Road   **4 B3**
China Street   **5 D3**
Chinatown   **4 C3**
Chinatown Complex **4 C4**
Chinatown Station   **4 C4**
Chitty Road   **3 E3**
Choon Guan Street   **4 C5**
Chulia Street   **5 D3**
Church Street   **5 D3**
Circular Road   **5 D3**
City Hall   **5 D2**
City Hall Station   **5 E2**
Clarke Quay   **4 C2**
Claymore Drive   **1 F2**
Claymore Hill   **1 F2**
Claymore Road   **1 F2**
Clemenceau Avenue **2 C4**
  continues   **4 C1**
Clemenceau Avenue
  North   **2 B2**
Clive Street   **3 D3**
Club Street   **4 C4**
Cluny Road   **1 D1** & **1 D2**
Coleman Street   **5 D2**
College Road   **4 A4**
Colombo Court   **5 D2**
Colonial Quarter   **4 B1**
Colonial Quarter Marina
  South   **5 D2**
Comcentre   **2 A4** & **4 B1**
Concorde Hotel   **4 A2**
The Concourse   **3 F4**
  continues   **5 F1**
Connaught Drive   **5 E2**
Conrad International
  Hotel   **3 E5** & **5 F2**
Cox Terrace   **2 C5** & **5 D1**
Craig Road   **4 C4**
Cross Street   **4 C3** & **5 D4**
Crown Prince Hotel   **2 A4**
Cuff Road   **3 D3**
Cumming Street   **4 C3**
Cuppage Plaza   **2 B4**
Cuppage Road   **2 B4**
Cuscaden Road   **1 E2**
Cuscaden Walk   **1 F2**

D

Delta Estate   **1 E4** & **4 A2**
Delta Road   **1 E4**
Derbyshire Road   **2 C2**
Desker Road   **3 E3**
Devonshire Road   **2 A4**
  continues   **4 B1**
Dhoby Ghaut
  Station   **2 C4** & **4 C1**

Dorset Road   **3 D2**
Draycott Drive   **1 F1**
  continues   **2 A3**
Draycott Park   **1 F1**
Dublin Road   **2 B4** & **4 B1**
Dunearn Road   **2 A1**
Dunlop Street   **3 D3**
Duxton Plain Park   **4 B4**
Duxton Road   **4 C4**

E

East Coast Parkway   **5 E5**
East Lagoon Link   **5 D5**
Edinburgh Road   **2 C3**
Egypt Embassy   **1 E3**
Elizabeth Hotel   **2 A3**
Elizabeth Link   **2 A3**
Emerald Hill Road   **2 B4**
Eminent Plaza   **3 F2**
Eng Cheong Tower   **3 F3**
Eng Hoon Street   **4 A3**
Enggor Street   **4 C5**
Environment Building **2 A2**
Erskine Road   **4 C4**
Esplanade
  Drive   **5 E2** & **5 E3**
Esplanade Park   **5 E3**
Esplanade–Theatres
  on the Bay   **5 E2**
Essex Road   **2 C1**
Eu Chin Street   **4 A3**
Eu Tong Sen Street   **4 B4**
  continues   **5 D3**
Evelyn Road   **2 B1**
Everton Park   **4 B5**
Exeter Road   **2 A4** & **4 B1**

F

Far East Plaza   **2 A3**
Far East Shopping
  Centre   **1 F2**
Farrer Park Fields   **3 D2**
Fernhill Close   **1 E1**
Fernhill Crescent   **1 E1**
Fernhill Road   **1 E1**
Finger Pier   **5 D5**
Finger Pier Building **5 D5**
First Hospital Avenue **4 A5**
Flanders Square   **3 E2**
Foch Road   **3 F2**
Fort Canning Park   **2 C5**
  continues   **4 C1**
Fort Canning Road   **2 C5**
  continues   **4 C1** & **5 D1**
Forum Galleria   **1 F2**
Four Seasons   **1 F2**
Four Seasons Park   **1 F2**
French Road   **3 F3**
Fu Lu Shou Complex **3 E4**
Fullerton Building   **5 E3**

G

Ganges Avenue	**1 F5**	
continues	**4 A2**	
Gentle Road	**2 A1**	
George Street	**5 D3**	
Gilstead Road	**2 B1 & 2 B2**	
Gleneagles Hospital	**1 D2**	
Gleneagles Medical		
Centre	**1 D2**	
Gloucester Road	**3 D2**	
Golden Landmark		
Hotel	**3 E4**	
Golden Mile Tower	**3 F4**	
Goldhill Avenue	**2 A1**	
Goldhill Centre	**2 C1**	
Goldhill Plaza	**2 B1**	
Goldhill Rise	**2 A1**	
Goodwood Hill	**2 A2**	
Goodwood Park		
Hotel	**2 A3**	
Grand Hyatt Regency		
Singapore	**2 A3**	
Grange Road	**1 E3**	
continues	**2 A4 & 4 A1**	
Guan Chuan Street	**4 A3**	

H

Hajjah Fatimah		
Mosque	**3 F4**	
Halifax Road	**2 C2**	
Hallpike Street	**5 D3**	
Hamilton Road	**3 F2**	
Hampshire Road	**3 D3**	
Handy Road	**2 C4**	
continues	**4 C1 & 5 D1**	
Havelock Road	**1 E5**	
continues	**4 A2**	
Havelock Square	**4 C3**	
Haw Par Glass Tower	**2 C5**	
continues	**4 A4**	
Heeren Building	**2 A4**	
Henderson Crescent	**1 E5**	
Henderson Road	**1 E5**	
Hertford Road	**2 C2**	
continues	**3 D2**	
High Commission of		
Brunei Darussalam	**1 D3**	
High Street	**5 D2**	
Hill Street	**5 D2**	
Hill Street Building	**5 D2**	
Hilton International		
Singapore	**1 F2**	
Hindoo Road	**3 D3 & 3 E3**	
Hock Teck See		
Temple	**5 D5**	
Hoe Chiang Road	**4 C5**	
Hokien St.	**5 D3**	
Holt Road	**1 E4**	
Hong Leong Building	**5 D4**	
Hong Lim Complex	**4 C3**	
Hong Lim Park	**5 D3**	

Hongkong Street	**5 D3**	
Hooper Road	**2 C2**	
Hoot Kiam Road	**1 F3**	
Horne Road	**3 F2**	
Hospital Drive	**4 A5**	
Hotel Asia	**2 A2**	
Hotel Phoenix	**2 B4**	
continues	**4 B1**	
Hotel Premier	**1 E2**	
House of Tan Yeok		
Nee	**2 B4 & 4 C1**	
Hullet Road	**2 B4**	

I

IBM	**4 C5**	
Immigration Building	**3 F3**	
Indian High Commission		
	2 A4 & 4 A1	
Indus Road	**1 F5**	
Intercontinental Hotel	**3 E5**	
continues	**5 E1**	
Irwell Bank Road	**1 F3**	
continues	**4 A1**	
Istana (President's		
Residence)	**2 C3**	
Istana Kampong		
Glam	**3 F4**	
Istana Park	**2 C4 & 4 C1**	

J

Jalan Arnap	**1 E3**	
Jalan Besar	**3 E3**	
Jalan Besar Plaza	**3 E3**	
Jalan Besar Stadium	**3 F2**	
Jalan Bukit Ho Swee	**1 E5**	
continues	**4 A3**	
Jalan Bukit Merah	**4 A4**	
Jalan Jati	**2 C1**	
Jalan Jintan	**2 A3**	
Jalan Kayu Manis	**2 A3**	
Jalan Kelawar	**1 E3**	
Jalan Korma	**2 C1**	
Jalan Kuala	**2 A5 & 4 A1**	
Jalan Kubor	**3 E3**	
Jalan Lada Puteh	**2 A3**	
Jalan Lembah Kallang	**3 F1**	
Jalan Minyak	**4 B3**	
Jalan Rumbia	**2 B5 & 4 C1**	
Jalan Sultan	**3 F3**	
Jalan Tan Tock Seng	**2 C1**	
Jalan Tupai	**1 E3**	
Jellicoe Road	**3 F3**	
Jervois Lane	**1 D4**	
Jervois Road	**1 D4 & 1 E4**	
Joo Avenue	**3 E1**	

K

Kallang Avenue	**3 F2**	
Kallang Bahru	**3 F2**	
Kallang Bahru		
Complex	**3 F2**	

Kallang Basin Estate	**3 F1**	
Kampong Bahru	**4 A5**	
Kampong Java Park	**2 C2**	
Kampong Java Road	**2 B2**	
KK Hospital	**2 C3**	
Kapor Road	**3 E3**	
Kay Poh Road	**1 F4**	
Kee Seng Street	**4 C5**	
Kelantan Lane	**3 E3**	
Kelantan Road	**3 E2**	
Kellock Road	**1 F4**	
Kempas Road	**3 F1**	
Keng Lee Road	**2 B2**	
Kent Road	**3 D1**	
Keong Saik Road	**4 C4**	
Keppel Towers	**4 C5**	
Khiang Guan Avenue	**2 B1**	
Killiney Road	**2 A5**	
continues	**4 B1**	
Kim Cheng Street	**4 A3**	
Kim Seng Road	**1 F4**	
continues	**4 A1**	
Kim Seng Walk	**1 F4**	
continues	**4 A2**	
Kim Yam Road	**2 B5**	
continues	**4 B1**	
King Georges Avenue	**3 F3**	
Kinta Road	**3 D2**	
Kirk Terrace	**2 C4**	
continues	**3 D4 & 5 D1**	
Kitchener Road	**3 E2**	
KK Women's & Children's		
Hospital	**2 C2**	
Klang Lane	**3 D3**	
Kramat Lane	**2 C4**	
Kreta Ayer Road	**4 C4**	
Kwan Im Tong Hood		
Che Temple	**3 D4**	
Kwong Wai Shiu		
Hospital	**3 E1**	

L

Lady Hill Road	**1 E1**	
Lan Street	**3 E4**	
Lau Pa Sat	**5 D4**	
Lavender Station	**3 F3**	
Lavender Street	**3 F2**	
Le Meridien/Singapore		
Shopping Centre	**2 B4**	
continues	**4 C1**	
Lengkok Angsa	**1 F3**	
Lengkok Merak	**1 E3**	
Leong San See		
Temple	**3 E1**	
Leonie Hill	**1 F3 & 4 A1**	
Leonie Hill		
Road	**2 A5 & 4 A1**	
Lermit Road	**1 D1**	
Liane Road	**1 D1**	
Liang Seah Street	**3 E5**	
continues	**5 E1**	

Lim Bo Seng		
Memorial	**5 E3**	
Lim Liak Street	**4 A3**	
Lim Teck Kim Road	**4 C5**	
Lincoln Road	**2 B2**	
Little India	**3 D2**	
Little India Arcade	**3 D3**	
Little India Station	**3 D3**	
Lloyd Gardens	**2 B5**	
continues	**4 B1**	
Lloyd Road	**2 B5 & 4 B1**	
Lower Delta Road	**1 E5**	
Lucky Plaza	**2 A3**	

M

MacAlister Road	**4 A4**	
MacDonald House	**2 C4**	
continues	**5 D1**	
MacKenzie Road	**2 C3**	
continues	**3 D3**	
Main Gate Road	**1 D2**	
Malacca Street	**5 D3**	
Malay Street	**3 E4 & 5 E1**	
Malaysian High		
Commission	**5 D2**	
Mandalay Road	**3 D1**	
Marina Bay Station	**5 E5**	
Marina Boulevard	**5 F5**	
Marina City Park	**5 F4**	
Marina Mandarin		
Hotel	**5 E2**	
Marina Park	**5 D5**	
Marina Place	**5 F5**	
Marina Square	**5 F2**	
Marina Station Road	**5 D5**	
continues	**5 F5**	
Maritime House	**4 B5**	
Market Street	**5 D3**	
Marne Road	**3 E2**	
Marriott Hotel	**1 F2**	
Martin Road	**4 B2**	
MAS Building	**4 C5**	
Maude Road	**3 E3**	
Maxwell Link	**5 D5**	
Maxwell Road	**4 C4**	
continues	**5 D5**	
McNair Road	**3 E1**	
Merchant Loop	**4 C2**	
Merchant Road	**4 C3**	
Mergui Road	**3 D1**	
Meritus Mandarin	**2 A4**	
Middle Road	**3 D4 & 5 E1**	
Middle Road		
Hospital	**3 D4**	
Millenia Walk	**3 F5**	
continues	**5 F2**	
Minden Road	**1 D2**	
Ministry of Education		
Teachers' Network	**1 F3**	
Ministry of	**4 C3**	
Manpower		

Mistri Road 4 C5
Mohamad Sultan
  Road 2 B5
  continues 4 B2
Mohammad Mustafa
  Centre 3 E2
Monk's Hill Road 2 B2
Monk's Hill Terrace 2 B2
Mosque Street 4 C3
Moulmein Rise 2 C1
Moulmein Road 2 C1
Mount Echo Park 1 D4
Mount Elizabeth 2 A4
Mount Elizabeth
  Hospital 2 A3
Mount Emily 2 C3
Mount Emily Park 2 C3
Mount Rosie Road 2 A1
Mount Sophia 2 C4
  continues 5 D1
Murray Street Food
  Alley 4 C4
Muthuraman Chetty
  Road 4 B2

N

Nagore Durgha 5 D4
Nankin Street 5 D3
Nanson Road 4 B2
Napier Road 1 D2
Narayanan Chetty
  Road 4 B2
Nassim Hill 1 D2
Nassim Road 1 D1
Nathan Road 1 E4
National Blood
  Centre 4 B4
National Library 3 D5
  continues 5 D1
National Skin Centre 3 D1
Neil Road 4 B5
New Bridge Road 4 B4
  continues 5 D3
New Park Hotel 3 E2
New World Park 3 E2
Newton Circus Hawker
  Centre 2 B2
Newton Road 2 B2
Newton Station 2 C1
Ngee Ann City 2 A4
Nicoll Highway 3 E5
Nile Road 1 F5
Niven Road 3 E4
Norfolk Road 2 C2
Norris Road 3 D3
North Bridge Road 3 E4
  continues 3 E5 & 5 E1
North Canal Road 5 D3
Northumberland
  Road 3 D3
Novena Station 2 B2

Nutmeg Road 2 A3

O

Ocean Building 5 E4
Office Ring Road 1 D2
Oldham Lane 2 C4 & 4 C1
One Fullerton 5 E3
One Tree Hill 1 E3
Ophir Road 3 E4 & 5 F1
Orange Grove Road 1 E1
Orchard Boulevard 1 E2
  continues 2 A4
Orchard Link 2 A4
Orchard Parade
  Hotel 1 F2
Orchard Plaza 2 B4
Orchard Point 2 B4
Orchard Road 1 F2, 2 A4
  continues 2 B4, 4 C1
  continues 4 C2 & 5 D1
Orchard Station 1 E2
Orchard Turn 2 A4
Ord Road 4 C2
The Oriental Hotel 5 F2
Outram Park 4 B4
Outram Park Station 4 B4
Outram Road 4 A3
Owen Road 3 D1
Oxford Road 3 D2
Oxley Garden 2 B5
  continues 4 C1
Oxley Rise 2 B4
  continues 4 C1
Oxley Road 2 B5
  continues 4 B1
Oxley Walk 2 B5
  continues 4 C1

P

Padang 5 E2
Pagoda Street 4 C3
Palmer Road 4 C5 & 5 D5
Pan Pacific Hotel 5 F2
The Paragon 2 A4
Park Crescent 4 C3
Park Mall 2 C5 & 4 C1
Parliament House 5 D3
Parliament Lane 5 D3
Parsi Road 4 C5
Paterson Road 1 F3
Pearl Bank 4 B4
Pearl's Hill City Park 4 B3
Pearl's Hill Terrace 4 C4
Peck Hay Road 2 A3
Peck Seah Street 4 C5
Pekin Street 5 D3
Penang Lane 2 C5 & 4 C1
Penang Road 2 B4 & 4 C1
Penhas Road 3 F3
People's Park
  Complex 4 C3

Perak Road 3 D3
Peranakan Place 2 B4
Percival Road 2 C5 & 5 D1
Perumal Road 3 E2
Petain Road 3 E2
Philip Street 5 D3
Pickering Street 5 D3
Plaza Hotel 3 F4 & 5 F1
Plaza Singapura 2 C4
  continues 4 C1
Prince Charles
  Crescent 1 D4
Prince Charles
  Square 1 D4
Prince Edward Road 5 D5
Prince Philip Avenue 1 D4
Prinsep Court 3 D4
Prinsep Street 3 D4
  continues 5 D1
The Promenade 2 A4
Purvis Street 3 E5 & 5 E1

Q

Queen Elizabeth
  Walk 5 E2
Queen Street 3 D5 & 5 E1

R

Race Course Lane 3 D2
Race Course Road 3 D2
Raeburn Park 4 A5
Raffles Avenue 5 F2
Raffles Boulevard 5 F2
Raffles City 3 D5 & 5 E2
Raffles Hospital 3 E4
Raffles Hotel 3 E5 & 5 E1
Raffles Landing Site 5 D3
Raffles Link 5 E2
Raffles Place 5 D3
Raffles Place Station 5 D3
Raffles Quay 5 D4
Raffles Quay Park 5 D4
Rangoon Road 3 D1
Rangoon Secondary
  School 3 E1
Read Street 4 C2 & 4 C3
Redhill Close 1 D5
Redhill Road 1 D5
Redhill Station 1 D5
Republic Avenue 3 F5
Republic Boulevard 3 F5
Ridley Park 1 D3
Ritz-Carlton Millenia
  Hotel 5 F2
River Valley Close 2 A5
  continues 4 B2
River Valley Grove 2 A5
  continues 4 A1
River Valley Road 1 E4
  continues 2 A5, 4 A1
  continues 4 C2 & 5 D2

Roberts Lane 3 D2
Robertson Quay 4 B2
Robina House 5 D4
Robinson 5 D4 & 5 D5
  Road
Rochalie Drive 1 D3
Rochor Canal 2 A2 & 3 D4
Rochor Canal
  Road 3 D4 & 3 E4
Rochor Centre 3 E4
Rochor River 3 F3
Rochor Road 3 E4 & 5 F1
Rodyk Street 4 B2
Rowell Road 3 E3
Royal Holiday Inn
  Crowne Plaza 1 F2
Rutland Road 3 D2

S

S.A.F.N.C.O. Club 3 E5
  continues 5 E2
Sago Lane 4 C4
Sago Street 4 C4
Saiboo Street 4 B2
Saint Andrew's
  Cathedral 5 E2
Saint Andrew's Road 5 E2
Saint Margaret's
  School 2 C4
Saint Martins Drive 1 E2
Saint Thomas Walk 2 A5
  continues 4 A1
Sam Leong Road 3 E3
San Centre 4 B3
Sarkies Road 2 A2
Saunders Road 2 B4
Scotts Road 1 F2 & 2 A3
Scotts Shopping
  Centre 2 A3
Seah Street 3 E5 & 5 E1
Second Hospital
  Avenue 4 B4
Selegie House 3 D4
Selegie Road 3 D4
Seng Poh Lane 4 A3
Seng Poh Road 4 A3
Serangoon Plaza 3 E2
Serangoon Road 3 E1
Shanghai Road 1 E4
Shangri-La Hotel 1 E1
Shaw Towers 3 E5 & 5 E1
Shenton House 5 D4
Shenton Way 5 D5
Sheraton Towers
  Singapore Hotel 2 A2
Sherwood Road 1 D2
Short Street 3 D4
Shrewsbury Road 2 C1
  continues 3 D1
Silat Avenue 4 A5
Sing Avenue 3 E2

Singapore Art
  Museum   3 D5
  continues   5 D1
Singapore Botanic
  Gardens   1 D1
Singapore Council of 2 C5
  Social Services   4 C1
Singapore Finance
  House   3 E5 & 5 E1
Singapore General
  Hospital   4 A4
Singapore History
  Museum   3 D5 & 5 D1
Singapore Indian
  Fine Arts Society   3 D2
Singapore International
  Convention & Exhibition
  Centre   3 E5 & 5 F2
Singapore National
  Eye Centre   4 B4
Singapore Philatelic
  Museum   2 C5 & 5 D2
Singapore Railway
  Station   4 B5
Singapore River   4 B2
  continues   5 D3
Singapore School
  for the Deaf   1 D4
Singapore Technologies
  Building   4 C5
Smith Street   4 C4
Somerset Road   2 A4
Somerset Station   2 B4
Sophia Road   2 C4
South Bridge
  Road   4 C4 & 5 D3
South Canal Road   5 D3
Specialists' Shopping
  Centre   2 B4
Spooner Road   4 A5
Spottiswoode Park   4 B5
Spottiswoode Park
  Road   4 B5
Sri Krishnan Temple   3 D4
Sri Mariamman
  Temple   4 C4

Sri Srinivasa Perumal
  Temple   3 E2
Sri Temasek   2 B4
Sri Veeramakaliamman
  Temple   3 D3
Stamford Road   3 D5
  continues   5 F2
Stanley Street   5 D4
Starlight Road   3 D2
Stevens Road   1 F1
Sturdee Road   3 E2 & 3 F2
Subordinate Courts   4 C3
Suffolk Road   2 C2
Sultan Mosque   3 F4
Sultan Plaza   3 F4
Sungei Road   3 D3 & 3 E4
Sungei Whompoe   3 F1
Suntec City   3 E5 & 5 F1
Supreme Court   5 D2
Surrey Road   2 B1
Swan Lake   1 D2
Syed Alwi Road   3 E3

T

Taman Serasi   1 D2
Tan Boon Liat
  Building   4 A3
Tan Quee Lan Street   3 E4
  continues   5 E1
Tan Tock Seng
  Hospital   2 C1
Tan Tye Place   4 C2
Tanglin Golf Course   1 D2
Tanglin Hill   1 D3
Tanglin Rise   1 D3
Tanglin Road   1 D3
Tanglin Shopping
  Centre   1 E2
Tanglin Walk   1 D3
Tangs   2 A3
Tanjong Pagar   4 C5
Tanjong Pagar
  Conservation Area   4 B5
Tanjong Pagar Road   4 C5
Tanjong Pagar
  Station

Tank Road   2 B5 & 4 C2
Teck Guan Street   4 C2
Teck Lim Road   4 C4
Tekka Centre   3 D3
Telok Ayer Park   5 D4
Telok Ayer Street   5 D4
Temasek Avenue   3 F5
  continues   5 F2
Temasek Boulevard   3 E5
  continues   5 F2
Temasek Tower   5 D5
Temple Street   4 C4
Terminal Avenue   5 D5
Tessensohn Road   3 C2
Tew Chew Street   4 C3
Thian Hock Keng
  Temple   5 D4
Third Hospital
  Avenue   4 A4
Thomson Road   2 B1
Times House   1 F4 & 4 A1
Tiong Bahru Plaza   1 E5
Tiong Bahru Road   1 D5
  continues   4 A3
Tiong Bahru Station   1 F5
Tiong Poh Road
                4 A4 & 4 A3
Tiverton Lane   2 A4
  continues   4 B1
Tomlinson Road   1 E2
Tong Building   2 A4
Tong Watt Road   2 B5
  continues   4 B2
Towner Road   3 E1
Tras Street   4 C5
Trengganu Street   4 C4
Tronoh Road   3 F1
Truro Road   3 D2
Tyrwhitt Road   3 E3

U

United Square   2 C1
Unity Street   4 C2
UOB Plaza   5 D3
UOL Building   2 A4
Upper Circular Rd   5 D3

Upper Cross Street   4 C3
Upper Dickson
  Road   3 D3
Upper Hokien
  Street   4 C3
Upper North Canal
  Road   4 C3
Upper Weld Road   3 E3
Upper Wilkie
  Road   2 C3 & 2 C4
USA Embassy   1 D2

V

Veerasamy Road   3 D3
Verdun Road   3 E2
Victoria Lane   3 E3
Victoria Street 3 D5 & 5 E1
Victoria Theatre
  & Concert Hall   5 E3
Viking Road   1 D5

W

Wak Hai Cheng
  Bio Temple   5 D3
Wallich Street   4 C5
War Memorial Park   3 F5
  continues   5 E2
Waterloo Street   3 D4
  continues   5 D1
Wee Nam Road   2 B2
Weld Road   3 E3
Whampoa West   3 F1
Wheelock Place   1 F2
Wilkie Road   2 C4
Winstedt Road   2 B2
Wisma Atria Shopping
  Centre   2 A4
Wisma Indonesia   1 E3

Y

Yan Kit Road   4 C5
York Hill Estate   4 A3

Z

Zion Close   1 E4 & 4 A2
Zion Road   1 F4 & 4 A2

General Index

Page numbers in **bold** type
refer to main entries.

A

Academy at-sunrice 54,
165
Action Theatre 152, 153
Acupuncture 171
Adelphi Shopping Centre
150, 151
Admission charges 168
Adventure sports clubs 162,
163
Affandi 49
Ailments 170
Air Canada 177
Air France 177
Air New Zealand 177
Airlines 177
Al Abrar Mosque 67
Albert Court 123
Alfred Dunhill 48
Ali Iskandar Shah, Sultan 78
Aljunied Brothers' House
of Batik 79, 148, 149
Alkaff Mansion 139
All Nippon Airways 177
Allan Chai 148, 149
Alley Bar 158, 159
Alliance Française de
Singapour 153, 156, 157
Alsagoff Arabic School 32,
72
Amara Hotel 123
American Airlines 177
American Express 171, 173
Amoy Street Food Centre
141
ANA Hotel 124
Anderson Bridge 38
Andhra Curry House 137
Anglo-Dutch Treaty 17
Ann Siang Hill **66**
Anna Sui 148, 149
Annalakshmi 134
Antiques and crafts 146,
148, 149
Anywhere 89, 159
Arab Street **79**
antiques and crafts 146
Ramadan stalls 22
shopping 73, 79, 145
textiles 147, 148
Arabs 30, 79
Archbishop's House 49
Archery Club of Singapore
162, 163
Armenian Church 18, 33, **58**

Arrival
arriving by air 176
arriving by rail 176
arriving by road 176
arriving by sea 176
Art and crafts 164
Art-house movies 156
ASEAN Sculpture Park 55
Asia Hotel 124
Asian Civilisations Museum
29, 47, **52–3**
Asiatropics 149
Atlas Hi-Fi 150, 151
Audio products 150, 151
Australian High Commission
169
Automated teller machines
(ATMs) 172–3
Avis 180, 181
Aw Boon Haw 19

B

Baghdad Street 78
Balaclava 158, 159
Ballet 153
courses 164
Ballet under the Stars 153
Banana Leaf Apollo 137
Bank notes 173
Bank of America 172, 173
Bank of China building 67
Banks and Banking Hours
172
Bar 159
Bar & Billiard Room 158,
159
Bar None 158, 159
Bar Opiume 158, 159
Bar Sá Vanh 158, 159
BarCelona 161
Bargaining 143
Bars **158–9**
Battle Box 29, 55
Beaufort 125
Beaujolais Wine Bar 160,
161
Bedok jetty 163
Bedok Swimming Complex
162, 163
Bendahara House 72, **78**
Benjamin Sheares bridge
116
Berjaya Duxton Hotel 65,
123
Bernie's BFD 139
Best Denki 150, 151
Beurel, Father Jean-Marie 49
Bhaskars Arts 153

Bicycle hire 164
Bidwell, J
Goodwood Park Hotel 89
Raffles Hotel 89
Big Bubble Centre 162, 163
Big Splash 116, 162, 163
BigO magazine 155
Bin House 148, 149
Bird (Botero) 38, 67
Bird sanctuaries 106, 116–17
Bird singing sessions 102
Bird-watching **95**
Pulau Ubin 107
Sungei Buloh Wetland
Reserve 92, 165
Bishan Swimming Complex
162, 163
Bishopsgate 110
Bisous 160, 161
Blue Cow 159
Blue Ginger 136
Blue Note 159
Blue Wave Sports 162, 163
Boat Quay 39, **67**
pubs 158
Bobby Rubino's 134
Bonsai 96
Books 150, 151
Boon Hi-Tech Superstore
150, 151
Borders 150, 151, 175
Bossini 149
Botero, Fernando 38, 67
Boutique hotels 121
Brahma 33, 64
Brannigan's 159
Brazil Churrascaria 139
Brewer, Frank 66
Brewerkz 136, 159
British Airways 177
British Council 156
British East India Company
15–18, 78
British High Commission
169
British India 149
British rule 17–20
Brix 161
Brown Rice Paradise 150,
151
Buddha statues 33, 80
Buddhism 32
Buddhist Lodge 23
Buddhist temples
see Chinese Temples
Budget car rental 180, 181
Budget hotels 121
Bugis Junction **79**

Bugis Village 79
Bukhara 134
Bukit Timah 36, 94
Bukit Timah Nature Reserve
36, **94**
mountain-bike track 164
Bulgari 89, 148, 149
Bumboats 17, 67
Buona Vista Swimming
Complex 163
Burberrys 149
Burkill, Isaac Henry 98
Burkill Hall 98
Buses 182
arriving by road 176
Business cards 169
Buskers' Festival 153
Bussorah Mall 73
Butterfly Park 104
Buzz booths 175

C

C K Tang **89**, 142, 148, 149
Cable car 37, 102, 113
Café Expresso 89
Café Iguana 136
Café Modestos 137
Caldwell House 18
California Pizza Kitchen 137
Calvin Klein 149
Camera Workshop 150, 151
Cameras 150, 151
Camping 121
Canadian High Commission
169
Canal, Singapore
(Lauvergne) 14
Car rental 180
Carlton 122
Carnegie's 159
Carpets 147, 148
Carrefour 59, 150, 151
Cartier 89, 148
Cathay cinemas 157
Cathay Pacific 177
Cathay Photo Store 150, 151
Cathedrals
St Andrew's Cathedral 46
Cathedral of the Good
Shepherd **49**
Cavenagh Bridge 38, 66
CDs and video 149
Cenotaph 47
Censorship 157
Central Fire Station 58
Central Sikh Temple 33
Centrepoint 87, **88**
Centro 160, 161

Challenger SuperStore 150,
151
Chan, Georgette 49
Chanel 149
Changi Airport 176, **178–9**
Changi Museum 107
Changi Prison 19, 92, **107**
Changi Sailing Club 163
Changi Village **106–7**
Chap goh mei 22
Chaplin, Charlie 50, 89
Charles & Keith 148, 149
Chatsworth Avenue 110
Chatsworth Road 110
Chatterbox 138
Chettiar Temple **53**
Chia Ann Siang 66
Chiamassie 15
Chihuly, Dale 49
Chijmes **48**
Caldwell House 18
chapel 26, 48
Chijmes Hall 48, 153
Children
facilities 168
restaurants 127
Children's Discovery Gallery
52
Chills Cafe 175
China Black 161
China Jump Bar and Grill
134, 161
China Square 141
Chinatown and the
Financial District **60–69**
cinemas 157
hotels 123
restaurants 135–6
Street by Street map 62–3
Street Finder, map 3
Chinatown Complex **65**,
141
Chinatown Point 12
antiques and crafts 146
Chinese **30**
Chinese cuisine **128–9**
Chinese dance 35
Chinese delicacies 147
Chinese dialect groups 30
Chinese festivals 32–3
Chap goh mei 22
Chinese New Year 22–3
Chingay Parade 23
Dragon Boat Festival and
Boat Race 23–4
Festival of the Nine
Emperor Gods 25
Hungry Ghosts Festival 24

Chinese festivals (cont.)
Mid-Autumn festival 24
Qing Ming Festival 23
Chinese Garden 36, **96**
Mid-Autumn festival 24–5
pagodas 36, 90
Chinese-language theatre 35
Chinese lion dances 153
Chinese medical halls 171
Chinese medicines 147
Chinese New Year 22–3
Gong Xi Fa Cai 22
markets 64, 65
Chinese opera 30, 34, 153
Chinese Opera Institute 34,
153
Chinese orchestral music 35
Chinese porcelain-making
97–8
Chinese Protectorate 18
Chinese religions **32–3**
Chinese temples
Da Bo Gong Temple 103
Hock Teck Ch'i Temple 67
Kiu Ong Yiah Temple 23
Kong Meng San Phor Kark
See Temple 33
Leong San See Temple **80**
Lian Shan Shuang
Temple 23
Sakya Muni Buddha Gaya
33, **80–81**
Sin Chor Kung Temple 32
Siong Lim San Si
Temple 33
Temple of A Thousand
Lights 33, **80–81**
Thian Hock Keng Temple
18, 32, 67, **68–9**
Tua Pek Kong Temple 25,
33, 103
Wak Hai Cheng Bio
Temple 32
Chinese Theatre Circle 153
Chinese Weekly
Entertainment Club 66
Chingay procession 23, 85
Chomp Chomp Food Centre
141
Chong Fah Chong 49
Christianity **33**
Christmas 25
Chua Mia Tee 49
Churches 33
St Andrew's Cathedral 46
Cathedral of the Good
Shepherd 49
St Joseph's Church 33

Churches (cont.)
  Armenian Church 18, 33, 58
  St George's Church 111
  Grace Methodist Church 112
Churchill, Sir Winston 92
Cinema **156–7**
Cineplexes 156
Citibank 172, 173
City Hall 45
CityCab 180, 181
Civic Plaza 89
Civil Service Club 111
Clarke, Sir Andrew 58
Clarke Quay 39, **58–9**
  market and stalls **142**, 149
Classical music 34, 54
Clifford Pier 67
Climate 168
Clothing 148, 149
Club Chinois 138
Club Street 66
Clubs **160–61**
Cluny Road 110
Coco Carib 155
Coins 173
Cold Storage 87, 150, 151
Coleman, George D
  Armenian Church 58
  Coleman Bridge 39
  Fort Canning Centre 55
  Istana Kampong Glam 74
  Old Parliament House 46
  St Andrew's Cathedral 46
Coleman Bridge 39
Colonial Core and Fort
  Canning **42–59**
  area map 43
  cinemas 157
  hotels 122
  restaurants 134–5
  Street by Street map 44–5
  Street Finder, map 3
Colonial houses 108,
  110–11, 112
Comedy 153
Comfort Taxis 180, 181
Communications **174–5**
Computers 150, 151
Concorde 123
Confucianism 32
Confucius 32
Conrad, Joseph 50, 67
Conrad International
  Centennial 122
Consumer rights 143
Contemporary music 154–5

Convent of the Holy Infant
  Jesus 48, 49
Conversion chart 169
Cooking classes 165
Cop Cafe 159
Copthorne Orchid 125
Costa Sands holiday chalets
  117
Courtesy campaign 168
Cowabunga Ski Centre 162,
  163
Coward, Noel 50
Crazy Elephant 155, 159
Credit cards 172
Crown Prince 124
Cruise ships 176
Cuppage Terrace 88
Currency and Banking
  172–3
Customs 177
Cyberarena 175
Cyberbyte 175
Cybercafés 175
Cyberia 175
Cyberstar Comcentre 175
Cycling 164
  East Coast Park 106, 116

D
Da Bo Gong Temple 103
Dali, Salvador 38, 67
Damenlou 123
Dan Ryan's Chicago Grill
  137
Dance 153
  Chinese 35
  modern 35
Dance Ensemble Singapore
  35
Dancing classes 164–5
Daniel Yam 149
Danish Seaman's Mission 112
Dbl O 161
Death houses 62, 65
Deepavali 25
Delhi 137
Delta Swimming Complex
  162, 163
Dempsey Road warehouses
  144, 148, 149
Dengue fever 170
Dentists 171
Department stores and
  shopping malls 142, 149
Development Bank of
  Singapore (DBS) 172, 173
Dhobies 88
Dhoby Ghaut **88**

Diners Club 171
Disabled travellers 171
Diving 162
Doc Cheng's 51, 134
Dome Café 49
Dragon Boat Festival and
  Boat Race 23–4
Drama groups 152
Driving 180
Drug-dealing 170
Duke of Windsor 89
Dutch East India Company
  16
Duxton Road 65
  shophouses 60, 65
Dyce, Charles 49

E
E J H Corner House 99
ez-link card 27, 182, 183
Early development 18
East Coast Park **106**
  walk **116–17**
East Coast Parkway 164
East Coast Recreation
  Centre 117
East Coast Seafood Centre
  117
Eastern & Oriental Express
  176
Ebenezer Chapel 111
Economic growth 21
El Papio 139
Electric City 150, 151
Electricity 169
Electronic goods 146, **150**,
  151
Electronic Road Pricing
  (ERP) Scheme 180
Elgin, Lord 39
Elgin Bridge 39
Elizabeth 124
Elvis Pub 159
Emage Multimedia Gallery
  49
Embargo 160, 161
Embassies and High
  Commissions 169
Embrace Dental Surgery 171
Emerald Hill **88**
Emergency numbers 171
Emirates 177
Empire Café 134
Emporio Armani 149
Empress Place **47**, 52
Empress Room 51, **134**
Eng Wah cinema 157
English-language theatre 152

Entertainment in Singapore
152–161
  booking tickets 152
  Chinese opera 153
  Cinema **156–7**
  comedy 153
  dance 153
  information sources 152
  international shows 152
  local theatre 152
  Music **154–5**
  musicals 152–3
  open-air entertainment 153
  Pubs and Bars **158–9**
  ticket outlets 153
  Wine Bars, Clubs and
    Karaoke **160–61**
Equinox 48, 135
ERP 180
Esmirada 138
Esplanade Park **59**
Esplanade–Theatres on the
  Bay 59, 152, 153
Ethnic music 154
Etiquette 168
  table 127
Eurasians **31**
Europa Ridley's 161
European powers 16

F

Fa Zhu Gong 68
Faber, Captain Charles
  Edward 55, 112
Faber Point 102, 112–13
Fabulous Fizz 158, 159
Fall of Singapore **92**
Family Attractions
  see Museums and
    Family Attractions
Far East Square 67
Farquhar, Colonel William
  17, 52
Farquhar Collection of
  Natural History Drawings
  52
Farrer Park Tennis Courts
  164, 165
Father Flanagan's 134, 158,
  159
Feng shui 32, 59
Ferries 176
Festival of Asian Performing
  Arts 152
Festival of the Nine
  Emperor Gods 25
Festivals
  Buskers' Festival 153

Festivals (cont.)
  Chinese New Year 22–3
  Chingay Parade 23
  Christmas 25
  Deepavali 25
  Dragon Boat Festival and
    Boat Race 23–4
  Festival of Asian
    Performing Arts 152
  Festival of the Nine
    Emperor Gods 25
  Hari Raya Haji 22, 32
  Hari Raya Puasa 23, 32
  Hungry Ghosts Festival 24
  Mid-Autumn festival 24–5
  Ponggal 22
  Qing Ming Festival 23
  Singapore Festival of Arts
    23, 152
  Singapore Food Festival 24
  Singapore International
    Film Festival 156, 157
  Thaipusam 22
  Thimithi Festival 25
  Vesak Day 23
  WOMAD Festival 153, 154
Film censors' ratings 156
Film festivals 156, 157
Films 156–7
Fishing 163
Five-foot ways 17
Flag & Whistle 159
Flea markets 142
Flower People 150, 151
Flowers 150, 151
Flying 164
Food 147, 150, 151
  etiquette 127
  Food courts 140–41
  Hawker Centres 141
  Where to Eat 126–7
Foot reflexology 171
Forbidden City 139
Fort Canning Centre 55
Fort Canning Park 37, **54–5**
  Ballet under the Stars 153
  open-air concerts 154
  open-air entertainment
    153, 154
Fort Siloso 104
Forum Galleria 86
Fountain of Wealth 59
Four Guided Walks **108–17**
Four Seasons Singapore 124
Friendly Transport Services
  180, 181
Friendly Water Seaports
  Services 162, 163

Fuk Tak Chi Museum 67
Fullerton Building 38
Funan the IT Mall 145, 150,
  151
Further Afield **90–107**
  area map 91
  hotels 125
  restaurants 139

G

Gaetano 136
Ganesh 81, 82
Gardens *see* Parks and
  Gardens
Garuda Indonesia 177
Gay World 114
Gems 148
Geylang and Katong
  114–15
Geylang Road 114
Geylang Serai 114–15
Ghorka Grill 135
Ghost Island 103
Giordano 149
Giorgio's 161
Girl on a Swing (Harpley) 98
Girl with Folded Arms
  (Chong) 49
Glass Hall 48
Gleneagles Hospital 171
Global Refund Cheque 173
Goethe Institute 156, 157
Gold 146, 148
Golden Bell 112
Golden Village cinemas 156,
  157
Golf 164
Goods and services tax 169,
  173
Goodwood Florist 150, 151
Goodwood Park Hotel **89**,
  125
Gordon Grill 138
Government House 18
Government tax 169
Grace Methodist Church 112
Grand Hotel de l'Europe 59
Grand Hyatt Singapore 124
Grand Plaza Parkroyal 122
Great Singapore Sale 24, 88
Great Southern Hotel 63
Greeting Cuts 150, 151
Grill on Devonshire 138
GST 169, 173
Guan Hoe Soon restaurant
  115
Gucci 48, 89, 148, 149
Guru Nanak 33

H

Hai Tien Lo 135
Hajjah Fatimah Mosque 73
Hanuman 83
Happy hours 158
HarbourFront Centre 103, 112, 163, 176
Hard Rock Café 138, 159
Hari Raya Haji 23, 32
Hari Raya Puasa 22, 32
Harpley, Sydney 98
Harrods 89
Harry's @ the Esplanade 158, 159
Harry's Bar 67, 159
Haw Par Villa 19, 28, **97**
Hawker Food **140–41**
Haxworth 92, 107
Health 170–71
Herb garden 96
Herbarium 98
Hertz Car Rental 180, 181
High Commissions 169
Hill Street **58**
Hill Street Building 58
Hilton Singapore 125
Hindu festivals 33
  Deepavali 25
  Ponggal 22
  Thaipusam 22
  Thimithi 25
Hindu temples 33
  Chettiar Temple **53**
  Sri Mariamman Temple 25, 33, 63, **64**
  Sri Srinivasa Perumal Temple 22, 25, **82–3**
  Sri Thandayuthapani Temple 22
  Sri Veeramakaliamman Temple 33, **81**
  Vinayakar Temple 33
Hinduism **33**
History of Singapore **14–21**
HMV Music 142, 149
Hock Teck Ch'i Temple 67
Holiday chalets 106, 117
Holiday Inn Park 125
Holland Road Shopping Centre 97
  antiques and crafts 146
  news stand 175
Holland Village **97**, 144
Homage to Newton (Dali) 67
Home ownership 21
Hongkong and Shanghai Bank 172, 173
Hospitals 171

Hotels 120–25
  boutique 121
  budget 121
  Choosing a Hotel **122–5**
  facilities 120, 121
  Hilton Singapore 125
  luxury 120
  mid-priced 120–21
  prices 121
  ratings 120
  reservations 121
  website directory 120
  Where to Stay **120–21**
Hour Glass 150, 151
House of Mao 137
House of Ong 159
Housing and Development Board (HDB) flats 21, 30
Hua Zhu 139
Hugo Boss 149
Hup Hin Bakery 115
Hungry Ghosts Festival 24
Hussein, Sultan 32, 72, 78

I

I-S magazine 152, 155
Ice Cold Beer 159
IDD calls 174–5
Images of Singapore 29, 105
Imitation goods 143
Immigrant influx 17–18
Immigration visa 177
Imperial Hot Wok 135
In-line skating 164
Independence 20–21
Indian classical dance 35, 153
Indian Cuisine **132–3**
Indian languages 31
Indian Orchestra 154
Indian Sepoy mutiny 19
Indians **31**
Indochine 136
Indochine Waterfront 135
Indonesian Embassy 169
Industrialization 20
Inn 123
Insomnia @ Chijmes 160, 161
Institute of Health 171
Inter-Continental Hotel 123
Internet access 175
Isetan 86, 142, 149
Iskandar 16
Iskandar Shah, Sultan 78
Islam **32**
Islands
  Kusu Island 103

Islands (cont.)
  Lazarus Island 106
  Pulau Brani 16
  Pulau Bukom 19
  Pulau Hantu 103
  Pulau Ubin 107
  Sentosa 104–5
  Sisters Islands 106
  St John's Island 106
Istana 18, 85
Istana Kampong Glam 72, **78**

J

J P Bastiani Wine Bar 161
Jackson, Lieutenant Philip 15
Jackson, Michael 50
Jade 146
Jamae Mosque 63
Japan Airlines 177
Japanese Garden 36, **96**
Japanese Occupation **19**, 92, 107
  memorials 47, 92
  Presbyterian Church 88
  Victoria Theatre and Concert Hall 47
Jasons 150, 151
Javanese control 15–16
Jazz 155
Jazz Jam 159
Jewellery 148, 149
Jim Thompson shops
Jinrickshaw Station 65
Jitterbugs Swingapore 164, 165
Joaquim, Agnes 58
John Little department store 86, 149
John 3:16 Photo Supplies 150, 151
Joo Chiat Complex 115
Joy Luck Club 161
Jubilee Hall 153
Juice magazine 155
Jurong Bird Park 28, **94–5**
Jurong Country Club 165
Jurong Reptile Park **95**
JusTanja 164, 165

K

Kali 81
Kallang Park 163
Kallang Squash and Tennis Centre 164, 165
Kallang Theatre 152
Kampong Glam and Little India **70–83**

Kampong Glam and Little India (cont.)
area map 71
cinemas 157
hotels 123
restaurants 137
Street by Street map 72–3
Street Finder, map 2
Kandahar Street 72, 78
Kandang Kerbau Market 80
Karaoke 161
Katong **114–15**
Katong Bakery & Confectionery 115
Katong Swimming Complex 163
Kempetai 19
Kenzo 149
Keppel Marina 163
Keramat 54
Keramat Kusu 103
Keyaki 135
Kinara 136
Kinokuniya 150, 151, 175
Kiu Ong Yiah Temple 25
KK Market 80
KLM Royal Dutch 177
Komala Villas Restaurant 81
Kong Meng San Phor Kark *see* Temple 33
Kota Rajah Club 78
Kranji War Memorial **92**
Krishna 25
Kuan Yin 68
Kusu Island **103**
Tua Pek Kong Temple 25, 33
Kwan Sisters 161

L
L'Aigle d'Or 136
La Forketta 138
Lagoon Rendezvous 141
Laguna National Golf & Country Club 164, 165
Land reclamation 21
Land Transport Authority (VEP) 177
Languages 168
Larry Jewellery 148, 149
LaSalle-SIA College of the Arts 164, 165
Lau Pa Sat **66**, 141
Lauvergne, Barthélémy 14
Law and penalties 170
Lazarus Island **106**
Le Meridien Changi 125
Le Meridien Singapore 124

Lee, Dick 153
Lee Hwa 148; 149
Lee Kong Chian 19
Lee Kuan Yew 20, 21
Lei Garden 134
Leong San See Temple **80**
Les Amis 138
Les Amis Wine Bar 161
Lian Shan Shuang Temple 23
Light Rapid Transit System 182
Lim Bo Seng Memorial 45, **47**, 59
Lim's Arts & Crafts 148, 149
Liquid Room, The 161
Literacy rates 21
Little India 70–83
area map 71
cinemas 157
Deepavali 25
hotels 123
restaurants137
Street by Street map 72–3
Street Finder, map 2
textiles 147, 148
Little India Arcade **80**
Little India Cultural Corner 80
Local bands and artistes 155
Local theatre 152
Loewen Road 111
Long Bar 50, 159
Losa-Ghini, Massimo 160
Louis Vuitton 89
Lox 161
LRT 182
Lucky Plaza 150, 151
Lufthansa 177
Lush 161

M
M-Hotel 125
M1 175
Ma Zhu Po 68
Mac Shop 150, 151
Macpherson, Lt-Col Ronald 46
MacRitchie, James 66
MacRitchie Reservoir 37, **93**
fitness parks 164
Madame Wong's 161
Made-in-Singapore Movies **157**
Madrasah 32
Mag's Wine Kitchen 161
Mahalo Hawaiian Beach Bar 159

Majapahit empire 16
Majestic Cinema 65
tilework 62
Majulah Singapura 30
Malacca sultanate 16
Malay Annals 16
Malay Cuisine **130–31**
Malay heritage centre 78
Malay Village 115
Malayan Railway 176, 177
Malays **30**
Malaysia Airlines 177
Malaysian High Commission 169
Mama Africa 136
Mandai Orchid Garden **93**
Mandarin Singapore 125
Maps
Central Singapore 12–13
Chinatown and the Financial District 61
Colonial Core and Fort Canning 43, 44–5
Kampong Glam and Little India 71
Museums and Family Attractions 28–9
Orchard Road 85
Parks and Gardens 36–7
Sentosa 104–5
Singapore 10–11
Singapore Botanic Gardens 98–9
Street by Street: Around the Padang 44–5
Street by Street: Chinatown 62–3
Street by Street: Kampong Glam 72–3
Street by Street: Orchard Road 86–7
Maracas Cocina Latina 158, 159
Mariamman 33, 64
Marina Deck 113
Marina Mandarin 59, 122
Marina Promenade 164
Marina Square **59**, 149
Markets and stalls **142**, 149
Marks & Spencer 88, 142, 149
Marmalade 135
Marsden Brothers Dive School 162, 163
Mass Rapid Transit System 182, 183
Mastercard 171
Maugham, Somerset 50
Maxwell, John Argyle 44, 46

Maxwell Road Food Centre 141
McNeice, Lady Yuen-Peng 99
McSwiney, D L 49
Medical Attention 170
Merchant Court 39, **122**
Meritus Mandarin 125
Meritus Negara 125
Merlion 38, 45, 105
Methodist Book Room building 53
Metro 142, 149
Metropole 122
Metropolitan Museum of Art (New York) shop 48
Mezza 9 138
Michelangelo's 139
Mid-Autumn Festival 24–5
lanterns 24
Milieu 161
Millenia Walk 59
Ming Village **96–7**
Ming's Cafe & Pub 161
Mitre 158, 159
Mobile phones 175
Modern Singapore 21
Mohamad Ali Lane 66
Molly Malone's Irish Pub and Grill 158, 159
Moneychangers 172
Moomba 136
Mooncakes 24
Morton's of Chicago 135
Mosques
  Al Abrar Mosque 67
  Hajjah Fatimah Mosque 73
  Jamae Mosque 63
  Sultan Mosque 13, 32, 72, **74–5**
Mount Elizabeth Hospital 171
Mount Faber 37, **102**
  birds 95
Mount Faber Park **112–13**
Mount Pleasant Road 110
Mountain-bike tracks 164
Movies 156–7
MPH 150, 151, 175
MRT 182, 183
Muddy Murphy's Irish Pub 155, 158, 159
Multicultural Singapore **30–31**
Mumtaz Mahal 137
Muruga 53, 81
Museums and Family Attractions **28–9**
  Asian Civilisations Museum 29, 47, **52–3**

Museums and Family Attractions (cont.)
  Battle Box 29, 55
  Changi Museum 107
  Fuk Tak Chi Museum 67
  Haw Par Villa 28, **97**
  Images of Singapore 105
  Jurong Bird Park 28, **94–5**
  Jurong Reptile Park **95**
  Night Safari 28, **93**
  Pewter museum 96
  Raffles Museum and Library 52
  Sentosa 104–5
  Singapore Art Museum 29, **48–9**
  Singapore History Museum 29, **52**
  Singapore Philatelic Museum **53**
  Singapore Science Centre 28, **96**
Music **154–5**
  Chinese orchestral music 35
  classical music 34, 154
  contemporary music 154–5
  ethnic music 154
  Indian classical music 35
  orchestral music 154
  world music 155
Musical Fountain 105
Musicals 152–3
Muslim festivals 32
  Hari Raya Haji 23, 32
  Hari Raya Puasa 22, 32
Mustafa Centre 150, 151
Muthu's Curry 81, 137
My Place Entertainment 161

N
Nagore Durgha Shrine 66, 67
Nanyang Academy of Fine Arts 164, 165
Narakasura 25
Nashville 161
Nassim Road 110
National anthem 30
National Council of Social Services (NCSS) 171
National Day 24
National flower 58, 93
National languages 30
National Museum
  see Singapore History Museum

National Orchid Garden 98
National Sailing Centre 163
National University of Singapore 52
Nature Society of Singapore 165
Nature watch 165
Necessary Stage 152
New migrants **31**
New Otani 122
New Zealand High Commission 169
Newspapers 175
Newton Circus Food Centre 141
Next Page 159
Ngee Ann City 85, 86, **88–9**, 144
Ngiam Tong Boon 50, 158
Night Safari 28, **93**
No. 5 155, 160, 161
Northwest Airlines 177
Novotel Apollo 123
Nox 161
Nrityalaya Aesthetics Society 153

O
OCBC Building 48
Office hours 168
OG Building 65
Oil storage depot 19
Old Parliament House 18, **46**
Omnimax Theatre 96
On Pedder 148, 149
Ong Ke Soa Kha 58
Open-air concerts 154
Open-air entertainment 153
Opening hours 168
  banks 172
Opera
  Chinese 34, 153
  Western 34
Orang laut 17
Orchard Hotel 124
Orchard Parade 125
Orchard Road **84–9**
  area map 85
  Christmas 25
  cinemas 157
  hotels 124–5
  restaurants137–9
  Street by Street map 86–7
  Street Finder, map 1
Orchestral music 154
Orchid Country Club 165
Ord, Harry St George 18
Oriental medicine 171

Oriental outfits 147
Oriental Singapore 59, 122
Original Sin 139
Orkestra Melayu 154
Orlina, Ramon 49
OUB Bank see Overseas Union Bank
Outdoor Activities and Special Interests **162–5**
Outward Bound Singapore 162, 163
Oversea-Chinese Banking Corporation (OCBC) 172, 173
Overseas Emporium 64
Overseas Union Bank (OUB) 67, 172

P
P & W MacLellan 66
Padang
  Street by Street map 44–5
Pan Pacific 59, 122
Pan Shou 29
Pan West Golf Shop 150, 151
Paradigm 161
Paragon 84, 86, 149
PARCO Bugis Junction 79
Park Mall 87
Parking coupons 180
Parks and gardens **36–7**
  Bukit Timah Nature Reserve 36, **94**
  Chinese Garden 36, **96**
  East Coast Park **106**, 116–17
  East Coast Parkway 164
  Esplanade Park **59**
  Fort Canning Park 37, **54–5**, 153, 154
  Japanese Garden 36, **96**
  Jurong Bird Park 28, **94–5**
  MacRitchie Reservoir 37, **93**
  Mandai Orchid Garden **93**
  Mount Faber Park **112–13**
  National Orchid Garden 98
  Pasir Ris Park 37
  St John's Island 37, **106**
  Singapore Botanic Gardens 36, **98–9**, 100–101
  Singapore Zoological Gardens 28, **93**
  Sungei Buloh Wetland Reserve 36, **92**
  Tiger Balm Gardens **97**
  VIP Orchid Garden 98
Parliament Complex 38

Pasir Ris Park 37
Pasta Brava 136
Patara 137
Paulaner Braühaus 159
Pei, I M 48
Pender Road 112
Peng Kwee 150, 151
Penny Black 158, 159
People of Asia 149
People's Action Party 20
People's Association 154
People's Park Complex 62
  Oriental medicine 171
  textiles 147, 148, 149
Perak Lodge 123
Peranakan house exhibit 52
Peranakan houses 88, 115
Peranakan Place 87, **88**
Peranakan theatre 35
Peranakans **31**
Percival, Lieutenant-General Arthur 19, 92
Performing Arts **34–5**
Personal Security and Health **170–71**
Perumal 82
Pewter Museum 96
Philippine Embassy 169
Phoenix 124
Phonecards 174
Phuture 160, 161
Pickering, William 18
Pickpockets 170
Picnic Scotts 141
Pierspoint Pub 158, 159
Pillai, P Govindasamy 82
Piracy 18
Pitstop Bistro Bar 159
Places of worship 169
Plaza Parkroyal 123
Plaza Singapura 12, 87
Polo, Marco 15
Pondok Java 73
Ponggal 22
Pop concerts 154
Poppy Fabric 148, 149
Porcelain-making 97–8
Port of Singapore 18–19
Porta Porta 139
Post Bar 158, 159
Postal services 175
Practical Information **168–9**
Precision Audio 150, 151
Prego 135
Presbyterian Church 88
Priest's House 49
Prime Camera Centre 150, 151

Promenade 86
Provignage The Wine Cave 161
Ptolemy 15
Pu-Luo-Chung 15
Public holidays 25
Public telephones 174
Public Transport **182–3**
Pubs and Bars **158–9**
Pugilistic Association headquarters 114
Pulau Brani 16
Pulau Bukom 19
Pulau Hantu **103**
Pulau Subar Darat 104
Pulau Subar Laut 104
Pulau Ubin **107**
  cycling 164
Pyramid 44

Q
Qantas 177
Que Pasa 160, 161
Queen Elizabeth Walk **47**, 59
Qing Ming Festival 23
Qu Yuan 23–4

R
Raffles, Sir Thomas Stamford 15–17
  Chinatown 61
  St John's Island 106
  school 48
  statue 46, 47
  town plan 15, 43
Raffles City 26, **48**
Raffles Country Club 164, 165
Raffles Culinary Academy 51, **165**
Raffles Grill 50, 135
Raffles Hospital 171
Raffles Hotel **50–51**, 122
  architect 52, 89
  Bar and Billiard Room 158
  Long Bar 158
  museum 51
Raffles Institution 48
Raffles' Landing Site 38, **46**
Raffles Marina 163
Raffles Museum and Library 52
Raffles Place **67**
  Bird (Botero) 38, 67
  Homage to Newton (Dali) 67
Raffles the Plaza 48

Rail travel 176
Rainfall 25
Ralph Lauren 48
Ramadan 22, 32
Ramlee, P 157
Red Bakery 115
Regent 124
Regent Singapore Bar 159
Religion **32–3**
Religious festivals 22–5,
  32–3
Republic of Singapore
  Flying Club 164, 165
Republic Plaza 67
Resident's Quarters 49
Restaurants **126–41**
  children 127
  Chinese Cuisine **128–9**
  Choosing a Restaurant
    134–9
  dining hours 126
  drinking 127
  food courts 140
  hawker food **140–41**
  Indian 80
  Indian cuisine **132–3**
  Malay cuisine **130–31**
  paying the bill 127
  reservations 126
  set meals 126
  smoking 127
  table etiquette 127
  types 126
  vegetarian 126–7
  Where to Eat **126–7**
Retail Promotions Centre 143
Retro Music Bar 159
Rice Table 137
Ridley, Henry 111
Ridley Park 111
Ristorante Bologna 165
Ritz-Carlton Millenia 59,
  122
River taxi service 67
River Valley Swimming
  Complex 162, 163
Riverside Point 39
Riverwalk Galleria 39
Robertson Quay 155
Robinsons 87, 88, 142, 149
Rolex 150, 151
Royal Peacock 121, 123
Royal Plaza 124
Royal Selangor 97
Royal Sporting House 150,
  151
Ruby Photo 150, 151
Running tracks 164

S
Sabana 15
SAFRA Seasports Centre 163
Sago Street 62, 65
Sai Baba movement 32
Sailing 163
St Andrew's Cathedral 33, **46**
St George's Church 111
St John's Island 37, **106**
St Joseph's Church 33
St Joseph's Institution 48, 49
Sakya Muni Buddha Gaya
  33, **80–81**
Salle, John Baptist de la 48
Sally Port 55
Salut 136
Salvatore Ferragamo 48, 89
San's Tours and Car Rentals
  180, 181
Sang Nila Utama 16
Santry, Denis 72, 74
Satay Club 59
Scandal Point 59
Scott, Charles 66
Scott's Hill 66
Scuba Connection 162, 163
Scuba Corner 162, 163
SDK Recreation 164, 165
Sea Breeze Adventure Club
  116
Sea Tackle 163
Seadive Adventures 162, 163
Seah Street Deli 51
Seasports Centre 163
Second Link 176, 177
Security 170
Seiyu 142, 149
Sejarah Melayu 16
Select Books 89, 150, 151
Seletar Country Club 164,
  165
Seletar Reservoir 163
Senbazuru 134
Sentosa **104–105**
  in-line skating 164
Sentosa Golf Club 164, 165
Sentosa Water Sports Centre
  162, 163
Serangoon Road **81**
  Deepavali 25
Service charge 169
Serviced apartments 121
Shanghai Sally's 161
Shangri-La Singapore 125
Shangri-La's Rasa Sentosa
  Resort 121, 125
Shaw Brothers cinemas 156,
  157

Shaw Foundation Stage 99,
  153, 154
Sheraton Towers 125
Shi (Pan Shou) 29
Ships 176
Shiva 33, 64, 81
Shoes 148, 149
Shophouse styles **65**
Shophouses
  Ann Siang Hill 66
  Duxton Road 60, 65
  Geylang 115
  Orchard Road 88
  Peranakan Place 87
  Temple Street 64
Shopping in Singapore
  142–51
  antiques and crafts 146,
    148, 149
  bargaining 143
  brand–name shops 48,
    148
  CDs and video 149
  clothing 148, 149
  consumer rights 143
  department stores and
    shopping malls 142
  directory 149
  Great Singapore Sale 143
  guarantees 143
  imitations 143
  jewellery 148, 149
  markets and stalls 142
  methods of payment
    142–3
  Orchard Road 85, 86–7
  sales tax 143
  shopping hours 142, 168
  Singapore's Best:
    Shopping Centres
    and Markets **144–5**
  Textiles **147, 148, 149**
  What to Buy in Singapore
    146–7
  Where to Shop **148–51**
Shopping malls
  Adelphi Shopping Centre
    150, 151
  Centrepoint 87, **88**
  Forum Galleria 86
  Funan the IT Mall 145,
    150, 151
  Holland Road Shopping
    Centre 97
  Liat Towers 86
  Lucky Plaza 150, 151
  Ngee Ann City 85, 86,
    88–9, 144

Shopping malls (cont.)
Paragon 86
Park Mall 87
Peranakan Place 87, 88
Plaza Singapura 12, 87
Raffles City 26, **48**
Sim Lim Square 150, 151
Sim Lim Tower 145, 150, 151
Specialist Shopping Centre 87
Tanglin Shopping Centre 86, **89**, 144
Tangs 86, 89
The Heeren 87
Wheelock Place 86
Wisma Atria 86, 149
Shui Hu 159
Sightseeing cruises 67
Sikh temples 33
Sikhism **33**
SilkAir 177
Sim Lim Square 150, 151
Sim Lim Tower 145, 150
Sin Chor Kung Temple 32
Sincere Watch 151
Singapore Adventure Club 162, 163
Singapore Airlines 177
Singapore Art Museum 29, **48–9**
Girl with Folded Arms (Chong) 49
Shi (Pan Shou) 29
Singapore Ballet Academy 164, 165
Singapore Board of Film Censors 157
Singapore Botanic Gardens 36, **98–9**, 100–101
open-air concerts 154
running track 164
Singapore Chinese Chamber of Commerce 58
Singapore Chinese Orchestra 35, 154
Singapore Cricket Club 18, 45
Singapore Cruise Centre 176
Singapore Dance Theatre 35, 55, 153, 164, 165
Singapore Discovery Centre **94**
Singapore Festival of Arts 152
Singapore Film Festival 157
Singapore Film Society 157
Singapore History Museum 29, **52**

Singapore Hotels Association 120
Singapore Immigration Department 177
Singapore Indoor Stadium 152, 153
Singapore International Film Festival 156, 157
Singapore Lyric Opera 34
Singapore Marriott 125
Singapore Philatelic Museum **53**
Singapore Repertory Theatre 152
Singapore River **38–9**
history 17, 18
night view 56–7
Singapore Road Safety School 116
Singapore Science Centre 28, **96**
Singapore Scout Association headquarters 110
Singapore Sling 50, 158
Singapore Stage Club 152
Singapore Stone 15
Singapore Street Directory 180
Singapore Symphony Orchestra 34, 154
Singapore Tennis Centre 164, 165
Singapore Time 169
Singapore Tourism Board (STB) 168, 169
Singapore Underwater Federation 163
Singapore Visitors Centre 168, 169
Singapore Yacht Club 163
Singapore Zoological Gardens 28, **93**
Singapore's Best: Parks and Gardens **36–7**
Singapore's Best: Shopping Centres and Markets **144–5**
Singapura 16
Singlish 168
SingTel 174, 175
Siong Lim San Si Temple 33
Sisters Islands **106**
SISTIC 152, 153
Sistina Gourmet Pizzeria 139
Small Claims Tribunal 143
Smoking 170
Somerset's Bar 159

South African High Commission 169
South Battery 55
South Bridge Road 62, 64
Souvenirs 146
Speak Mandarin campaign 30
Special Needs 121
Specialist Shopping Centre 87
Spice garden 54
Sport Entertainment 164, 165
Sports goods 147, 150, 151
Sri Mariamman Temple 33, 63, **64**
Thimithi Festival 25
Sri Srinivasa Perumal Temple **82–3**
carving 70
Sri Srinivasa Perumal Temple (cont.)
Ponggal 22
Thaipusam 22
Thimithi Festival 25
Sri Thandayuthapani Temple 22
Sri Veeramakaliamman Temple 33, **81**
Starhub 175
Steeple's Deli 89
Straits Settlements 17, 18
Streets of Kampong Glam **78**
Stuart Anderson's Black Angus 138
Studio City 157
Subramaniam 22, 53
Substance 148
Substation 153, 164, 165
Sugar 159
Suits 147
Sultan Mosque 13, 32, 72–**5**
administrative building 76–7
Sultan of Swing 160, 161
Sun Yat Sen 19, 102, 112
Sun Yat Sen Nanyang Memorial Hall 102
Sun Yat Sen Villa **102**
Sungei Buloh Wetland Reserve 36, **92**
Sunset Bay 159
Sunsport Centre 164, 165
Suntec City **59**
Fountain of Wealth 59
Singapore Visitors Centre 168
Superbowl Golf & Country Club 164, 165
Supermarkets 150, 151

Supreme Court 18, 44
  facade 42
  frieze 13
Survival Guide **168–83**
  Communications **174–5**
  Currency and Banking
  172–3
  Personal Security and
  Health **170–71**
  Practical Information
  168–9
  Travel Information **176–83**
Swan and Maclaren 52
Swan Lake 98
Swatch Stores 150, 151
Sweet Aromas 175
Swimming 162
Swiss International Airlines
  177
Swissôtel the Stamford 48
Symphony Lake 99
Syonan-To 19

T
T'ai 161
Takashimaya 142, 149
Tan Boon Liat 112
Tan Chee Sang 18
Tan Hoon Siang Mist House
  99
Tan Kah Kee 19
Tan Kim Seng fountain 43,
  47, 59
Tan Swie Hian 49
Tanah Merah Ferry Terminal
  176
Tange, Kenzo 67
Tanglin Mall markets 142,
  149
Tanglin Police Station 171
Tanglin Shopping Centre
  86, **89**, 144
  antiques and crafts 146,
  148, 149
  jade 146
Tango 161
Tangs **89**, 142, 148, 149
Tanjong Pagar Conservation
  Area **65**
Tanjong Pagar dock 19
Tanjong Pagar Railway
  Station 176
Tanjong Pagar Road 65
Tao Nan School 52
Taoism 32
  Festival of the Nine
  Emperor Gods 25
Tat Chuan Audio 150, 151

Taxis 180–81
  booking 181
  airport 176, 178
Tea Chapter 150, 151
Tekka centre 80, **145**
Tekka market 80
Telok Ayer Market 66
Telok Ayer Street **66–7**
Telok Blangah Hill 112
Temasek 16, 17
Temenggong Road 113
Temple of A Thousand
  Lights 30, **80–81**
Temple Street **63**, 64
Temples
  Central Sikh Temple 33
  Chettiar Temple **53**
  Da Bo Gong Temple 103
  Hock Teck Ch'i Temple 67
  Kiu Ong Yiah Temple 25
  Kong Meng San Phor Kark
  See Temple 33
  Leong San See Temple **80**
  Lian Shan Shuang Temple
  23
  Sakya Muni Buddha Gaya
  33, **80–81**
  Sin Chor Kung Temple 32
  Siong Lim San Si Temple 33
  Sri Mariamman Temple
  25, 33, 63, **64**
  Sri Srinivasa Perumal
  Temple 22, 25, **82–3**
  Sri Thandayuthapani
  Temple 22
  Sri Veeramakaliamman
  Temple 33, **81**
  Temple of A Thousand
  Lights 33, **80–81**
  Thai Buddhist Temple 23
  Thian Hock Keng Temple
  18, 32, 67, **68–9**
  Tua Pek Kong Temple 25,
  33, 103
  Vinayakar Temple 33
  Wak Hai Cheng Bio
  Temple 32
Tengku Mahmoud 78
Tennis 164
Teutonia Club 19, **89**
Textiles 147, 148, 149
Thai Airways 177
Thai Buddhist Temple 23
Thaipusam festival 22, 53,
  82
Theatre
  Chinese-language 34
  English-language 34

Theatre (cont.)
  Peranakan 35
Theatreworks 34, 55, 152
Thian Hock Keng Temple
  18, 32, 67, **68–9**
Tan Tock Seng 68
Thimithi festival 25, 64
Thomson, J T 16, 49
Thrifty 180, 181
TIBS 180, 181
Ticket outlets 153
Ticketcharge 152, 153
Tierney's Gourmet 150, 151
Tiffany & Co. 89, 148, 149
Tiger Balm 19
Tiger Balm Gardens **97**
Tiong Bahru **102**
Times the Bookstore 150,
  151, 175
Tipping 169
Toilets 171
Toll charges 176
Tomlinson Antique House
  148, 149
Tong Heritage Bar 159
Top of the M 139
Top Ten Attractions 27
Tourist Information 168
Tourist Information Centre
  168, 169
Tourist maps 180
Tower Records 142, 149
Toy Factory 152
Trade 18, 19
Traders 124
Traffic and parking 180
Trains arriving by rail 176
Tran Trong Vu 49
Transvestites 79
Travel Information **176–83**
Travellers' cheques 172
Travellers' Health and
  Vaccination Centre 170, 171
Travellers' Needs **120–65**
Travelling Around
  Singapore **180–81**
Travelling by Air **178–9**
Trengganu Street 62
Tua Pek Kong Temple 25,
  33, 103
Turtle Island 103
Tuscany Ristorante 134

U
Ulu Pandan Boys' Brigade
  Mountain Bike Track 164,
  165
Underwater World 104

United Airlines 177
United Overseas Bank
  (UOB) 172, 173
University Cultural Centre
  152
Unkai 139
UOB Plaza 38, 67
Urbane 161
US Embassy 169

V
V-8 Movies 150, 151
Vaccinations 170
Vanda Miss Joaquim orchid
  58, 93
Vehicle Entry Permit (VEP)
  177
Velvet Underground 160, 161
Vera Wang 148, 149
Vesak Day 23
Victoria, Queen 47
Victoria Memorial Hall 44, 47
Victoria Theatre & Concert
  Hall 44, **47**, 153, 154
Vinayakar Temple 33
VIP Orchid Garden 98
Visa credit card 171
Visas 177
Vishnu 33, 64, 82, 83
Volcanoland 105
Vuttisasara 80

W
Waikiki Dive Centre 162, 163
Wak Hai Cheng Bio Temple
  32
Wakeboarding 162
Wala Wala 159
Walks **108–117**
  colonial houses **110–11**
  East Coast Park **116–17**
  Geylang and Katong
  114–15
  Mount Faber Park **112–13**
Wan Qing Yuan 102
War Memorial Park **47**
Watches 146, **150**, 151
Waterskiing 162
Whampoa 18
Wheelock Place 86
Where Singapore 152
Why Pay More? 150, 151
William Water Sports Centre
  162, 163
Windsurfing 163
Wine Bars, Clubs and
  Karaoke **160–61**
Williams, Robbie 50
Wisma Atria 86, 149
WOMAD (World of Music,
  Art and Dance) Festival

  153, 154
Wong Hoy Cheong 49
Wong San's 158, 159
Woo, Raymond 96
Woodlands Causeway 176,
  177
Woolner, Thomas 46
World music 155
World War I 19
  memorial 46, 47
World War II 19
  memorials 46, 47, 92
  see also Japanese
  Occupation
Worship 32–3
  etiquette 169

Y
Yard 159
Yingthai Palace 137
YMCA 88, 164, 165
Youth Flying Club 111
Youth Park 155
Yue Hwa Chinese Products
  Store 62, 145, 150, 151
Yuen-Peng McNeice
  Bromeliad Collection 99
Yusof Bin Haji Moh 78

Z
Zai Si Xian Hej 68
Zouk 160, 161

Acknowledgments

DORLING KINDERSLEY would like to thank the following people whose contributions and assistance have made the preparation of this book possible.

MAIN CONTRIBUTORS

Jill Laidlaw worked as an editor of highly illustrated non-fiction in London publishing before moving to Singapore in 1995. She specialized in project-managing large-format photographic books with Southeast Asian themes. In 1998, she began writing full-time on Southeast Asian art and culture for local and international publications.

Kathy Khoo is a freelance writer, contributing to local and regional travel and lifestyle magazines.

Julia Pasifull Oh is a freelance writer and researcher with special interest in the history, art and culture of Singapore. She is a co-author of *Nineteenth Century Prints of Singapore* (1987), National Museum.

Rufus Bellamy is a journalist and film-maker who specializes in the environment. He has published and broadcast with a wide range of local and international magazines and television companies.

Ben Munroe is the Senior Editor of *IS* magazine, a Singapore city and entertainment guide. He has contributed to publications in Bangkok, Hong Kong, Singapore and the United Kingdom, writing on the subjects of art, travel, wining and dining.

Joan Koh is the Associate Editor of *WHERE* Singapore, a city and entertainment guide.

ADDITIONAL CONTRIBUTORS

Robert Conceicao lectures in public relations and writes for regional publications, with special interest in history, politics, travel and culture.

Lim Kim Seng is the author of *Birdwatching in Singapore* (1999) and co-author of *Birds: An Illustrated Field Guide to the Birds of Singapore* (1997). He is an active member of the Nature Society (Singapore).

FOR DORLING KINDERSLEY

MANAGING ART EDITOR Kate Poole
SENIOR MANAGING EDITOR Louise Bostock Lang
CARTOGRAPHIC EDITOR Dave Pugh
PRODUCTION Mel Allsop, Sarah Dodd, Marie Ingledew, Michelle Thomas
EDITORIAL DIRECTOR Vivien Crump
ART DIRECTOR Gillian Allan
MANAGING DIRECTOR Douglas Amrine

ADDITIONAL EDITORS

Tim Jaycock, Susan Gallagher, Samantha Hanna, Kok Kum Fai, Christine Chua.

PROOF READER AND INDEXER

Kay Lyons.

SPECIAL ASSISTANCE

Dr Yam Tim Wing and Karen Bartolomeusz of the National Parks Board; Kua Soon Khe of Thian Hock Keng Temple; Mr Lingam, Hindu Endowments Board, and Mr Ramesh, secretary, Sri Srinivasa Perumal Temple; Liew Kim Siong, Elaine Olivia Chong and the staff of the Public Affairs department, Sentosa Development Corporation; Daing Mohd. Farhan Hashim, chairman, Trustees of Masjid Sultan, and Hj Abdullah of the Sultan Mosque; May Ang, Gina Tan, Renu Nair and Juliana Chong of Raffles Hotel; Uma Devi of the National Archives; Helen Ng and Chua Li Koon of the Singapore History Museum; Suenne Megan Tan of the Singapore Art Museum; Juniper Chua of the Asian Civilisations Museum; Chan Miang Boon and staff of the Public Affairs department of Transitlink; Han Liang Yuan of the Land Transport Authority; David Lim of the Mandai Orchid Garden; Christine Tan of the UOB PLaza; Ray Parry of the Duxton Hotel; Lee Tee Mui, food stylist; Karmila Kamuri of the Singapore Tourism Board library; Diana Lim of Sin Kee Arts & Crafts; Celia Low and Katherine Ho of the Singapore Symphony Orchestra; Louise Phua of the Singapore Dance Theatre; Natasha Pat Lim of the Singapore Chinese Orchestra; Elsa Lim and Felina Khong of Action Theatre; Ruby Khoo of the Singapore Repertory Theatre; Traslin Ong and Lucilla Teoh of Theatreworks; Foo Mei Ling of the Toy Factory Theatre Ensemble; Radha Vijayan of Nrityalaya Aesthetics Society; Mrs Yasotha of the Singapore Indian Fine Arts Society; Dr Chua Soo Pong of the Chinese Opera Institute; Sherine Wong of the Singapore Lyric Opera; Guo Xiong of The Practice Theatre; Isaac Chan of Gunung Sayang Association; Vivian Ong of the Singapore Indoor Stadium; Seow Sher Yen of The Substation; Seet Tze Ching of Esplanade, Theatres on the Bay; Amy Tay of Raintree Pictures; Pam Oei of Fringe Films; Mabelyn Ow of Zhao Wei Films; Michael Cheah of BigO; Mr Chua of Dance Ensemble Singapore; Priscilla Goh of National Youth Council; Steven Cheong of the Singapore Police Force; Edward Goh of the CIAS Auxilliary Police, Ong Pei Ling of the Civil Aviation Authority of Singapore; Seow Beng Lan of Su Yeang Design; Rick Clements of Singapore Airlines; Linda Teo of the Singapore Science Centre; Morten Strange of Nature's Niche; Chan Wee Lee of the Battle Box; Stanley Leong of Worldstage Pte Ltd, for WOMAD; Robin Cheong of the Board of Commissioners of Currency; Vivien Kim of Words Worth Media Management.

PHOTOGRAPHY PERMISSIONS

DORLING KINDERSLEY would like to thank the following for their assistance and kind permission to photograph at their establishments or during performances: Imperial Hot Wok Chinese Bistro; Hong Reng Tang Imperial Herbal Kitchen; Bukhara restaurant; Raffles Hotel; Lagun Sari restaurant; Dance Ensemble Singapore; Singapore Dance Theatre; Gunung Sayang Association; Singapore Symphony Orchestra; Singapore Chinese Orchestra; Chinese Opera Institute; Nrityalaya Aesthetics Society.

PICTURE CREDITS

t = top; tl = top left; tlc = top left centre; tc = top centre; tr = top right; cla = centre left above; ca = centre above; cra = centre right above; cl = centre left; c = centre; cr = centre right; clb = centre left below; cb = centre below; crb = centre right below; bl = bottom left; b = bottom; bc = bottom centre; bcl = bottom centre left; br = bottom right; d = detail.

Every effort has been made to trace the copyright holders and we apologize in advance for any unintentional omissions. We would be pleased to insert the appropriate acknowledgements in any subsequent edition of this publication.

Photographs and drawings have been reproduced with the permission of the following copyright holders:

© Bill Haxworth 92bl; © Trustees of the Imperial War Museum, London 19tr, 20tl, © Tan Kok Kheng 19tl; © Lee Hin Ming 19bc; © Ministry of the Information and the Arts 20r, 21 tl.

The publisher would like to thank the following individuals, companies and picture libraries for permission to reproduce their photographs:

ACTION THEATRE: 152br; AMOS WONG: 72tr, 72tl, 72bl, 73t, 73c, 78c; ARTWORDS: 12tl, 85t; ASIAN CIVILISATIONS MUSEUM, NATIONAL HERITAGE BOARD: 29tr; TIMOTHY AUGER: 54ca, 55br, 59b.

BATTLE BOX 29br; BES STOCK: © Alain Evrard 5c, 46tl; 76–7, 118–9, 166–7; BIG SPLASH MANAGEMENT PTE LTD: 162b.

EARTH SATELLITE CORPORATION/SCIENCE PHOTO LIBRARY: 11tr.

FRINGE FILMS, COURTESY OF TIGER TIGER PRODUCTIONS: 157r.
COURTESY OF LTA: 183crb

EDITIONS DIDIER MILLET: 3t, 9t, 13b, 16c, 17bl, 18bl, 18r, 18br, 19br, 50lc; 41t.

NATIONAL ARCHIVES: 16tr, 16bl, 17bc, 19tr, 19tl, 19bc, 20tl, 20cr, 21tl, 92bl, 167t.

PHOTOBANK: 2–3, 40–41, 56–7, 60, 84, 88bl, 90, 100–101; PRACTICE THEATRE 34bl.

COURTESY OF SENTOSA ISLAND: 105ca; SINGAPORE ART MUSEUM, NATIONAL HERITAGE BOARD: 29c, 49bl; SINGAPORE HISTORY MUSEUM, NATIONAL HERITAGE BOARD: 8–9, 14, 15t, 15b, 16b, 16br, 17br, 119t; SINGAPORE INDOOR STADIUM: 154tr; SINGAPORE LYRIC OPERA: 34cl; SINGAPORE REPERTORY THEATRE 152c; SINGAPORE SYMPHONY ORCHESTRA: 34br; SINGAPORE TOURISM BOARD: 22b, 23tl, 23tr, 23bl, 23br, 24b, 25tl, 25bc, 25r, 30c, 52tl, 82b; MORTEN STRANGE: 95bl.

THEATREWORKS 34tr; TOY FACTORY THEATRE ENSEMBLE: 34tld.

VISION PHOTO AGENCY: 2, 42.

GOH GEOK YIAN: 19bl.

Front Endpaper: Special photography except © PHOTOBANK Ll, Lr, Rbl; VISION PHOTO AGENCY Rbr.

JACKET:
Front - DK PICTURE LIBRARY: Peter Chen l; FTUP PTE. LTD., SINGAPORE: c; MASTERFILE UK: Didier Dorval main image; PICTURES COLOUR LIBRARY: Picture Finders r. Back - DK PICTURE LIBRARY: b and t. Spine - MASTERFILE UK: Didier Dorval.

Glossary

ARCHITECTURE

bungalow: term with colonial connotations for house usually surrounded by a verandah

five–foot way: covered walkway running in front of a row of shophouses

godown: warehouse

gopuram: tapering tower of Hindu temple *(see p83)*

HDB: Housing and Development Board

mihrab: niche in mosque, framed by decorated arch, facing Mecca *(see p74)*

mimbar: podium in a mosque from which the priest delivers his sermon *(see p74)*

minaret: slender tower of mosque with one or more balconies from which people are called to prayer *(see p74)*

shophouse: terrace house with business premises on the ground level and living quarters above

CULTURE

feng shui: Chinese geomancy

hong bao: red packet containing money given for good luck at Chinese New Year

kavadi: metal cage with spikes carried by Hindu devotee during Thaipusam *(see p22)*

Peranakan: term applied to descendants of Straits-born Chinese men ("Babas") and local Malay women ("Nonyas") *(see p31)*

wayang: traditional Southeast Asian theatre, from Chinese opera to shadow-puppetry

DRESS

baju kurung: traditional long-sleeved, brightly coloured top worn by Malay Muslim women

cheongsam: traditional silk dress with Mandarin collar worn by Chinese women

samfoo: traditional Chinese women's working garb

sarong: length of cloth wrapped around the waist (for men) or around the chest (for women)

songkok haji: symbolic white cap worn by male Muslims who have completed their pilgrimage to Mecca

tudung: traditional headscarf worn by Malay Muslim women

FOOD

ayam: chicken *(see p131)*

char siew pau: steamed minced pork bun

char kuay teow: stir-fried flat noodles with egg *(see p128)*

curry puff: deep fried pastry containing curry, egg, potatoes and chicken *(see p131)*

dhosai: Indian paper-thin bread with various sauces *(see p132)*

ice kachang: dessert with crushed ice topped with red beans, sago, jelly, maize, evaporated milk and coloured syrup *(see p129)*

ikan: fish

kambing soup: mutton soup

keropok: fish or prawn crackers

kopi tiam: traditional coffee ("kopi") shop ("tiam")

kopi-o: coffee taken with sugar and no milk

kopi peng: iced coffee

murtabak: Indian omelette pizza with minced mutton and onions *(see p132)*

nasi: rice

nasi padang: rice served with a variety of dishes

nonya kueh: sweet, starchy cakes of various flavours

or luat: oysters fried with eggs *(see p128)*

rojak: salad of turnip, dried cuttlefish, pineapple and beancurd

roti prata: fried, flat bread served with curry *(see p132)*

satay: barbecued mutton, chicken or beef *(see p130)*

sotong: squid

tau hu: beancurd

teh: tea with milk and sugar

teh-o: tea with sugar, no milk

udang: prawn

won ton mee: noodles with roasted pork slices and dumplings

yu sheng: raw-fish salad taken during Chinese New Year for good fortune *(see p129)*

LOCAL SLANG

ang moh: Caucasian

Ah Beng: Chinese male with flashy, tasteless style of dress

Ah Lian: female equivalent of Ah Beng

buaya: lecherous male

cheng hu: local government

five Cs: Cash, Credit card, Car, Condominium and Country club: the Singaporean dream

give face: show respect

ke tor lok: "where are you going to?"

kiasu: "afraid of losing"

lah: locals often end a sentence with "lah". For example, "this dress cost only $20, lah!"

mama shop: newsstand selling everything from newspapers to cigarettes

mat: Malay youth

mat rock: Malay youth who is a fan of heavy metal music

mina: female counterpart of "mat"

mina rock: female counterpart of "mat rock"

Sarong Party Girl (SPG): local girl with preference for Caucasian men (derogatory)

shiok: expression of appreciation: "shiok" food tastes "brilliant"

Singlish: form of English spoken in Singapore; full sentences are rare, words are repeated for emphasis, and slang rules *(see p168)*

tai-e-long loanshark

MISCELLANEOUS

AYE: Ayer Rajah Expressway

CAAS: Civil Aviation Authority of Singapore

CBD: Central Business District

chettiar: Indian money-lender

COE: Certificate of Entitlement (needed as a condition of owning a car)

CTE: Central Expressway

dhoby: Indian laundryman *(see p88)*

ECP: East Coast Parkway

ERP: Electronic Road Pricing

GST: goods and services tax

istana: palace; the Istana is the President of Singapore's offical residence *(see p18)*

jalan: street; walk**PIE:** Pan Island Expressway

LRT: Light Rapid Transit *(see p182)*

MRT: Mass Rapid Transit *(see p182)*

NS: national service

padang: field *(see p44-5)*

PAP: People's Action Party

pasar malam: night market

PIE: Pan Island Expressway

sinseh: Chinese physician who prescribes medicine from his shop *(see p171)*

STB: Singapore Tourism Board

URA Urban Redevelopment Authority

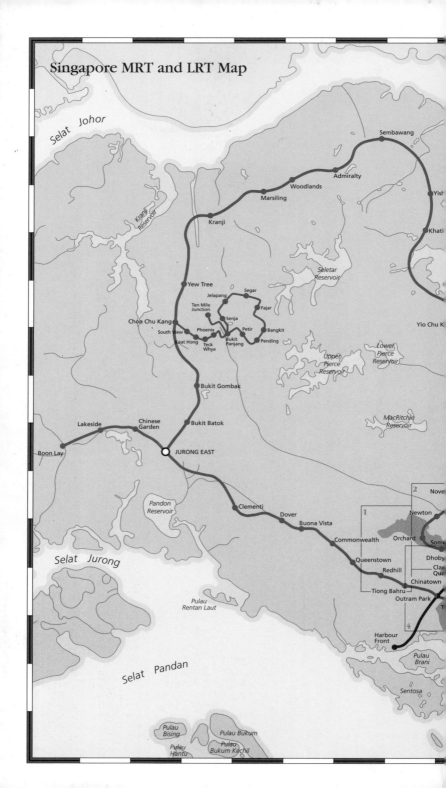

Singapore MRT and LRT Map

Selat Johor

Kranji Reservoir

Sembawang

Admiralty

Woodlands

Marsiling

Yish

Khati

Kranji

Seletar Reservoir

Yew Tree

Yio Chu K

Jelapang

Segar

Ten Mile Junction

Fajar

Senja

Choa Chu Kang

Phoenix

Petir

Bangkit

South View

Keat Hong

Teck Whye

Bukit Panjang

Pending

Lower Pierce Reservoir

Upper Pierce Reservoir

Bukit Gombak

MacRitchie Reservoir

Lakeside

Chinese Garden

Bukit Batok

Boon Lay

JURONG EAST

Pandon Reservoir

2

Nove

Clementi

Newton

Dover

1

Buona Vista

Orchard

Some

Commonwealth

Dhoby

Selat Jurong

Queenstown

Clar
Qua

Redhill

Chinatown

Tiong Bahru

Outram Park

Pulau Rentan Laut

Selat Pandan

4

Harbour Front

Pulau Brani

Sentosa

Pulau Bising

Pulau Bukum

Pulau Hantu

Pulau Bukum Kechil